Multinational Risk Assessment and Management

MULTINATIONAL RISK ASSESSMENT AND MANAGEMENT

Strategies for Investment
and
Marketing Decisions

Wenlee Ting

QUORUM BOOKS

New York • Westport, Connecticut • London

Library of Congress Cataloging-in-Publication Data

Ting, Wenlee.
  Multinational risk assessment and management.

  Bibliography: p.
  Includes index.
  1. Risk management—Political aspects.
2. International business enterprises—Management.
3. Investments, Foreign—Political aspects—Evaluation.
4. Political stability—Evaluation.   5. Country risk.
I. Title.
HD61.T56   1988   658   87-5970
ISBN 0-89930-175-4 (lib. bdg. : alk. paper)

British Library Cataloguing in Publication Data is available.

Library of Congress Catalog Card Number: 87-5970
ISBN: 0-89930-175-4

First published in 1988 by Quorum Books

Greenwood Press, Inc.
88 Post Road West, Westport, Connecticut 06881

Printed in the United States of America

The paper used in this book complies with the
Permanent Paper Standard issued by the National
Information Standards Organization (Z39.48-1984).

10 9 8 7 6 5 4 3 2 1

To Liyu, Michael, and Ralph

Contents

Illustrations

Tables

Preface

As international trade and investment proliferated over the previous decades, the specter of country risks has always pervaded the consciousness of the international decision makers. Risks in all their manifestations—political, technological and cultural—stood as perhaps the last psychological as well as practical barriers to further attempts at true globalization of business. As I was researching and doing business in the newly industrializing countries of Asia, I began to realize that many of the risk perceptions held by Western businessmen center on perceptions of a bygone era of political and ideological conflicts.

In many of the newly industrializing countries, East Asian as well as in Latin American, the wide range of relevant risks tends to stem from industrial policies, regulatory restraints and commercial restrictions imposed on foreign business. These restrictions are probably motivated more by rational industrialization and technological needs than by ideological considerations.

This book is therefore a tentative and preliminary attempt at "setting the records straight," especially for the international business decision makers in focusing on the relevant risks affecting their business activities abroad. The broader objective is to contribute, in a small and tentative way, to a better understanding of the approaches and paths that will lead us to what is perhaps a greater integration and globalization of international business.

I am greatly indebted to Elizabeth Guia, Masood Ariz, Charles Grover,

Ken Ang, Harold Edwards and David Wolf in providing research assistance at different stages of writing the book. Special thanks go to my wife, Liyu, for her support and valuable comments. As usual, the sole responsibility for any remaining errors in the book rests exclusively with this author.

Existing Approaches to Political Risk Assessment

The level of political consciousness of international business tends to fluctuate with major and dramatic developments such as wars, revolutions, insurrections, and other political conflicts. Corporate awareness of political risks in business, for instance, remained high with the most recent major wave of nationalizations and expropriations, particularly of extractive and natural resource projects in the late sixties and early seventies. This level of interest, however, has not been constant and has not always been matched by a commensurate level of effectiveness in risk analysis. The Iran and Nicaragua revolutions, especially the former, caught corporate planners unprepared. The lapse into a moment of unguardedness drastically rekindled intense attention among both the multinationals and the political risk analysts. Many dimensions of political risk analysis are now measured in terms of the Iran and Nicaragua watersheds. The post-Iran and post-Nicaragua era, therefore, saw a rapid growth in political risk analysis not only among academics, who are natural constituents of the subject, but also among government bureaucrats. This renewed interest sparked by Iran and Nicaragua turned many foreign and intelligence services officials into purveyors of instant risk assessments for anxious clients in Corporate America.[1]

The fixation on the two events overshadowed other positive as well as negative developments in the international risk horizon toward the early and mid-eighties. The post-Iran era also saw the development of less noticed events that forebode well for the health of international business. Developments such as the waning of the oil power of OPEC, the rise to prominence of newly industrializing Asia, and the gradual democratization of parts of Latin America all contributed favorably to the climate for international business. On the other hand, old problems, although temporarily abated, remained in suspended animation. The shaky international financial system, beset by the continuing debt burden and the surprising strength of the dollar, is a case in point. In other areas, the economic disruptions in many parts of sub-Saharan Africa and political turmoil in the Middle East, South Africa, and the Philippines will continue to loom significantly in the risk scenarios for the rest of the eighties and perhaps well into the nineties. The state of international political risk analysis seems to reflect and correlate with the ongoing risk developments. Just how they are doing this is the subject to which we now turn.

EXISTING APPROACHES: CONCEPTS, FRAMEWORKS, AND MODELS

The broad spectrum of political risk analysis ranges from political science-oriented approaches that remain on the broad conceptual level to empirical based forecasting services providing quantitative but largely subjective risk forecasts. This broad spectrum also includes other international business-oriented analyses appearing in the form of frameworks and models as well as a wide body of literature focusing on foreign exchange risks and management. A perspective on the wide-ranging approaches can best be provided by viewing them in terms of the "three plus one" categories of instabilities. The three major broad categories of risks faced by international business are political instability, policy instability, and exchange-rate instability; a fourth category is strategy instability.

Political instability is usually associated with drastic changes in the political regimes of host countries, including war, revolution, and other political turmoil. *Policy instability* refers to the uncertainties surrounding the host government's policies, especially those affecting international investments, such as exchange controls, local contents, and indigenization requirements. *Exchange-rate instability* refers to the firm's exposure to the various effects of foreign exchange fluctuations and the resulting loss of profitability. The fourth category is internal rather than external to the firm. It stems from the deliberate strategic decisions on the part of multinationals in constantly reviewing their investment portfolios in terms of profitability. This implies that a company may divest or withdraw from certain host countries on the basis of strategy or profitability considerations alone. Although such divestitures have essentially nothing to do with the host country's actions and solely reflect the firm's portfolio adjustments, they nevertheless constitute a source of uncertainties for the firm. A fifth category of risks can perhaps be postulated, although no satisfactory mechanism exists to deal with its analysis not to mention any possibility of assessment. This category consists of purely random occurrences such as the Union Carbide poison gas leak incident in Bhopal, India. Such a residual and chance occurrence cannot lend itself to any satisfactory analysis.

The following sections discuss the various approaches to risk analysis that correspond approximately to the first three "instabilities."

MACRO-SOCIOPOLITICAL APPROACHES

The macro-sociopolitical approaches focus on political instability as a major variable in risk analysis. Political events can shape and affect the development of economic and business conditions in host countries at basically two levels. First, they can drastically alter the prevailing system, especially when systemic upheavals such as those in Iran and Nicaragua establish entirely new environments. Second, in countries with somewhat less cataclysmic changes, the prevailing political structure and forces also directly and indirectly exert an influence on the general business environment. However, in this scenario, the linkages between political and business changes are somewhat more difficult to delineate. Nevertheless, in certain countries, it is apparently possible to identify the business ideologies inherent in the prevailing political structure of the host country, such as the attitudes to foreign investors that various contending factions espouse. In this case, it is still possible to project the resultant risk scenarios for international investors. For instance, the continuation in power of the reformist groups in mainland China would reinforce the current liberalizing trends in the investment and business climate. The causal process in the second scenario involving less drastic change is somewhat more likely to be on a continuum and therefore to allow more degrees of continuity for the risk analysts. The discontinuities in the more drastic change scenario, on the other hand, imply less accurate and less precise risk assessment.

In any event, the major premise of the macro-sociopolitical approaches to risk analysis is that the complex array of developments in the host country's sociopolitical environment leading to political instability tends to bring about expropriatory actions by the host government. The key "outcome" variable of most of these macropolitical approaches is thus the expropriation or other expropriatory acts directed at foreign business and investment.

A Note on Macropolitical Instability

A brief discussion about the dynamics of political instability would be helpful in providing a background perspective on the macro-sociopolitical approaches to risk analysis. Tensions and stresses leading to political instability in a host country result from a vast intertwining and interacting web of ideological, religious, racial, and economic factors. The competition among factions and groups espousing contending ideologies, religions, and economic views leads to a realignment and change in the country's balance of power and the mechanism of national control. The emergent political structure essentially determines the risk scenarios for the foreign investors.

Based on the conventional perspective, the traditional source of political tension in most developing Third World countries is ideology, particularly the left versus the right. The rise of Marxist-oriented states are cases in point. In other situations, most notably in Iran, the source is a combination of religious factors and conflicting perceptions about the desirability and speed of economic modernization. The rapid course of modernization initiated by the shah's regime clashed with the more nationalistic and traditional values of the Moslem clerics. The modernization-versus-tradition issue was thus exacerbated by factionalism arising from religious and personal differences. The ensuing competition for power and control between the modernizing and traditional elements led ultimately to the final convulsion and the fall of the shah's regime. In the majority of countries, however, the stresses brought about by the conflicts between opposing forces are often resolved through relatively less catastrophic means.

In Iran and in other areas, the emergent pattern of political development is now superimposing new dimensions on traditional global geopolitics. The two major new dimensions, the resurgence of religious fundamentalism and separatism, are beginning to blur the conventional ideological division between left and right. For instance, it is difficult or perhaps even inappropriate to label the revolutionary regime in Iran as left or right. Factional conflicts and separatist movements such as those of the Catholics in Northern Ireland, the Basque in Spain, the Moslem insurgents in the Philippines, and the religious fratricide in Lebanon are other cases in point. Resurgent fundamentalism and separatism are now increasingly the factors behind political instability. Even in the context of the old ideological division, the implication of recent developments is not altogether unambiguous for international business. Conventional wisdom tends to characterize leftist revolutionary changes as inherently unstable and hostile and hence posing potential risks for international investment. However, the recent experimentation by socialist countries, from China to Mozambique, to attract foreign investment and encourage private enterprise is increasingly complicating the ideological line of division.

The Macro-sociopolitical Models

The macro-sociopolitical (MSP) models essentially offer a macrolevel perspective of risk analysis. The focus is on the broad social, ideological, and economic forces in the host country and their causal relationships with the dynamics of political instability. The MSP models are therefore based on political instability as a key variable in risk analysis. Although some attempts are made to establish a certain degree of linkage between political instability and business variables, the emphasis remains on political dimensions. The key relationship in most of these models is to express the political instability dimension as a function of various economic, ideological, and social forces. The MSP models and frameworks provide a relatively comprehensive and broad overview of the potential for change and instability in the host country's systems that may result from various social, ideological, and economic forces. Whereas some MSP models tend to focus on this key relationship between the environmental factors and political instability, others are further developed in terms of relating political instability to risks such as expropriation. Figure 1.1 depicts the generic paradigmatic outline of most MSP models.

FIGURE 1.1
Generic Paradigm of Macro Socio-Political Models

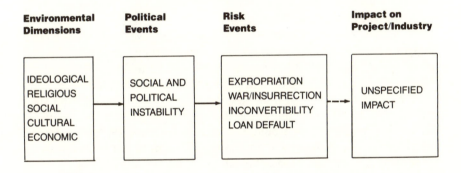

Insensitivity to the differential impact of risks. The MSP models are detailed and well conceptualized in explaining the causal process between the macroenvironmental factors and the resultant political instability, reflecting an expert grasp of political-science-type relationships. Also, there is often no serious conceptual problem in postulating some relationship between political instability and the likelihood of expropriation. However, the major shortcoming of the MSP approaches is the lack of specificity either in relating the impact of expropriation or the effect of political instability to actual investment projects or business ventures. There is very little or no analysis of the linkage between either the expropriation variable or the instability variable and specific business or industry types. Many crucial questions are left unanswered. For instance, does expropriation fall equally on all projects or on specific ones? Given available evidence suggesting that risk impact is often industry- or even firm-specific, one can appreciate the problems presented by the MSP models.

Even the frequently taken-for-granted relationship between instability and expropriation is now increasingly becoming questionable given the emerging global geopolitical matrix noted previously. For instance, revolutionary societies are often characterized as politically unstable and therefore adverse to international investment. "Revolutionary" Nicaragua, for example, still hosts many of the best-known multinationals. This unexpected coexistence, if not cooperation, between revolutionary Marxism and multinational business extends to Marxist Angola and Mozambique. In Angola, for instance, Western multinational corporations (MNCs) such as Chevron, Gulf, and Conoco run oil exploration and agricultural projects under the unlikely protection of Cuban and Marxist Angolan troops while the country as a whole has instituted a policy of attracting foreign investments.[2]

One of the major criticisms against these approaches is that they are too broad and general to provide linkages to any actual impact on business activities and operations. In short, the models are silent on how system instability leads to actual risks for the firm's operations. They assume that each firm or even each project in a given host country faces the same level of risks. Although one of the models discussed in this section does attempt to integrate macrorisks into management decision making, most stop short of offering any basis for firm- or project-level decision making. As one noted observer commented, "Political scientists have done considerable research on the subject of political instability in the form of revolutions. But they still disagree significantly on how to define political stability or instability, on how to measure the phenomenon and on what are the causal forces. Furthermore, the political scientists' principal focus of interest is not likely to produce the answers needed for international business."[3]

Despite some of the reservations enumerated above, many of the political science-oriented approaches contributed significantly to our present understanding of political risks. However, the fact remains that no single discipline is or will be able to provide a complete explanation of the political risk phenomenon entirely by itself. Current and future conceptual advances in the field will have to depend on the insights and contributions of many disciplines including that of political science.

The following sections examine some selected and more noteworthy examples of the political science-oriented approaches. Although some of these approaches may claim to be international business-oriented or multi-disciplinary approaches, the variables they deal with, their macrolevel treatment of the phenomenon, and their common focus on political instability or its equivalent would be sufficient for them to be classified as political science-inspired approaches.

Johnson Uneven-Development/National Power Model

Howard C. Johnson's risk-analysis model is based on a theory of power competition and national development.[4] The model, therefore, falls under the category of a macro-sociopolitical approach to risk analysis. His central hypothesis is that political risk, expropriation in his example, stems essentially from the interactions between uneven development in a country and its national power. Uneven national development was expressed as a function of five major environmental factors: political development, social achievement, technical advancement, resource abundance, and domestic peace. The author theorized that uneven development results from the difference and inconsistency between the levels of progress in the five environmental areas. The power dimension represents the combined economic, military, and diplomatic powers of the country. In terms of the generic MSP paradigm in Figure 1.1, the equivalent measure for "political instability" in Johnson's model is his key variable for uneven development. Therefore, in relating political instability (uneven development) to environmental factors, the author's approach is similar to that in other MSP models that are discussed in the ensuing sections.

In addition, the Johnson model examines the sociopolitical processes underlying the five major environmental dimensions. Although the model shows the direction of the relationship of these processes to the environmental variables, there is no specific exposition of the nature of the relationships. The underlying sociopolitical processes are the following:

Identity—National integration and feeling of common bond

Legitimacy—The general acceptance of a central government

Penetration—The authoritative effectiveness of the government

Participation—Involvement and influence in the process of representative government

Distribution—The sharing of economic and political resources among the population.

Country scores were computed for both the uneven-development and power dimensions. A 2 × 2 matrix was then developed by superimposing the uneven-development scale onto the power-dimension scale. The sample countries are then classified into the four resultant quadrants according to their scores on the uneven-development/power scales. The four categories are weak/even, weak/uneven, strong/even, and strong/uneven. *Weak/even countries* are characterized as stable, traditional, agrarian societies; *weak/uneven countries* are inherently unstable since those countries are at earlier stages of economic and political development. Coups and revolutions often accompany the rapid societal changes in the weak/uneven countries. *Strong/even countries* are usually the mature industrialized countries with relatively stable sociopolitical environments.

The highest probability of political risks exists in the *strong/uneven countries* because of the inconsistent progress among the major sociopolitical variables. Political aspirations often fall far short of economic and technical advances and hence generate a greater tendency of perceiving the foreign investors as scapegoats for the national frustrations.

Probability estimates of expropriation risk, based on relative frequencies of occurrence in the sample countries, were developed for the four quadrants. Countries in the strong/even and weak/even groups show the lowest probability of expropriation whereas a moderate level of expropriation probability exists for weak/uneven countries. Strong/uneven countries show the highest relative probability of expropriation. The Johnson model is one of the macro-sociopolitical approaches that provides "objective" probability estimates of expropriation according to country characteristics. Johnson's exposition also suggests an interesting approach to company-risk assessment. He classified political risks as three types:

Business risk—Negative variation in operating income resulting from both market and nonmarket risks.

Financial risk—Negative variations in income available for profit remittances and debt-service payments outside the country, that is, transfer risks such as foreign exchange controls and other repatriation restrictions.

Catastrophic risk—Termination of business by direct government actions such as expropriation, nationalization, confiscation, or forced divestment.

The author suggested that evaluation of political risks should be conducted on a sequential basis. For instance, cash-flow adjustment should first be done for nonexpropriation business risks, followed by an adjustment for expropriation risks; finally, an evaluation is performed for transfer risks. This is justified by the fact that nonexpropriation sets the necessary precondition for transfer or repatriation risks.

Johnson accomplished a comprehensive, relevant, and systematic analysis to arrive at his risk model, especially in terms of his examination of the sociopolitical processes underlying the environmental variables. Again, like the other MSP approaches, his model stops short of addressing the relationship of the risk event to its specific impact on firm-level decisions, although an unconnected section on cash-flow adjustment was included in his exposition.

Knudsen National Propensity-to-Expropriate Model

Knudsen's model is based on an "ecological" or environmental approach and could thus be classified as an MSP-oriented model. Like the Johnson model, it makes an attempt to link political instability to the propensity to expropriate. Both the Johnson and Knudsen models, therefore, go one step beyond the Political System Stability Index (PSSI) framework that is discussed in the next section. Knudsen's approach is based on a statistical study of a sample of Latin American countries, and it examines several national or "ecological" dimensions that were hypothesized to measure a country's frustration level.[5] The propensity-to-expropriate model is shown in Figure 1.2.

FIGURE 1.2
The National Propensity to Expropriate Model

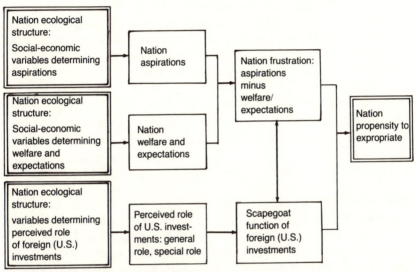

Note: Double line denotes measurable entities

Source: Harald Knudsen, "Explaining the National Propensity to Expropriate: An Ecological Approach," *Journal of International Business Studies,* Spring 1974, p. 54. Reproduced with permission.

Knudsen hypothesized that the interactions between the country's frustration level and a substantial presence of U.S. investment will explain its national propensity to expropriate. The national frustration level is derived from the difference between what the author conceptualized as the nation's level of aspirations and the level of welfare and expectations level. These levels were postulated to represent the nation's ecological structure. Proxy socioeconomic variables such as literacy rate, newspaper readership, natural resource endowment, infant mortality, health care, and per capita GNP were used to measure the levels of aspirations, welfare, and expectations. The author, however, did not adequately justify his selection of the various socioeconomic variables as a measure of these ecological levels. An additional dimension was derived to measure the perceived role of U.S. investment. The implication of Knudsen's model is that the country's frustration level will be high when its welfare and economic expectations are low in relation to its aspirations level. A high national frustration level coupled with a high degree of presence of foreign investment suggests that foreign investment tends to be a scape-goat for national frustration and hence may be expropriated.

Statistical procedures involving factor analysis and discriminant analysis were used to analyze the data. The analysis was able to "discriminate" or classify correctly nineteen of the sample of twenty-one countries into predetermined groups of countries that were ranked according to their propensity to expropriate. The following list shows the group of countries that were classified on the basis of 1968-71 data on observed or actual propensity to expropriate U.S. investment, and the model was able "correctly" to place nineteen of the twenty countries:

High propensity to expropriate: Chile, Bolivia, Peru

Medium/high propensity to expropriate: Guyana, Mexico, Venezuela

Medium/low propensity to expropriate: Colombia, Ecuador, Guatemala, Panama

Low propensity to expropriate: Argentina, Brazil, Costa Rica, Dominican Republic, El Salvador, Haiti, Honduras, Jamaica, Nicaragua, Paraguay, Uruguay.

In terms of the generic MSP paradigm, the "political instability" equivalent in Knudsen's model is his national frustration level. Similarly, his ecological dimensions of the aspirations, welfare, and expectations levels correspond to the environmental forces in the generic paradigm. It is one of the MSP models that had managed to establish empirical substantiation for the model relationships through the use of statistical procedures. In short, methodologically, the author did an excellent job in explaining the relationship of political dynamics to expropriation based on a region-specific sample (Latin America). Although he succeeded in his attempt to link expropriation with political instability as measured by the level of national frustration, the model still falls short of industry-specific political risks. The model was appropriate during an era when nationalistic Latin American countries fearing U.S. domination were perceiving that their sovereignty was at bay. However, given that expropriation is often selective and industry-specific, it therefore lacks an explanation of risks on a microlevel, that is, the act of expropriation directed at specific investment projects of multinationals.

Haendel-West-Meadow's Political System Stability Index

The Political System Stability Index, developed by Dan Haendel, Gerald T. West, and Robert G. Meadow, was intended to be a "quantitative" framework for measuring political risks.[6] It is one of the earlier large-scale models that use objective numerical data rather than attitudinal data as indicators of political risks. Since it deals with macropolitical events, the PSSI belongs to the macro-sociopolitical approach to risk analysis. The framework's key variable is the political system stability index (see Figure 1.3). The PSSI is

FIGURE 1.3
Formation of Political System Stability Index (PSSI)

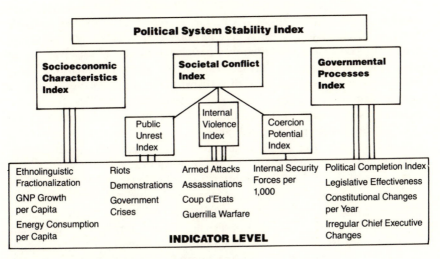

Source: Dan Haendel, *Foreign Investments and the Management of Political Risk.* Boulder, Co.: Westview, 1979, p. 108. Reproduced with permission.

formed from three major component indices: the country's socioeconomic characteristics index, a societal conflict index, and a governmental processes index. The societal conflict index, in turn, is composed of three subindices: the public-unrest index, the internal violence index, and the coercion-potential index. Each of these major component indices are measured by fifteen underlying indicators: ethnolinguistic factionalization, per capita GNP growth, and per capita energy consumption (socioeconomic index); riots, demonstrations, and government crises (public-unrest index); armed attacks, assassinations, coup d'etats, and guerrilla warfare (internal violence index); internal security forces per thousand people (coercion index); political competition, legislative effectiveness, constitutional changes per year, and irregular chief-executive changes (governmental processes index). Data on the fifteen indicators are obtained from published secondary sources such as yearbooks, government documents, and political data banks.

A few interesting variables are worth mentioning. The relationship of the per capita energy-consumption variable to system stability appears to be ambiguous. Although this variable is a relevant indicator of risk in terms of the country's ability to supply sufficient amounts of energy for economic growth, the PSSI did not distinguish between domestic and foreign sources of energy supply. If foreign sourcing constitutes a predominant proportion of the energy usage, the system's stability would be exposed to greater risk. On the other hand, a greater proportion of domestic sourcing would imply a more secure system stability. The inclusion of the "internal-security-forces per-thousand" factor as an indicator of the coercion level and in turn the societal conflict index appear to be highly validated by actual events in unstable dictatorial regimes. A case in point is Iran before the fall of the shah. The country at that time was permeated almost at all levels by the shah's secret police, the Savak. This shows that the intensity of the repression level seems to vary directly with the explosive potential of a regime toppling over. Apart from one or two other variables, the PSSI is generally sound and in accordance with the prevailing wisdom of the political science approach to risk analysis.

The PSSI, in terms of its structure, conforms generally to the generic MSP approach shown in Figure 1.1. Its political system stability index is the equivalent of the political instability variable in the generic MSP paradigm, whereas its component indices (socioeconomic, societal, and government processes) are the equivalent environmental variables. One of the major shortcomings of the PSSI is the absence of any linkage of the system-stability index to risk variables. The failure to address how system stability or instability is related to risk for international business and investors results in its lack of practical applicability for risk assessment and management. In short, it is silent on what happens after it has measured political system stability and fails to suggest how the decision maker should proceed with this information. In addition, the PSSI, unlike the Knudsen's model discussed in the previous section, is not validated by any appropriate statistical procedures despite its claim of being quantitative in approach Although the framework is intuitively appealing and generally conforms to the conventional wisdom of political science, the inclusion of variables and the postulated relationships have not been empirically tested. The PSSI would therefore be appropriate for an initial screening of potential host countries rather than for precise industry-level risk analysis.

Other Political Stability Indexes and Measures

Various studies of political instability have been developed by political scientists and international relations scholars that were not intended for international investment decisions. They belong to that class of political risk approaches that are purely political science both in focus and purpose without the pretense of having any international business implications. However, given the availability of this large body of both conceptual and empirical work that has been done on foreign political behavior and international politics, the relatively new discipline of political risk analysis can readily borrow and integrate the results of this work into risk assessment. Some of the more prominent examples range from comprehensive studies of international politics such as Charles A. McClelland's World Event Interaction Survey and Current World Stress Studies, which monitored both intra- and international threats situations, and Edward Azar's Conflict and Peace Data Bank to political instability measures studies such as the Banks and Textor measure and the Feierabend measure. The Banks and Textor and the Feierabend political studies provided the conceptual foundations for many of the political risk models that were developed for international business.[7]

The Bank and Textor measure classified governmental stability into four categories of degree of stability on the basis of a number of factors measuring changes in the institutions of government. Feierabend's political instability measure was developed from a list of thirty political risk events weighted according to their degree of destabilization. These risk events include strikes, riots, demonstrations, arrests, assassinations, executions, terrorism, sabotage, guerrilla warfare, coups d'etats, and revolts. It was seen earlier that the Political System Stability Index, a large-scale quantitative study discussed in the preceding sections, used many of the indicators of political stability that are similar to the Feierabend's variables. However, it seems apparent from this brief discussion that political instability measures by themselves are severely limited in any potential application to international business decision making. Many business people and managers are not trained to interpret the implications of such measures for decision making. In addition, they obviously do not offer any specific guidelines for project or firm-level investment decisions.

INTERNATIONAL BUSINESS-RISK ANALYSES

International business-risk approaches are more specific to international business decision making in both their focus and purpose. Risk-analysis studies that can be classified as being international business inspired consist of conceptual paradigms, risk-classification frameworks, decision-making-based approaches, and empirical based risk-forecasting approaches.

Robock's Macro and Microrisk Dichotomy

One of the earlier conceptual advances in the discipline of political risk assessment was the distinction between "micro" and "macro" risks proposed by Stefan Robock. Robock categorized political risks into macro and microrisks.[8] *Macrorisks* refer to general political events and government actions that tend to be broad and pervasive, such as regime changes, revolutions, warfare, and sectarian conflicts, and which broadly affect all foreign investment or business operations. *Microrisks* are those actions and events that selectively affect certain fields of investment or business activities. Distinguishing microrisks from macrorisks is an important step in recognizing that most political risks are industry- or project-specific. Expropriations in the seventies, for example, were mainly directed at extractive industries, whereas manufacturing projects are less vulnerable. This distinction allows a more precise identification and hence assessment of the risks relevant to a particular foreign enterprise in the host country.

Robock also suggested that at any time it would be possible to rank types of business activity and investment projects according to their degree of vulnerability to political risks. Extractive industries, especially in petroleum and metals, public utilities, and financial services tend to top the list in terms of being most vulnerable to political risks. These fields of business are characterized by their perceived lack of value-added contribution to the local economy. On the other hand, a manufacturing project, particularly a high-technology one, tends to be perceived as contributing more to the economy in skill and technology transfers.

It was noted that vulnerability to micropolitical risks are constantly changing and that they are dynamic. Even manufacturing projects could be subject to increasing vulnerability over time as the local firms begin to accumulate capital and gain management and newly acquired technical know-how. The expanding role of the indigenous firms in the same industry would begin to erode any initial technological and managerial advantage the foreign firm might originally possess. A strategic implication suggested by this phenomenon for multinational firms is to keep ahead of local competition by continuously injecting new technology.

Simon's Risk-Classification Framework

The macro-microrisk dichotomy was recently extended and refined by Jeffrey Simon into a more general and comprehensive risk-classification framework.[9] Besides making the "macro" and "micro" distinction, he distinguished between whether the source of the risk is internal or external. In additon, both macro and microrisks are in turn subdivided into societal related and governmental related risks. This results in an eight-cell classification scheme (see Figure 1.4). Simon's multidimensional classification scheme clarifies some of the previous confusion in defining risks and allows a more exact focus both on the nature of the risk events as

FIGURE 1.4
A General Framework for Political Risk Assessment

	Macro		Micro	
	Societal-related	**Governmental-related**	**Societal-related**	**Governmental-related**
Internal	Revolution Coup d'etats Civil war Factional conflict Ethnic/religious turmoil Widespread riots/terrorism Nationwide strikes/protests/boycotts Shifts in public opinion Union activism	Nationalization/expropriation Creeping nationalization Repatriation restrictions Leadership struggle Radical regime change High inflation High interest rates Bureaucratic politics	Selective terrorism Selective strikes Selective protests National boycott of firm	Selective nationalization/expropriation Selective indigenization Joint venture pressure Discriminatory taxes Local content/hiring laws Industry-specific regulations Breach of contract Subsidization of local competition Price controls
External	Cross-national guerilla warfare International terrorism World public opinion Disinvestment pressure	Nuclear war Conventional war Border conflicts Alliance shifts Embargoes/International boycotts High external debt service ratio International economic instability	International activist groups Foreign MNE competition Selective international terrorism International boycott of firm	Diplomatic stress between host and home country Bilateral trade agreements Multilateral trade agreements Import/export restrictions Foreign government interference

Source: Jeffrey D. Simon, "Political Risk Assessment: Past Trends and Future Prospects", Columbia Journal of World Business. Fall 1982, p. 67. Reproduced with permission.

well as the probability of these events impacting on the firm's assets and operations. For instance, his microgovernment-related internal risks provides a useful delineation for industry- and project-specific risks and opens the way for a more specific integration of risk analysis into investment decision making. Although the inclusion of individual risk items—for instance, market-related risks like interest rate and inflation—may be questionable, the framework nevertheless provides a good workable basis for recognizing specific risks. Many of the previously discussed MSP approaches suffered from the shortcoming of dealing with only general macrorisks without being able to offer any specific guidelines on the nature of risk for different types of investment and industries.

In the context of his classification framework, Simon offered the following definition: *political risk* can be viewed as governmental or societal actions and policies, originating either within or outside the host country and negatively affecting either a select group of, or the majority of, foreign business operations and investments.[10]

Simon also suggested setting up a company-based political risk-assessment system to monitor both macro and microrisks. His proposal for such a system, which he called the "early-warning system," consists of an in-house structure that will be able to monitor both country-specific and industry-specific conditions. The early-warning system should also be able to process vast amounts of diverse economic and political information generated by the multinational's worldwide scanning capability and constantly to update and revise the rapidly changing conditions. The system's microrisk data are to be collected and processed by the company's network of foreign subsidiaries in the respective host countries while corporate headquarters will perform a separate macrorisk assessment. Both macro and microassessment are then coordinated and correlated to see if they are mutually reinforcing. Inconsistencies between the macro and microassessments are then reconciled by revising the data and analysis. Simon suggested that a unit at corporate headquarters should be given the responsibility for the early-warning system and its functions in coordinating, analyzing, and disseminating the risk forecast to the different divisions concerned.

Decision-Making-Based Approaches

Robert Stobaugh's probability framework is one of the earlier decision-based approaches to risk assessment. He surveyed forty international firms about their assessment of foreign investment climates and then classified the corporate decision process into (1) go-no go, (2) premium for risk, (3) range of estimates, and (4) risk analysis.[11]

The "go-no go" approach reduces the entry decision to one or two more visible variables. For instance, the company might approve or reject an investment in country X on the basis of its imminent currency devaluation or some major economic disruption or political upheavals such as a coup. The premium-for-risk approach is more rigorous. The decision criterion is that the proposed investment projects in countries with poor investment climates should be capable of producing higher return on investment (ROI) than comparable projects in countries with better investment climates. Stobaugh found that some of the firms' methods in country evaluation and determination of the amount of premium to add on to the required rate of return ranged from subjective and informal to a formalized rating scale for ranking the countries. Normally, a risk premium of about 4 to 5 percent is added on to the required after-tax ROI. The major problem with the premium-for-risk approach is the assumption that the degree of risk is constant or uniform over the investment horizon of the project. It therefore ignores the timing of the differential risk impact in different years of the project.

Two more "sophisticated" approaches are the range-of-estimates approach and the risk-analysis approach. In the range-of-estimates approach, major factors that will affect the project's profitability are identified. The decision maker then assesses and estimates their values over the time horizon of the project, and a resultant cash flow based on these estimates is computed. Sensitivity analysis of the cash flow can then be performed by using a range of estimates for each of these variables. Some of the variables that are commonly used to adjust the cash flows include income tax rates, depreciation-allowance rates, loan cost and availability, exchange controls, and currency fluctuations. The range-of-estimates method of adjusting the project's cash flow allows a more precise and accurate assessment of foreign investment risks.

The risk-analysis approach is based on an application of the probability theory. The technique essentially consists of developing a Bayesian type of conditional probability "decision tree" for the occurrence of a risk in the target country. The approach consists of arriving at the probability of different outcomes under various assumptions of certain political events occurring in the host country. Conditional probability "branches" are developed for each of the risk events. For example, the probability that the new regime will be left wing is 0.600. If the new regime is left wing, there is a 0.500 probability that the plant will not be nationalized, whereas if the new government is right wing, there is a 0.800 probability that the plant will not be nationalized. In the right column, the summary outcome for each branch is obtained by multiplying all of the probabilities along the branch. In addition, the outcomes for each event can be regrouped to obtain the overall probability for that event. For example, the overall probability of the plant not being nationalized is 0.810. Although the assignment of explicit probabilities contributes to more precise decision making than informal hunches by the analyst, the approach is still based on the subjective probability distribution or risk-preference function of the decision maker.

Other approaches that directly integrate risk analysis into decision making include the application of game theory to risk assessment and forecast and the modifying of conventional capital budgeting procedures to take into consideration the political risks. In the game-theory application, Michael P. Sloan suggested the use of what he termed the "multiple political futures" technique. This method involves developing an information bank of multiple future political-economic scenarios to evaluate a series of investment strategies. A game-theory type of decision matrix of expected profit is developed by cross-tabulating the proposed strategies with several projected future political-economic scenarios. The decision maker can then use game-theory criteria such as the maximin or minimax solutions to arrive at optimal investment strategies. Sloan suggested that the large-scale processing of data necessary to evaluate as many as three thousand political-economic future scenarios is now made feasible by the use of computers.[12]

Of the many decision-based approaches to risk analysis, the most widely mentioned is the integration of risk analysis into capital budgeting procedures. Although risk-adjusted capital budgeting methods are addressed in greater detail in Chapter four, a brief survey of these procedures is presented here. The capital budgeting adjustment methods include but are not limited to the following: adjusting the projected cash flow of the project, adjusting (usually increasing) the discount rate, shortening the payback period, adjusting the cost of capital to reflect local interest rates, and adjusting the exchange rates for local currency conversion.

Discount-rate adjustment appeared to be the most widely applied method of dealing with political risks. This is essentially similar to the premium-for-risk technique discussed by Stobaugh in the previous section. The discount rate is adjusted upward by adding an arbitrary risk premium to the required rate of return for foreign projects to reflect the additional political risks of the host country. As stated, this approach assumes that risk is constant or uniform over the time horizon of the project. Adjusting the discount factor upward therefore does not take into account the differential impact of the uncertainties on each period's cash flow. Furthermore, the choice of a risk premium that is, the magnitude of upward adjustment of the discount factor, is arbitrary. A similar approach regularly practiced by firms in their foreign investment assessment is to vary the cost of capital, usually through the use of a higher cost of capital or the cost of capital of the host country in question. Varying or shortening the payback period is another popular technique for evaluating foreign investment risk. Like discount-factor adjustment, an arbitrary variation of the payback period assumes that risk is constant over the project's life. The practical advantage of these two approaches is that they are straightforward to use and are less time consuming than other more precise risk-evaluation methods.

Conceptually, the most accepted approach is cash-flow adjustment. This method allows a more precise consideration of the particular impact of each period's risk on the cash flow. It also requires a greater and more careful search for information regarding the projected cash flow. However, considering the fact that vast amounts of resources have to be committed to foreign investment ventures, the additional time and effort required for cash-flow adjustment seems justified. In a variation of this technique one computes the internal rate of return from the risk-adjustment cash flow. The difference between this risk-adjusted rate of return and the firm's normal required rate of return is then a measure of the magnitude of the risk premium. Other variations in capital budgeting technique to incorporate risks include the employment of projected exchange-rate estimates in adjusting cash flow. Regardless of the actual method used, capital budgeting procedures involving discounted cash-flow analysis are versatile enough to allow many variations of the standard methodology.

Surveys of firms over time showed an interesting pattern of risk adjustment in capital budgeting procedures. In a survey, it was found that 13 percent of the respondent U.S.-based multinational firms varied their cost of capital by using local costs and local prime interest rates, and about 32 percent of the firms reported varying the rate of return and payback period in their foreign investment evaluation. More recent surveys appear to confirm a similar pattern of risk adjustment in foreign investment assessment. The studies showed that half or more of the responding multinationals adjusted their discount rate by adding an arbitrary risk premium to the required rate of return on foreign projects. Among these firms, 30 to 40 percent adjusted their rate subjectively whereas about 44 percent either used a local weighted average cost of capital or some worldwide weighted cost of capital in determining the discount rate.[13]

Empirical Based Forecasting Services

Toward the late seventies, mainly as a result of the 1979 Iranian revolution, and into the early eighties, with the continuing political turmoil in Central America and elsewhere, intense interest in political risk assessment for international business rapidly gained momentum among the multinationals. Riding this crest of interest and attention on political risks, several companies began to establish or expand regular political risk-assessment services for corporate and other interested subscribers. Examples of these general surveys of investment climates include the following:

Business Environmental Risk Information (BERI)

Frost and Sullivan's World Political Risk Services (WPRS)

Business International's Country Assessment Service (CAS)

Euromoney Country Assessment Reports

International Country Risk Guide

The key features of these syndicated risk-forecasting services are their regular periodic updates and their quantitative approach. Frost and Sullivan's WPRS, for instance, surveys more than eighty countries every month, and Business International's assessment service surveys seventy-one countries twice yearly. Furthermore, all of them use numerical or alphabetical indices to rank countries on several macrolevel risk dimensions. For example, the WPRS employs a twelve-grade system, A + to D −, to rank countries on the three risk dimensions of finance, investment, and export risks. Similarly, Business International uses a one-hundred-point scale to rank countries on a weighted combination of risk factors.

Unlike the foregoing conceptually oriented approaches, the empirical risk-assessment approaches are not based on any conceptual foundations derived from the various relevant disciplines. Most of them consist of systematic collection and quantification of expert-generated data to produce the risk indices. The so-called expert data in the Business International case are generated by an international research staff and in the WPRS case, by canvassing a panel of experts in the government, business, and academic sectors. Their methodology essentially consists of "quantifying" what are in fact subjectively derived data and what therefore presents readers with an illusion of objectivity. The major achievement or failure, depending on ones perception, is the attempt to use a reductionist line of thinking in risk analysis. A mass of amorphous country data is mechanically reduced to a single number or alphabetical grade. As one observer noted, "Still others, and this includes perhaps a large number of companies . . . , enlist the aid of specialized services which attempt to provide numerical risk ratings on a country-by-country basis. This latter approach to political risk analysis is highly structured and its success of acceptance derives from our propensity to try to reduce our thinking to the absolute."[14]

The commentator further observed:

There is no proof that these highly organized approaches to risk taking enable the decision maker to function any better. However they do expand one's range of vision and because decision making remains a highly intuitive art, this contribution is important. . . . Forecasts which reduce selective probabilities to cold numbers may appear impressive, but this quantitative approach implies a degree of accuracy—and confidence—which may not be warranted. Moreover it contains the failing of not being able to distinguish between probabilities relating to specific industries. . . . the risk factor inherent in investment in natural resource would be far greater than investment in a project that is perceived locally as nonexploitative.[15]

Thus an additional criticism against the risk-forecasting services is their macrolevel analysis. A broad and general ranking of a country's investment climate or stability cannot take into account the variation in risk exposures of different types of investment. Various types of investment and even individual firms are exposed in fundamentally different ways to political risks. For instance, while petrochemicals companies were divesting from their investments in many countries in the late seventies, pharmaceutical and high-technology electronics firms were finding favorable investment climates in the same countries. A more detailed treatment of the syndicated risk-forecasting services and how they fit into corporate-risk assessment is presented in Chapter seven.

POLICY INSTABILITY: MICRORISK APPROACHES

The third major category of risks tends to focus more on the specificity of risks facing investment projects and business ventures. In other words, it provides at least some basis for drawing a certain degree of relationship between the risks themselves and their potential impact on a particular project. The macro-oriented approaches on the other hand, as noted, presume that the same risk, for example, expropriatory actions by the host government, falls identically on all projects. They stop short of making any distinction between the differential vulnerability of different projects to a given political risk.

Several recent approaches appear to have pursued a different perspective in risk assessment by emphasizing more the potential risk actions that have project-specific implications. Most of these micro-oriented risks stem from regulatory and policy changes made by the host government with respect to foreign investment projects and business ventures. Studies by Raymond Vernon (1980), Thomas Brewer (1981, 1983), Jeffrey Simon (1982), and Wenlee Ting (1985, 1986) focused on the host country's attitude, policy, and regulations affecting foreign investors. These approaches attempted to relate the host-country dimensions to specific investment projects.

The Vernon Obsolescing Bargain Factor

Raymond Vernon's significant contribution to risk analysis went beyond the usual macro-sociopolitical and economic environments to focus on the relative bargaining position between the multinational investor and the host country in terms of technological and managerial systems.[16] He proposed a scenario whereby the initial, considerable power and dominance of the multinationals are gradually eroded by changes in the international markets for capital, technology, and management expertise. The erosion of foreign investors' bargaining position, or the obsolescing bargain, stems from a general process of gradual deterioration in the investor's initial clearly defined technological and management positions. The foreign investor usually commences operation with 100 percent ownership and a decisive edge in technology and managerial expertise, but this leading edge begins to fade almost immediately. Changes in the world markets such as the increased availability of capital financing, widespread proliferation of technology, competition from other multinationals, and acquisition of managerial expertise by local nationals all have contributed to and accelerated the obsolescing bargain of the initial investment. As the local nationals gained managerial and technical expertise and with greater and easier access to technologies and capital made available by other multinational suppliers, pressures began to build on the investor to adjust to the new conditions. Some firms chose to maintain their competitive edge by upgrading and moving into more difficult technologies, whereas others acceded to unbundling pressures by the host country to dilute equity and management control and enter into more ambiguous arrangements. These arrangements included increasingly popular forms such as joint ventures, management contracts, and coproduction. Vernon noted that as the bargaining position of the firm began to deteriorate, the dangers (risks) to the investor were likely to increase even if the sociopolitical conditions of the host country remained unchanged.

In a recent study, Brewer appears to have confirmed this observation. He noted a lack of a strong and systematic relationship between political instability and policy instability.[17] In other words, the kinds of pressure and policy shifts brought on by the obsolescing phenomenon has very little to do with sociopolitical instability. Furthermore, contrary to common assumptions about developing countries, political instability may not lead to policy changes. It was speculated that politicians are more preoccupied with political happenings and tend to neglect less dramatic policy areas. It was also conjectured that a new political leadership may tend to maintain policy continuity in some sectors as a reassurance to the foreign investors. This type of microrisk scenario is a radical departure from the conventional sociopolitical approaches that tend to cast foreign investors and multinationals in a scapegoat role in times of political turmoil. This microrisk scenario is also a marked departure from Vernon's own earlier work, which highlighted the sovereignty-at-bay relationship between the host country and the then dominant multinationals.[18]

Other studies proceeded along similar lines of development. Taking off from Robock's macro/microdichotomy, Simon's classification framework attempts explicitly to identify and categorize risk events into macro and microdimensions, which then are further refined by additional internal/external and societal/government-related dimensions. The increased specificity of Simon's framework allows a more precise identification and hence an assessment of the risks. By focusing on the internal microgovernment-related risks, for example, a company would be in a position to monitor risks such as selective nationalization, selective indigenization, local content laws, and contract frustration that would have a special relevance for its project. In a more recent analysis, Simon proposed another classification of risk based on a macrolevel perspective. This more recent framework, which attempts to classify risk according to the stage of economic development (industrialized/developing) and the degree of openness in the sociopolitical system of the host country, falls far short of his original micro/macro and societal/governmental framework in providing a better understanding of political risks.[19]

The arbitrary division into industrialized and developing countries critically missed out on an important development in the global economic scene. The emergence of the newly industrializing countries and a new set of psychoeconomic dynamics invalidate the traditional thinking on the MNC/host-country interactions in terms of the industrialized/developing dichotomy. Many of these newly industrializing countries (NICs), especially in East Asia, have established industrial policies and investment-management systems that both facilitate and control the inflows of foreign investments. The new set of psychoeconomic attitudes, combined with an innovative investment-policy structure, produces an operating scenario that many multinationals have not hitherto had to face.

The Ting Obsolescing Demand Model

In a recent attempt to develop a risk-analysis framework, this author proposed an approach that takes into consideration both the obsolescing bargain phenomenon and the related trend of setting up industrial policy structures and investment-management systems among the NICs and, increasingly, other host countries.[20] This author noted that as many of the countries that are attractive for investment, especially the Asian NICs, rapidly industrialize and advance in most areas of their socioeconomic development, they acquire greater legal sophistication. Hence for a wide range of industrially aspiring countries, the tendency toward more outrageous behavior such as expropriation and confiscation may be almost inconceivable and highly unlikely. For these countries, firm- and industry-specific risks resulting from policy shifts are more relevant to the decision maker than sociopolitical inspired risks such as expropriation and confiscation. These risks, which stem from economic rather than political nationalism, may intensify as these countries' industrial aspirations become more ambitious, particularly in terms of mounting a competitive challenge to Japanese and Western multinationals in the global markets.

In light of the rapid rise of competitive economic nationalism and the waning of sociopolitical risks, I formulated a risk-assessment and management model focusing on industry- and company-specific risks, especially for firms operating in the newly industrializing areas of East Asia and Latin America.[21] The model is based on industrial policy dimensions and the obsolescing bargain concept. *Obsolescing bargain* is the perceived decline or deterioration in the bargaining position of a multinational firm in an investment project because of loss in technological edge and rising competition from other multinationals. In extending the generic obsolescing bargain concept, an obsolescing curve expressed in the form of a demand curve may then be defined for each investment. The curve would measure the perceived worth of and hence the demand for the project over time from the standpoint of the host country. The perceived worth of a project was postulated as a function of several key factors that are significant to the continued attractiveness of the investment project:

1. The industry in which the investment belongs
2. The number of local firms in the industry
3. The market share of the local firms in the industry
4. The project's local market share
5. The priority of the industry in national plans
6. The project's innovation and technological lead
7. The project's relative export performance

Although the list of the aforementioned factors is not exhaustive, it nevertheless constitutes some of the major determinants of how desirable the project is perceived to be from the point of view of the host country's decision makers. These major dimensions could therefore be conceived as demand-side determinants of the value of a specific investment project. Their magnitude would provide the investing company an indication of the worth of the project at any time. Since risk is frequently industry-specific, the type of industry in which the project belongs is a significant variable in setting the initial level of risk. Extractive projects and banks are perceived to be more exploitative than manufacturing, for example, which is seen as contributing more to the local economy.

The size of the role of indigenous firms in the same industry in which the foreign investor operates also affects the degree of risk exposure for the company. If the importance of the local firms increases in terms of numbers and market share, especially in countries that are rapidly industrializing, the greater will be the risk exposure and vulnerability for the multinationals as they and the local firms jostle for dominance in the industry. Similarly, the importance attached to a specific industry in the national development plan will influence the risk configuration for the multinationals that are operating or hope to operate in it. A case in point is Brazil's setting aside of its important computer sector as a "reserved market" for local Brazilian firms. Any existing foreign firm operating in such protected markets is subject to immense restrictions. The industry priority, however, is contingent on or moderated by the innovation and technological lead of the foreign multinational. Thus even if a high-technology industry like the computer industry is a high priority of the country's industrial policy and if only the foreign firms presently can adequately meet the industry's needs, the resultant risk will be lower. Indeed, one of the most effective risk-reduction strategies for foreign investors is continuously to inject a new infusion of technology into the industry to maintain a bargaining edge. Finally, the better the average export performance of the multinational in contributing to the balance of payments, the stronger will be its desirability to the host country. Many nations now include the export ratio of a project's output as a mandatory issue in preentry negotiations. Some foreign exchange-scarce countries are requiring as much as 80 percent of the investment project's output to be exported.

The combined effects of the above factors will cause the perceived worth of the investment project to decline over time. Curve A in Figure 1.5 represents the normal rate of obsolescence in the perceived project's value over time if no actions are taken by the firm to influence the rate of decline.

FIGURE 1.5
The "Demand" Curve for an Investment Project in the NIC Context

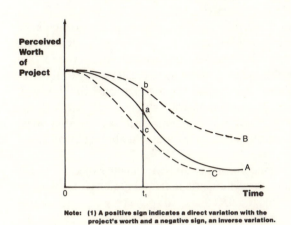

"Demand" Determinants[1]

1. Industry Type ($+, -$)
2. Number of Competing Local Firms ($-$)
3. Market Share of Local Firms ($-$)
4. The Project's Market Share ($+$)
5. Industry's Priority ($-$)
6. Project's Technology Lead ($+$)
7. Project's Balance of Payment Contribution ($+$)

Indirect "Demand" Determinants

8. Number of Multinationals of other Nationality ($-$)
9. Ease of Acquisition of Non-MNC Technology ($-$)
10. Corporate Image ($+$)
11. Compliance with Interface System ($+$)

Note: (1) A positive sign indicates a direct variation with the project's worth and a negative sign, an inverse variation.

Source: W. Ting, Business and Technological Dynamics in Newly Industrializing Asia (Westport, Connecticut: Quorum Books, 1985), p. 57. Reproduced with permission.

Thus at time t_1, allowing for normal attrition, the project will have a perceived value of a. In addition to the demand determinants already enumerated, a set of indirect host-country dimensions may influence the position and shape of the project's demand curve:

8. Number of multinationals of other nationalities in the same industry
9. Ease of acquisition of comparable non-MNC-based technology
10. Corporate image of the multinational
11. Compliance with the entry-management system of the host country

Factors 8 and 9 have important risk implications for an investment project. The available supply of competitive investments and technologies, as seen earlier, is rapidly multiplying for a host country. The increasing competition among multinationals from Japan, Europe, and the newly industrializing countries has immensely widened the range of options available to a recipient country. Just as a company may pursue a strategy of diversifying into different markets, host countries are increasingly seeking to diversify the national sources-of-technology supply. A broad range of competing offerings in technology and industrial processes are readily available from a wide variety of multinationals from different countries. As the host country's options multiply, the perceived value of an individual project may correspondingly decline since any previous advantage held by the investor will gradually be eroded by the upsurge in easily accessible alternate sources of technology. This trend is further compounded by the fact that many newly industrializing countries are beginning to enter into self-sustained indigenous technology development and innovation. All of these developments combine to diminish any strategic edge an individual investment may have in the host country.

Two additional factors, the firm's corporate image and its compliance with the entry-management system, affect the project's perceived worth and hence its vulnerability to risks. Both dimensions are well within the foreign investor's control, and certain actions taken by the company can serve to enhance the perceived value of the project. The multinational could project a good-corporate-citizen image and demonstrate strict compliance with the requirements of the entry-management system such as meeting local contents requirements, accelerating indigenization, and abiding by other tax and legal regulations.

Once the obsolescing demand curve for an investment project has been defined in terms of the major determinants, it can be used as a framework for preentry evaluation and negotiations and for postentry risk assessment and management. At the preentry stage, the firm can assess the magnitude of the role of the local firms in terms of the potential competitive and legal risks they pose for the project. A thorough evaluation of the project's technological edge relative to the local technological capability, the strategic importance of the industry the company is proposing to enter, and the export-contribution ratio can substantially improve the multinational's negotiation position. At the postentry stage, the framework can be used as a basis for monitoring the risk exposure and can suggest the necessary risk-management strategies. By projecting and tracking the eleven variables over time, an indication of the project's worth can be determined. Once the risk configuration for a specific investment is determined, a risk-management program can be formulated. I suggested that risk management can be classified generally as either integrative or defensive. *Integrative risk management* is basically a proactive risk-reduction strategy involving the management of some of the project's demand factors, especially through appropriate compliance and interactions with the entry-management system. *Defensive risk-management techniques,* on the other hand, involve the reduction of risks independent of the investment activities such as the purchase of political risk insurance coverage.

Referring to Figure 1.5, a successful integrative risk-management program can slow the decline in the perceived value of an investment project by shifting the obsolescing demand curve from A to B. Thus at time t_1, the project would have a higher perceived value of *b* instead of *a*, at the normal attrition rate. Essentially, to maintain the project's perceived worth at an above-normal attrition rate, the firm has direct control over several of the demand variables: the project's relative technological lead, the project's export-contribution ratio, the company's corporate image, and the degree of the firm's compliance with the entry-management system. An integrative risk-management program, therefore, would consist of a continuous infusion of technology and maintenance of a high export ratio to keep the project attractive; efforts to cultivate and enhance the company's image in the host country; appropriate compliance with entry-management requirements such as local content, indigenization, and equity sharing (planned divestment); and generally abiding with other rules and regulations.

Although the multinationals can, to the extent mentioned above, raise the perceived worth of an investment project by pursuing integrative risk-reduction techniques, forces beyond their control may tip the balance toward greater risk exposure. For instance, the rapidly expanding indigenous sector in the host country could intensify the competitive threats in the same industries that the foreign firms have invested in heavily. This and the ease of accessibility of the host country to a wide range of technologies further accelerate the erosion of any initial edge a project may have. It is a phenomenon that is already materializing in some sectors of the newly industrializing countries, especially in electronics with its rapidly decaying technologies, thus resulting in greater pressures and restrictions on the multinationals. Therefore, over time, a faster-than-average growth of the indigenous firms and accelerated local technological development will hasten the decline of the demand curve even more rapidly to C and bring about a higher degree of risk exposure for the foreign investors.

EXCHANGE-INSTABILITY APPROACHES

A separate category of risks for international business involves repatriating funds and the receipt of money from foreign sources. *Foreign exchange risk* refers to the uncertainty surrounding the act of bringing money back to the home country because of exchange instability. Such "repatriation" risks can be divided into the policy-related risks of exchange controls and restrictions imposed by the host country and the market-related risks of exchange-rate fluctuations. The former are generally accepted as political risks because they are the result of direct government action; they are also called inconvertibility risks. The latter category of risks is not normally considered a political risk since the risks relate to exchange-rate instability or fluctuations that stem predominantly from market forces. They nevertheless constitute a major source of host-country-associated risks and should be considered as an integral part of international risk assessment and management.

Exchange-Rate Fluctuations

The instability of a host country's exchange rate leads to a series of financial and payment-related risks or the risk of currency exposure for the multinational investor and trader. The exchange-rate uncertainties that give rise to these payment-related risks could stem from a variety of changes in the host country. Exchange-rate changes could be due to temporary disturbances in the country's balance of payments such as short-term trade imbalances and speculative capital movements. Exchange instability could also be a consequence of long-run and more basic changes in the host country's economy, including changes in interest rates, inflation, production, employment, and the foreign sector. For instance, countries facing chronic disequilibrium in their external balance such as serious payment deficits and excessive debt burdens habitually suffer from volatile exchange-rate fluctuations, and their currencies tend to decline constantly in value.

The financial and payment-related risks stemming from foreign exchange instability can be classified as economic, transaction, and translation exposures. Both transaction- and translation-related exposures deal with the phenomenon of relatively short-run exchange-rate changes. *Economic exposure,* on the other hand, refers to a possible impact on the future cash flow of the firm's subsidiary resulting from an unexpected variation in a country's exchange rates due to economic changes in the economy.

Transaction exposure refers to positive or negative changes in the settlement of an international transaction involving foreign exchange. It therefore consists of payment-related risks such as meeting contractual obligations involving international payments after a shift, both favorable and unfavorable, in the exchange rates has taken place. For example, an exporter expecting a ninety-day receivable denominated in a foreign currency will suffer a foreign exchange loss if that currency depreciates within ninety days. Conversely, if the foreign currency appreciates, the exporter will be in a position to profit from the foreign exchange gain.

Translation exposure refers to the accounting procedures of converting and consolidating the financial statements of a foreign subsidiary with those of the parent firm after a change in the host country's exchange rate. Translation exposure therefore relates to how foreign currency financial statements are to be reported in the consolidated financial statement. This process of translating foreign currency assets, liabilities, revenues, and expenses is a function of accounting rules and conventions of the home country. Presently, the FASB-52, which replaced the controversial FASB-8 in 1981, is the set of rules governing translation procedures for U.S. firms and is issued by the Financial Accounting Standards Board.[22] The old FASB-8, which was based on the monetary/nonmonetary or temporal method of translation, lost favor with the multinationals because of its inability to reflect the realities of a strong dollar and constantly shifting exchange rates. Under the monetary/nonmonetary method, all monetary items such as cash, accounts receivable, current liabilities, and long-term debt of the subsidiary are translated at current exchange rates, that is, those in effect at the time of reporting; all other nonmonetary assets and liabilities such as inventory, plant, and equipment are translated at historical rates or those in effect at the time of acquisition. In an era of a strong dollar, this has resulted in major currency-translation losses as foreign earnings and net assets denominated in a depreciated currency are converted back into dollars. The major objection to FASB-8 is the inclusion of these currency-translation losses (and gains) in the income statements of the parent company regardless of the actual performance of the subsidiary. Thus many multinationals have to report losses in the consolidated income statement arising from currency translation even though the subsidiary's performance is excellent.

To be more responsive to the needs of multinationals operating under a strong dollar and in a world of constantly fluctuating exchange rates, the current-rate method was adopted for FASB-52. Under the current-rate method, all assets and liabilities are translated at the current rate or the rate in effect at the balance-sheet date, and income-statement items are translated at a weighted-average exchange rate for the period. The current-rate method assumes all foreign assets and liabilities are exposed to the risk of currency fluctuations. FASB-52 removed the major complaint against FASB-8 in that currency-translation gains or losses are no longer included in calculating the net income of the parent firm. Instead, gains and losses from translating the subsidiary's balance sheet are reported as an adjustment item in the parent firm's equity account. Another new feature is the adoption of the concept of a "functional currrency" as opposed to the "reporting currency." To reflect the fact that a foreign subsidiary is relatively self-contained and generates its cash flow in specific operating environments, the financial performance of the subsidiary should be based on the currency of its primary operating environment or its functional currency. The functional currency will usually be the currency of the host country in question, and the reporting currency is the home or parent country's currency. The adoption of the all-current-rate approach and the use of a functional currency under the FASB-52 has contributed to preserving the local currency relationship of foreign financial statements even after translation. It also allows the company to concentrate on managing economic and transaction exposure instead of being preoccupied with balance-sheet hedging to avoid translation losses.

Even under the FASB-52, the impact of translation exposure on a firm's balance sheet is still an important consideration. The extent of translation exposure depends on the mix of the company's foreign assets and liabilities and on the extent of its hedging against currency shifts. Companies that have a large net-assets position and a significant amount of foreign currency receivables but little local liabilities such as sales subsidiaries and leasing and franchising operations are most vulnerable to currency exposures. Manufacturing subsidiaries with sizable local liabilities and foreign currency debts are more likely to end up as gainers when the dollar strengthens against the foreign currencies. Balance-sheet or operating hedging techniques include matching local assets and liabilities, incurring local currency debt when available, speeding up the collection of receivables, quickly repatriating the cash, and rewriting purchase contracts with payment denominated in weakening local currencies.

The favored technique in hedging against currency exposure is the forward-exchange market hedge. This involves the use of currency futures to cover any exposed asset or liability position. For example, to protect its receivables in French francs, a U.S. multinational could enter into a contract to sell an equivalent amount of francs forward for dollars at an agreed-upon price. Although the firm can be assured of a certain amount of dollar receipts if the franc weakens against the dollar, the company would have to forego any foreign gains if the dollar/franc exchange rate shifts favorably. Currency-futures hedging has recently expanded with the advent of long-term forward-exchange markets that have gone beyond the traditional one-year limit. Multinational companies and banks can now hedge against currency exposures for as many as five years into the future. Almost all international banks now routinely offer one- to five-year quotations for major world currencies. Some multinationals forward hedge in as many as thirty currencies with maturity periods ranging from one to five years.[23]

Even with all available hedging strategies, multinationals such as IBM, Monsanto, 3M, and Caterpillar still have realized substantial currency losses. In the case of IBM in one recent year, its equity rose marginally only because its retained earnings were slightly higher than the $763 million currency loss for that year. For other companies whose retained earnings were not sufficient to offset the huge currency losses, stockholders' equity actually declined. Furthermore, many multinational firms prefer not to hedge their currency exposures for a variety of reasons, particularly cost-benefit considerations. Some companies find that the cost of forward-exchange hedges in the form of contract fees paid to banks cannot justify the amount of protection bought. Others see foreign exchange exposures as a possible source of speculative gains if the rates move in their favor.[24]

Foreign Exchange Controls and Inconvertibility

The imposition of foreign controls by a host country is an accepted form of political risk that is in fact insurable by political risk insurance companies. Such inconvertibility risks arise because the host country is either unwilling or unable to convert local currency earnings into the multinational's home currency or into other hard currencies. Usually, the unwillingness stems from broader-based restrictive monetary policies of the country such as the constant need to regulate and restrict capital flights and other outward flow of funds. At other times many host countries are simply unable to meet demand for foreign exchange conversion because of a lack of sufficient foreign exchange reserves.

Exchange-control rules and regulations are imposed in many forms. In some countries like Venezuela and Belgium, a multi-tiered exchange-rate structure is instituted. Transactions contributing to the economic interest of the country are accorded favorable rates such as the importation of critical equipment and materials for a high-priority or export-oriented project, and more adverse rates are accorded to low-priority transactions like profit remittances of foreign firms. Other countries like Brazil impose progressive surcharges on profit and earnings remittances exceeding certain percentages of registered capital. Taiwan and South Korea, for instance, exercise the principle of matching the inflow and outflow of funds; that is, companies must earn the right to obtain foreign exchange by generating a compensatory amount of foreign exchange revenues through exporting, for example. In most of these examples, foreign exchange controls are instituted as part of the host country's industrial policies and entry-management systems. When exchange controls are applied selectively, they can be considered as microrisks that are project- or even firm-specific.

Even when foreign exchange conversion is allowed by exchange rules, the country may impose what is known as passive blockage or administrative impediments in the repatriation process. Passive blockage of repatriation may be part of a deliberate restrictive policy, or it may be simply the result of bureaucratic inefficiencies. Companies are required to wait in line in the government foreign exchange queue for repatriation approval, which may extend to several years. A variety of techniques are available in dealing with exchange controls and inconvertibility. They include negotiating to advance up the government-approval queue, enlarging the investment base on which profit repatriation is computed, arranging mutual currency swaps, or engaging in countertrade. The countertrade technique involves the acceptance of payment in the form of goods that can be sold later for freely convertible hard currencies.

TOWARD A DEFINITION OF POLITICAL RISK

Defining Political Risks

It is apparent that there is no general consensus on the definition of political risks. The terminological confusion stems from the widely diverse approaches to risk analysis, and its meaning therefore varies with the discipline and the approach on which it is predicated. Not the least of the definitional difficulties stems from the frequent confusion between an event that has the potential of becoming a risk and its uncertain impact on a business or investment outcome. A simple example illustrates this confusion. A change in the ruling regime of a host country is frequently considered a potential risk event that may or may not lead to an expropriation of an investment project. Here, an event perceived as a risk may be confused with an uncertain outcome, that is, the act of expropriation.

On the other hand, there are other more specific events that could directly cause an uncertain outcome for business activities. For instance, an imposition of exchange controls by the host government will directly block or delay the transfer of funds out of the country. Therefore, the degree of specificity of the risk event in relation to the business outcome is an important requirement in clarifying the definition of political risks. It was seen that the macro/microdistinction and its later refinements have to some extent been able to provide more specific linkages between the risk events and their impact on international business.

Another consideration in arriving at a definition of political risks has to do with the generic definition of the term itself. For instance, the conventional statistical approach is to define risk as the uncertainty surrounding the outcome of an event. Since risk in this context is viewed as a "variance" around an expected outcome, both positive variation (better than expected) and negative variation (worse than expected) in outcomes are considered permissible. Negative variation is known in financial circles as "downside" risk and is also the generally accepted layperson's version of risks.

The insurance industry usage of the term also considers risk as a negative variation. *Risk* in this context is defined as an exposure to a peril or a loss. The connotation is that of a negative outcome. Until recently insurance coverage was normally extended to "loss" risks and excluded speculative risks that might result in gains as well as losses. This partially explains why inconvertibility risks (possible losses) are insurable whereas foreign exchange fluctuations (possible gains and losses) are not insurable by political risk insurance companies. Both the statistical "variance" and the "loss" approaches to the definition of risk are used in this book.

Three dimensions are essential for arriving at a definition of political risks. First, since political risk for international business is both specific and selective in its impact, the person, firm, or project bearing the risks has to be specified. The risks facing a manufacturing investor are different from those facing an exporter or a lender. Second, a valid definition of political risk should also identify the source of the risk events in the host country. The three instabilities—political, policy, and exchange (inconvertibility)—could be used as a basis for classifying the risk events. Third, the definition of political risks should include only nonmarket risks, that is, risks that stem primarily not from market forces but from direct and overt government actions. In the light of these considerations, political risks can then be defined as: the nonmarket uncertainties or variation surrounding the desired business outcome (revenues, costs, profit, market share, continuation of the business, and so on) for an international project or a venture that may stem from instabilities in the host country's political, policy, and/or foreign exchange systems.

Types of Risk by Nature of the Business

The following sections examine types of risk according to the kind of business in which the international firm engages.

Investors. Multinationals, especially those with capital and technology-intensive manufacturing investments abroad, have to deal with a more complex array of risks in the host-country operating environment. These investors have both fixed assets and cash-flow exposures. Relevant risks would therefore include property damage sustained as a result of war and insurrections and partially compensated or uncompensated nationalization and expropriations. The multinational firm by virtue of its investment is also subject to the whole range of policy risks such as local contents requirements, indigenization, and joint-venture pressures. Finally, the investor has to face the inconvertibility or transfer risks of exchange controls and blockage of funds.

International lenders. International banks and other financial services firms have to be concerned with both financial assets and cash-flow exposures. Most international banks conducting international lending and borrowing activities focus their attention on the so-called country risks. *Country risks* are normally defined among banking circles as the exposure of the bank to a potential loss, when conducting international lending, that results from events in a particular country that are caused by the country's government and not by individuals or a private enterprise. Events that could lead to country risks, therefore, would include both economic as well as sociopolitical conditions. Country risks in terms of action taken by the sovereign borrower include the following:

Repudiation or default. Deliberate and intentional cessation of debt-service payments because of inability or unwillingness to pay. Repudiation or nonrecognition of the debt is extremely rare.

Technical default. Temporary failure, either due to unwillingness or inability, to meet one or several debt-service payments. The nonpayment is temporary and could be due to administrative delays, inefficiencies, or a temporary lack of foreign exchange.

Rescheduling. The lengthening of the term of the loan by lowering the annual repayments of principal and spreading the payments over a period of years longer than originally agreed. The originally agreed-upon interest remains in force.

Moratorium. The altering of the terms of the loan by allowing a grace period before the repayment of principal is resumed.

Blocked repatriation of funds. The firm is prevented from repatriating its funds because of the imposition of foreign exchange controls by the host government. These risks are also known as transfer risks. Normally, exchange risks due to fluctuations in the exchange rates are not considered a country or political risk since these risks stem from market forces and are not the result of arbitrary government actions.

All of the above risks facing the international lenders result in an opportunity loss as well as administrative costs in rescheduling or in enforcing the collection payments.

Exporters and traders. Relative to the international investors and lenders, the risks facing the international trader are more easily definable because they are confined to a narrower range. The usual risks include cash-flow exposures due to exchange controls and inconvertibility, contract frustration, bureaucratic inpediments, and perhaps damage to and confiscation of goods resulting from acts of war, insurrection, and military blockages. The following are definitions of some of the more frequently used risk-related terms in this book.

Risk events/factors. Any events or actions that could potentially result in a loss of assets, income, and/or any negative business outcome that necessitates the incurring of costs or expenditures. Risk events may or may not actually result in the incidence of risk impacting on a specific project or company.

Risk analysis. The general process of identifying, specifying, and describing the risk factors and risk events and attempting to relate these risk dimensions to their possible causes and to their possible impact on business activities. Risk analysis therefore includes most of the conceptual paradigms, framework, and models discussed in the foregoing sections.

Risk assessment. The general process of collecting, generating, and producing information and/or prescriptions, for business use, on the various risk factors and their relationships as determined in the risk analysis.

Risk measurement. The systematic coding and quantification of the collected risk data and information collected. Risk measurement, therefore, is an integral part of risk assessment. The measurement of the risk variables enable the risk-analysis frameworks and models to be "operationalized." Risk measurement could range from nonparametric scaling and ranking procedures to statistical and probability estimates.

Risk management. The general process of planning for, controlling, and reducing the impact of the incidence of risk as well as activities and events that could lead to the occurrence of the risk. Risk management, therefore, would include both preventive as well as remedial actions regarding the risk. Integrative risk management is preventive, and it includes actions taken to minimize or even prevent the possibility of the occurrence of the risk events. Defensive risk management is remedial, and it includes actions taken to minimize the impact of the incidence of risks.

Toward a General Political Risk-Assessment Framework

The earlier discussions show the extent and diversity of approaches to risk assessment and analysis. Consequently, there is no consensus or generally accepted conceptual approaches to risk analysis and assessment. Some of the reasons inhibiting the development of a general theory or even framework reside in the nature of the discipline itself as well as operational difficulties in applying the concepts. The range of risks facing international firms are so multifaceted in origin that any attempt at conceptualizing a general theoretical framework may be difficult. Herein lies the central paradox in political risk analysis: the need to consider the diversity of risks and the specificity of their impact at the same time. On the "supply" side of the discipline, the diverse background of political risk analysts would impede any consensus on a generally acceptable political risk theory. As was seen earlier, risk analysts, coming from a wide range of disciplines, include political scientists, economists, business-school professors, former diplomats and ex-foreign service officers, and sociologists. On the demand or user side of the equation, the need for specific decision-based information precludes the use of conceptually derived and academically oriented frameworks. As a result, unsatisfactory measures such as the arbitrary quantifying of subjective data are employed to bridge the concept-user gap. Thus these quantitative but macrolevel approaches are still lacking in their ability to meet the specificity need of international business decision making. All of the above factors have contributed to the impasse in the development of the political risk-assessment discipline.

Since the major objective is to improve international business decision making in terms of political risk assessment and management, it might be more appropriate to integrate the diverse approaches in terms of a user-based framework. By working backwards from the user's need rather than from any a priori conceptualizing, the various risk approaches could then be integrated into a firm- and project-specific decision framework. The suggested model should be able to incorporate the "three plus one" instabilities and should relate directly to the multinational firm's objectives in the host country. The objective function could be the maximization of the risk-adjusted net present value of the cash flow from the venture or project. The risk-adjustment process would follow from the risk-assessment and management analyses. The model could be divided into integrative and defensive risk assessment. The integrative sequence would focus on microlevel risks along the lines of the obsolescing demand model described earlier, whereas the defensive sequence would focus on macro-sociopolitical risks such as expropriation. A detailed formulation of the proposed model plus a political risk information system are presented in Chapter 5 as part of corporate risk assessment.

NOTES

1. The New York Times, August 7, 1983, p. F 23.

2. The Wall Street Journal, November 13, 1985, p. 34.

3. Stefan H. Robock, "Political Risk: Identification and Assessment," Columbia Journal of World Business, July-August 1971, p. 8.

4. Howard C. Johnson, "An Actuarial Analysis," in Richard Ensor, ed., Assessing Country Risk (London: Euromoney Publications, 1981), pp. 31-48.

5. Harald Knudsen, "Explaining the National Propensity to Expropriate: An Ecological Approach," Journal of International Business Studies, Spring 1974, 51-71.

6. Dan Haendel, Foreign Investment and the Management of Political Risk (Boulder, Colo.: Westview Press, 1979); Dan Haendel, Gerald T. West, and Robert G. Meadow, Overseas Investment and Political Risk (Philadelphia: Foreign Policy Research Institute, 1975).

7. See, for example, Arthur S. Bank and Robert B. Textor, A Cross-Polity Survey (Cambridge, Mass.: MIT Press, 1963); Ivo K. Feierabend and Rosalind L. Feierabend, "Aggressive Behavior in Politics, 1948-1962: A Cross-National Study," Journal of Conflict Resolution, Fall 1966, pp. 249-271.

8. Robock, "Political Risk," pp. 6-20.

9. Jeffrey D. Simon, "Political Risk Assessment: Past Trends and Future Prospects," Columbia Journal of World Business, Fall 1982, pp. 62-71.

10. Ibid., p. 68.

11. Robert B. Stobaugh, Jr., "How to Analyze Foreign Investment Climates," Harvard Business Review, September-October 1969, pp. 100-108.

12. Michael P. Sloan, "Strategic Planning by Multiple Political Futures Techniques," Management International Weekly, Vol. 5, No. 1 (Westport, Conn.: Concorde Group International), pp. 4-17.

13. Arthur Stonehill and Leonard Nathanson, "Capital Budgeting and the Multinational Corporation," California Management Review, Summer 1968, pp. 39-54; David J. Oblak and Roy J. Helm, Jr., "Survey and Analysis of Capital Budgeting Methods Used by Multinationals," Financial Management, Winter 1980, pp. 37-41; Vinod B. Bavishi, "Capital Budgeting Practices at Multinationals," Management Accounting, August 1981, pp. 32-35.

14. Robert E. Ebel, "The Magic of Political Risk Analysis," in Mark B. Winchester, ed., The International Essays for Business Decision Makers, Vol. 5 (Houston: The Center for International Business, 1980), p. 292.

15. Ibid., p. 292.

16. Raymond Vernon, "The Obsolescing Bargain: A Key Factor in Political Risk," in Winchester, International Essays, pp. 281-286; idem, Storm Over the Multinational: The Real Issues (Cambridge: Harvard University Press, 1977).

17. Thomas L. Brewer, "The Instability of Governments and the Instability of Controls on Funds Transfers by Multinational Enterprises: Implications for Political Risk," Journal of International Business Studies, Winter 1983, p. 147.

18. Raymond Vernon, Sovereignty at Bay: The Multinational Spread of U.S. Enterprises (New York: Basic Books, 1971); idem, Sovereignty at Bay after Ten Years," International Organization, Vol. 35, No. 3, Summer 1981, pp. 517-530.

19. Jeffrey D. Simon, "A Theoretical Perspective on Political Risk," Journal of International Business Studies, Winter 1984, pp. 123-143.

20. Wenlee Ting, "New Perspectives on Risk Assessment and Management in the Asia Pacific: A Host Country Dynamics Approach," Proceedings of the Academy of International Business South East Asia Meeting, Taipei, Taiwan, June 1986, pp. 778-795.

21. Wenlee Ting, Business and Technological Dynamics in Newly Industrializing Asia (Westport, Conn.: Quorum Books, 1985), pp. 51-59. See relevant sections on economic nationalism, macro and microrisks, risk management, and the obsolescing demand model.

22. Financial Accounting Standards Board, Foreign Currency Translation, Statement of Financial Accounting Standards No. 52, December 1981 (Stamford, Conn., 1981).

23. "A Forward Market's Long Reach," Business Week, November 23, 1981, p. 103.

24. "How Companies Are Coping with the Strong Dollar," Fortune, November 26, 1984, pp. 116-124.

2

Host-Country Dynamics: Policy, Technological, and Financial Risks

EMERGENCE OF HOST-COUNTRY DYNAMICS

Transformation in the International Risk Environment

The prevailing approach of international business to political risks can be viewed as being predicated on two underlying premises or scenarios. The first and still the more predominant scenario involves a presumption that both the multinational and the host country adopt a mutually antagonistic stance vis-à-vis the other. This stance could be appropriately termed the "sovereignty-at-bay" syndrome. The second scenario involves a presumption that a more technocratic and cooperative problem-solving attitude underlies the relationship between the multinationals and the host country. The latter scenario could be more appropriately termed the "host-country dynamics" approach. Multinational corporate-risk assessment adopts a perspective based on either or both of these scenarios.

The sovereignty-at-bay syndrome, following the scenario rendered by Raymond Vernon in his noted study, describes an era in the 1960s and early 1970s in which hostile actors were pitted against one another for control of economic resources and political dominance.[1] Economic and political independence of host countries were depicted as being imperiled by the powerful multinationals. Both perceived as well as actual destabilization activities of the multinationals in turn sparked extreme reactions by the host countries. Confiscation, expropriation, nationalization, terrorism, and so on marked the experiences of that era. The host of expropriations in Latin

America, Asia, and Africa in the 1960s and 1970s is now part of the classical folklore in political risk literature.

The sovereignty-at-bay syndrome thus emphasizes the more drastic and adverse actions taken by the host countries against foreign investors for political and ideological reasons. Although the sovereignty-at-bay scenario dominated political risk thinking in the 1960s and 1970s, it still permeates the current corporate perceptions of political risks, especially in view of the ongoing adverse political changes in the more volatile trouble spots of the Third World. In particular, the Iranian and Nicaraguan revolutions, not to mention the ongoing Middle East and Persian Gulf conflicts and other flash points around the world, have substantially reinforced this view of political risk surrounding international business. The dominant mindset of corporate as well as professional political risk analysts in the United States continues, therefore, to focus on the adverse political dimensions of the multinationals' interactions with the host countries. The tremendous growth in corporate demand for political risk insurance seems to bear out this line of thinking.

Concurrently, however, the international investment environment is also being transformed by another set of forces emerging in the host countries and creating an entirely new risk scenario for the multinational investors. The transformed environment involves interactions between the multinationals' interactions with the host countries. The tremendous growth ideological level to a more sophisticated and fine-tuned level, especially in the newly industrializing countries (NICs) of Asia and Latin America. Host countries as well as the multinationals are now operating in what has come to be known as the host-country-dynamics (HCD) scenario in which a more rational and equitable balance of forces now appears to govern the investment process.[2]

The term *host-country dynamics* incorporates the entire set of forces that accompany a country's industrialization and economic development, including especially the rapid transformation of the technological structure and the growing power and sophistication of the local technocrats and business elites in interacting with the multinationals and foreign investors. Nothing better exemplifies the emerging importance of host-country dynamics than the adoption of formal industrial policies and the conscious and deliberate setting up of entry-control and management systems to deal with foreign investment and business.

Under the host-country-dynamics scenario, therefore, the critical risks tend to stem predominantly from policy interactions between the multinational investors and the host country. This implies a need to shift the risk-assessment focus to policy risks affecting foreign investment such as the host country's industrial policies, laws, and regulations pertaining to economic, industrial, and technological development. Such risks are less dramatic and more gradual and subtle, comparatively, than the ideologically oriented risks that preoccupy the perceptions of many corporate-risk analysts. As a result, such risks are also more difficult to "manage" by the company since they are an inherent part of the legal and policy framework formulated in the context of the host country's laws governing foreign investment and trade.[3]

Emergence of Host-Country Dynamics

The rise of host-country dynamics in the transformed international investment environment may be attributed to several major trends or developments. These developments contributed to and accelerated the transformation of the international investment environment. Some of the more prominent of these forces include the following:

1. Industrialization and initiation of industrial policies
2. Proliferation of technology
3. Rising technological and management expertise
4. Emergence of raw materials cartels
5. Stresses in the international financial system

First, one of the most prominent forces leading to the emergence of the host-country dynamics is the process of rapid industrialization taking place in many of the host countries. Following Japan's phenomenal industrial success, many host countries have also began to adopt similar industrial policies and have formulated investment programs aimed at both regulating and supporting the multinational investors in the countries' industrial development efforts. Rapid industrialization and also the simultaneous increase in the sophistication of their technocratic structure brought about a new attitude on the part of the host country toward the international investors. Multinationals and foreign investors with their accompanying technology and access to the world markets are now increasingly seen as a vital instrument in the host country's industrial policies. While being welcome, the incoming investments and technologies, however, are molded and shaped strictly according to the host country's industrial designs.[4]

Many host countries, for instance, as part of their industrial policy objectives, have also instituted programs to enlarge the industrial role of the local firms in the economy, frequently at the expense of the foreign investors. This tendency by the host country to discriminate in favor of local firms would obviously undermine the position of a foreign investment project or venture operating in the same industry as the favored local firms. The expanding role of the indigenous firms causes structural changes in the market, which in turn adversely affects the marketing as well as the production operations of the multinational's investment venture and hence increases its degree of risk exposure. Thus multinationals are frequently caught between the host country's dual desires to attract foreign investment and the concurrent need to promote local firms competing against the foreign investors. For instance, Dow Chemical's withdrawal from South Korea in the early eighties and Weyerhauser's divestment from Indonesia stemmed partially from the desire of the local partners to increase their role in the respective ventures. Both companies suffered heavy losses from these unplanned divestments mainly because the rate of obsolescence or the declining worth of the ventures was perhaps more rapid than anticipated.

Second, what is perhaps the most crucial factor contributing to the rise of host-country dynamics is the extensive international proliferation of technology, especially to the newly industrializing countries, and the resultant increase in competition between technology suppliers.[5] With the multitude of technological options available, host countries are no longer technologically dependent on any single dominant multinational firm and one single source of supply. Not only are the traditional multinationals from the United States, Japan, and Europe competing intensively for entry into recipient countries, newly emerging multinationals from countries like South Korea, Taiwan, and Brazil are also aggressively joining the game. Given the increased range of options available, some host countries have in fact developed a conscious and deliberate strategy of diversifying their sources of technology supply. China, for instance, spread its investment projects among firms from different countries in order to maintain its bargaining leverage. In addition to the increased competition among technology suppliers, the spread of technology has produced other risks such as the loss of proprietary technology due to lack of technological protection and the rapid gains made by endogenous technology development in the host country. The emergence of technological risks and its implications for the international investor are examined in greater detail in the next major section.

The rapid and widespread international diffusion of technology, perhaps more than any other factor, has brought about the ascendance of the host-country-dynamics environment. This in turn has created an entirely new category of risks for international business. These risks stem essentially from a more rational and organized approach to decision making and implementation by the host countries and less from ideologically motivated reasons. The major concern of most host countries today is the maximization of benefits from international investment and technology transmissions and the creation of means to best achieve it. Control and management systems are thus increasingly being set up to maximize technological and other benefits from the foreign investors.

The third major development contributing to the emergence of host-country dynamics is the rapidly rising capability of the host-country nationals in the fields of technology, management, and interactions with the multinationals. Some observers have described this phenomenon as improvement along the learning curve. Increased exposure to the demands of international business and a rising educational level in the technical and managerial fields have contributed to an enhancement of the capability of the host country in dealing with the multinational investors. Advancing along the learning curve is nowhere better demonstrated than in the rise in negotiation skills. Foreign investors are beginning to find that they are facing not only tough but also skillful and knowledgeable negotiators in host-country counterparts. The emergence of entry-management systems also contributed to providing a framework in guiding the host-country negotiators in interfacing with the foreign investors. Improvement along the learning curve is therefore one critical aspect of the heightened technocratic orientation of the host-country decision makers.[6]

The increasing technical and managerial capability of the host country combined with the intensified competition among technology suppliers significantly influenced the mode of market entry by the multinationals. Although the traditional integrated and wholly owned investment package is still permitted by many host countries, the dominant trend is toward a preference for "unbundled" arrangements. *Unbundling,* as the word implies, refers to the process of breaking up the traditionally wholly owned investment package into ownership sharing and disaggregating the various dimensions such as technology, marketing, and even management into separate components. Thus unbundled market-entry modes such as joint ventures, licensing, management contracts, and other types of contractual arrangements are increasingly used as the preferred entry vehicles.[7]

Joint ventures are preferred by the host country because they not only allow an ownership stake in an investment project but also open up opportunities for local nationals to participate in management. In the case of licensing, the technology and production know-how come unencumbered by foreign control and thus further reinforce the technical and managerial independence of the local licensees. Complementing the process on the host-country side, unbundled arrangements are also increasingly preferred by the multinationals as an appropriate means of integrating themselves into the transformed investment environment in the host country. Joint ventures, for instance, are seen by many multinationals as a way to diffuse nationalistic sentiments and also allow the company to take full advantage of the skills and expertise of the local partners. Licensing, among other advantages, allows the licensor company to establish a foothold in tough and complex markets without incurring a high degree of equity exposure.

Among the forces that have contributed to the advent of host-country dynamics is the increasing attempt of raw material-producer countries to organize themselves in dealing with the multinationals and the consumer nations.[8] Efforts by the producer nations to improve production, pricing, and marketing terms for their products often lead to organizations approaching that of cartels. This is particularly true in the case of OPEC and other natural resource and extractive projects such as in mining, timber, and agricultural commodities. Aside from the obvious shift in ownership arrangements in favor of the producer nations, these countries are also better and more effectively organized vis-à-vis the world markets, especially in pricing and supply conditions. In addition, the learning-curve phenomenon and the proliferation of technology also have reinforced the shift of power from the multinationals to the producer host countries. The rise in competitive technologies and increased negotiating leverage of the producer nations have contributed to improving the terms of a project for the host country. Although, raw materials cartels are presently on the wane because of worldwide deflation, the cyclical nature of the business may yet turn the markets again in favor of the producer countries.[9]

Recent developments in the international financial system, particularly the massive external debts of many developing countries in Africa, Latin America, and Asia, also have contributed to the shift in the bargaining balance of power in favor of the debtor nations. Debtor countries are beginning to question their obligations to honor their external debts.[10] Venezuela, Argentina, and other Latin American countries have met collectively to adopt a united stand with respect to their financial plight. The debt movement has raised the possibility of adopting severe measures, which include the mention of imposing debt moratoriums and increasing restrictions on the flow of funds and on international trade and investments within their jurisdictions. All of these possibilities obviously contribute to further magnifying the uncertainties and exposures the foreign investors already face in these countries. Another section of this chapter provides additional perspectives on the various dimensions of international financial risks and the impact on international business.

Assumptions of the Host-Country-Dynamics Approach

The central philosophy underlying the host-country-dynamics approach is the belief that international investment and technology transfers constitute a nonzero-sum game and possibly a positive-sum game in which each player can gain without doing so at the expense of the other. The synergistic interactions between the host country with its resources and opportunities and the foreign investor with its technology and know-how are able to generate a greater magnitude of benefits than in the absense of the investment project. This appears to contrast with the more traditional investment scenario in which the dominant side exerts a more one-sided claim on the resources and output of the investment process, frequently to the detriment of the counterparts on the other side. Each side perceives the other as wanting to seize dominant control of the project. It is not surprising that both the multinationals and the host countries began to resort to extreme self-protective and preemptive actions. For instance, redistributive measures taken by the host countries like nationalization, expropriation, and other confiscatory practices were essentially zero-sum-game actions taken to forestall the perceived dominance of the foreign investors.

The host-country-dynamics scenario, on the other hand, in addition to its positive-sum-game assumptions, reflects a more technocratic and problem-solving approach on the part of host countries toward the international investors. The foreign investment project is seen as a positive contributor to the country's industrial objectives. At the same time, there is a greater willingness on the part of the host country to allow greater leeway to the foreign investors. Thus instead of an ambivalent and defensive attitude, the host country tends to view the investment more rationally and hence to evaluate each investment venture on a case-by-case basis in terms of the benefits and contribution generated by a specific project.[11]

However, there is a negative aspect to the emergence of host-country dynamics. Concurrent with the willingness to welcome foreign investment, host countries are also more willing to impose restrictions on low-priority foreign projects and ventures. Restrictive factors and other adverse measures aimed selectively at certain projects, known collectively as policy risks, are increasingly being imposed on projects seen as making little or no contribution to the host country. Under the host-country scenario, policy risks, particularly at the project level, have emerged as the dominant set of risks facing foreign investment. Such policy risks include measures ranging from restrictive taxes to stringent production and marketing restrictions aimed at the foreign investment project. Unlike the more traditionally perceived and ideologically oriented political risks, however, risks arising from policy interactions with the host country have largely failed to capture the attention of Western risk analysts.

This lack of recognition of the emergence of project-specific policy risks may be attributed to the fact that the policy restrictions involved are technically complex and usually relate more to the legal and financial disciplines. In addition, since most of these restrictions are established within the host country's legal framework, the risk impact is more subtle and less clear-cut than, for example, the outright confiscation of the foreign project. However, with the rapid emergence of policy risks as a dominant aspect of host-country dynamics, neglecting their existence could seriously jeopardize the company's overall risk-management efforts. In essence, because of its more subtle nature, the final impact of policy risks on foreign investment could be even greater than that of the more dramatic and visible kinds of political risk such as expropriation and other confiscatory actions. For instance, policy restrictions such as indigenization, local contents, and countertrade requirements of host countries may raise the cost of operations to such a level as to force the firm to consider divestment. Such "due-process" divestment is certainly no better than forced expropriation of the company's assets for which at least insurance coverage may be available.

Accelerated Obsolescence of Investment Projects

The rapid international spread of technology combined with the improving technological skills of the host country have tended to cause an acceleration in the obsolescence of the perceived technological value contributed by a foreign investment project. As noted, there is a greater willingness on the part of the host country to phase out an investment project when it is perceived to be no longer making any worthwhile contribution, technologically or managerially. It is the host country's perception of the worth or value of a specific project, therefore, that essentially determines the level and rate of risk exposure faced by a project. As the perceived worth declines, the level of project risks increases, particularly in the form of intensified restrictions and other selective discriminations taken against a project. Raymond Vernon first referred to this phenomenon as the "obsolescing bargain" associated with natural resource projects over time.[12] However, this phenomenon may also be broadened into a more generic concept and extended to other investment projects. The obsolescing bargain as seen from the host-country side is the perceived decline in the worth of a project as a result of a variety of forces. The obsolescing bargain concept when applied to most investment projects would include time obsolescence, physical obsolescence, and technological obsolescence.[13]

Time obsolescence could occur purely as a function of the passage of time and may be considered as a sort of perceived "staleness" from the prolonged presence of a project. Physical obsolescence, the actual wearing out of the physical assets of a project, may also contribute to its declining worth. Technological obsolescence is perhaps the most vital aspect of project obsolescence. Technological obsolescence tends to set in as a result of the rapid spread of technology and the improvement in the host country's technological capability along the learning curve. The increasing availability of competing technologies may also contribute to a speedier decline in the worth of a specific project. The increased availability and competitive supply of a technology allows the host country a greater degree of choice among alternative upgrades of the technology, a broadened range of technological choices tends to enhance the bargaining power of the host countries and cause them to place a lesser value on an existing project and its technology. Countries like China, Brazil, and South Korea have implemented deliberate strategies to diversify their sources of technology supply. Therefore, instead of putting all of their investment eggs in one basket, these countries are allocating investment projects among U.S., European, and Japanese multinationals and increasingly among multinationals from the newly industrializing countries.

Structural Forces of Obsolescence

The perceived worth of a project from the standpoint of the host country is assumed to decline or decay at some "normal" rate as a result of the above obsolescing factors inherent in the project. However, additional factors on the part of the host country and the multinational itself can further accelerate or slow the rate of decline. These actions include the host country's industrial policies, especially those aimed at foreign investment and technology development; the promotion of indigenous industry and business; the activities of the multinational itself; and the combined effects of these factors on the degree of restrictiveness of the entry-management and control systems of the host country. Changes and developments in the above factors in addition to the various obsolescence forces could lead to a reevaluation of a project by the host country. A possible reduction in the perceived worth could bring about a greater likelihood of tightened regulations and additional pressures on the project. A more restrictive entry-management system therefore directly translates into increased risk exposure for the project. Chapter five develops an investment-risk model incorporating the combined impact of these host-country forces on the risk profile of an investment project.

TECHNOLOGICAL RISKS

A crucial and integral component of the emergence of host-country dynamics is the intensified and extensive spread of technology. The rapidity of the technological proliferation process has led to a rush by the host countries to acquire technology and production know-how for a wide range of industrial products by whatever means is at their disposal. The acquisition process has not always been strictly legal, particularly in the newly industrializing countries in Latin America and Asia. In their intense desire to advance up the technological ladder and to obtain even the slightest technological advantage, many of these countries have openly condoned the most expedient way to acquire technology. As a consequence, the widespread and increasing infringement of intellectual property rights has emerged as an urgent international problem among the international business community. In the latest forthcoming round of the multilateral negotiations within the General Agreement on Tariffs and Trade (GATT), member countries, especially the industrialized nations, are giving the issue top priority and will be striving for an agreement on an international code for the protection of intellectual property rights.[14]

Classes of Intellectual Property Rights

Intellectual property is a generic term covering all forms of technological know-how and information such as inventions, literary works, and computer software and all other forms of intellectual creation registered with government authorities for sale and use by the owner. Intellectual rights may also include other proprietary information and knowledge not formally registered such as trade and technical secrets and confidential data essential to preserving the integrity of the business. Formalized intellectual property includes patent, trademark, service mark, and copyright. A *patent* conveys certain rights to an inventor or the owner for a stipulated period. They include the right to manufacture the invention, the right to enjoy the use of and profit from the sale of the invention, and the authority to assign the rights of use to other parties. Under U.S. laws, a patentholder is entitled to enjoy these rights for a period of seventeen years, after which the patent expires and reverts to the public domain. A *trademark* confers the right to use any word, name, or symbol to identify and distinguish a product. It includes brand names to identify products (e.g., Coke), service marks to identify services e.g., McDonald's Hamburgers and American Express Card), and certification marks to identify products and services meeting certain standards or using certain materials (e.g., the natural "Cotton" mark and logo on apparel). For a marketing-oriented company, a trademark may be its most valuable asset. The Coca Cola company, for instance, is believed to value its various marks at well over $1 billion. Aside from illegal copying, one of the major trademark risks is the danger of a brand name falling into usage as a generic term. Xerox, Nylon, and Kleenex, are examples of well-known brand names that have fallen into generic use.

A *copyright* confers certain rights to an author of a literary, dramatic, musical, or artistic work and, most recently, computer software. Just as in the case of patents, the rights include the right to profit from and enjoy the use of the work, to assign the rights of use and profit to others, and to have protection against copying. Under current U.S. laws, a copyright is valid for the life of the author plus fifty years, after which the copyright reverts to the public domain.

An additional area of possible infringement of business property rights is unfair competition or imitation. It refers to a broad area of trade practices that may possibly violate established legal standards of business conduct. Provisions under unfair competition include protection against the simulation of the trademark, brand name, logo, or packaging of other companies and the misappropriation of trade secrets. *Simulation* refers to the use of a mark or name similar to but not identical to an already registered mark with the intention of misleading the consumers.

Appropriability of Technology

Perhaps among the most important motivations for firms to engage in international investment and trade is the maximization of returns from exploiting product innovations and technologies worldwide.[15] The ability of an innovating firm to capture worldwide returns from its innovation and technology is known as *appropriability*. The ability to appropriate returns from a technological innovation depends on several factors such as the technological complexity of the innovation, the stage in the technology cycle, the vehicle of transmission to the recipient, and, perhaps most critical, the existence of an effective and well-enforced technology-protection system. International appropriability of technology, therefore, can be ensured only through the maintenance by the host country of a system of protection of intellectual property rights. The existence of an international protection system for intellectual property rights and technological appropriability is crucial to the process of continuous innovations. Increased risk of nonprotection, both domestically and internationally, may seriously undermine the willingness of firms in undertaking expensive R&D because they may be precluded from enjoying returns from their innovations in the international markets.[16]

Companies that stand to lose most from loss of appropriability due to nonprotection are usually high-technology and innovative firms. Such companies spend enormous amounts of money on R&D, and the loss of appropriability has grave repercussions on the viability of their future innovation activities. The degree of appropriability tends to vary along the stages in the product-technology cycle. The stages in the technology cycle consist of invention, innovation (R&D), creation of the production function, commercial launching, market growth, maturity, and standardization. Appropriability for the innovating firm appears to the highest at the earlier stages of the cycle mainly because the know-how is still new and therefore unique to the company. Apart from patent protection, there are barriers to acquisition of the innovative know-how, especially the firm-specific information, by competing firms. Loss of appropriability usually begins to occur at the later stages of the technology cycle, particularly at the standardization stage. At the later stages of the cycle, information concerning the product's technology has been so extensively diffused that competing versions begin to flood the market.

In the late-cycle stages, particularly at the standardized stage, the process of international diffusion begins. According to conventional product-cycle hypothesis, marketing saturation and intense competition at the late stages of the cycle tend to lead to rising product and marketing costs and falling if not constant prices. The resulting profit squeeze usually causes the firm to seek production and markets in the foreign countries. The commencement of the international spread of technology is therefore motivated by a company's desire to escape a domestic profit squeeze and hence extend appropriability of the technology in the international markets.[17]

Recent developments in the dynamics of technological innovations, however, have began to undermine this conventional view of a gradually evolving and sequential diffusion of technology overseas. Instead, with the advent of more rapid continuous innovations, especially in the high-technology electronics field, product cycles are getting increasingly shorter. For instance, each new generation of personal computers tends to have an ever shorter product cycle. The original and earlier CPM-based personal computers (PCs) lasted for about four years before being overtaken by the newer MS-DOS machines. The original MS-DOS version with 64-K of memory was even more quickly supplanted by faster, more powerful, and better performing PCs, such as IBM's XT (extra technology) and AT (advanced technology) series. In less than a year and a half, the technology of even these latest innovations has spread so extensively that the PC market today is flooded with IBM-compatible XT and AT units or "clones." Most of the clones originate in countries like Taiwan, Hong Kong, and South Korea.

Technological developments such as the above example of personal computers constitute what essentially is an almost instantaneous diffusion of technology to the foreign countries superceding the conventional view of a slow and gradually evolving diffusion in the technology cycle overseas. In addition, most of the international transmission of technology now seems increasingly to bypass the multinationals, which are traditionally perceived as the vehicles for intrafirm technology transmissions under the conventional product-cycle framework. The conventional view is that technology is mainly transmitted abroad by MNCs via direct investment in wholly owned subsidiaries in the foreign markets. Instead, most of the transmissions, especially to the newly industrializing countries such as Taiwan and Korea, are non-MNC transfers carried out on a relatively arm's-length basis between independent firms. Thus recent transmissions have been carried out mainly in the form of technology-consulting and assistance agreements, licensing, and original equipment manufacturer (OEM) arrangements between, for example, a U.S. technology supplier and a recipient Taiwan manufacturer. In short, the increasingly important pattern in international transmissions is now essentially in the form of "unbundled arrangements" between suppliers and buyers in the open and nonintrafirm international technology markets.[18]

Modes of Technology Transmissions and Diffusions

As the pattern of transmission has moved from the traditional intrafirm MNC-based transfers to independent, arm's-length and unbundled arrangements, technological risks correspondingly have been increasing. Technology risks basically involve a loss of appropriability, that is, the firm's ability to capture returns from its innovations and technology. Traditionally, intrafirm transfers via wholly owned and controlled subsidiaries offers maximum protection for appropriability of technological returns. But with the rise of unbundled arrangements, transmissions are now taking place on a relatively unprotected and uncontrolled basis. The resultant technological risks, that is, reduction or loss of appropriability, may stem from technology transmissions that are both legal as well as illicit.

Legal transmissions include arrangements ranging from equity joint ventures, licensing, OEM transfers, technical assistance agreements, and high-technology consulting to imitation of nonproprietary know-how and mandatory licensing. Licensing and joint ventures constitute relatively protected means of transmissions whereby, presumably, the transferring firm would have adequately incorporated a high degree of appropriability in these arrangements. Sections in Chapter three further explore how licensing and joint venture can be set up as an appropriate low-risk means of market entry.

OEM transfers usually occur in the context of international purchasing and consist of the transmissions of designs and specification know-how from the purchaser to the OEM. In a typical OEM transfer, a buyer from the purchasing country, usually a major retail chain or multinational corporation (MNC) from, for example, the United States, provides design and other technical know-how to independent manufacturers in, for instance, Taiwan and reimports the parts or finished products for marketing under its own brand name in the U.S. market. Companies such as Sears, Roebuck, General Electric, and Chrysler have been involved in OEM transfers and purchasing in products ranging from computers to household appliances to cars to furniture. Appropriability risks for the purchasing firm that originates the technology in an OEM transfer appear to be minimal because for most part the transmitted product knowledge is protected either by trademark or license. In many other instance, such as with videocassette recorders and a wide range of electronics items, the OEM itself is the technology innovator, and hence this would imply the absence of any technological exposure on the part of the purchasing firm.

Other legitimate international transfers of technology include imitation of nonproprietary know-how, mandatory-licensing and technology-assistance agreements, and consulting. *Imitation of nonproprietary know-how* refers to a process in which the recipient firm attempts legally to copy parts of a product with the exception of the protected proprietary component. For instance, IBM-compatible personal computers provide an interesting case in point. The recent flood of legitimate IBM-compatible units or clones was essentially made possible by the fact that the majority of the parts can be copied legally except for the patented basic input/output system (BIOS), which is proprietary and protected. Legally simulated BIOSs, however, have enabled clone units to reach almost 99 percent IBM compatibility.

Technology-assistance and consulting transmissions refer to a legally sanctioned transfer of technology and know-how to the transferee firm. The process usually involves providing technical help in the research and development of a product or a system. As in the case of licensing, appropriability of returns for the technology supplier presumably would have been built into the transfer agreement. *Mandatory licensing* refers to the legal requirement of the host country that provides for the compulsory licensing of the technology to local firms if the foreign patentholder does not exercise the patent within a stipulated period. Thus if the patentholder desists from producing and marketing the product within a reasonable time, the patent registration will be invalidated, and local firms will be licensed to commercialize the product. In more stringent cases, mandatory licensing to local firms after a stipulated period is required regardless of whether or not the original patentholder exercises the patent.

International Product Piracy and Counterfeiting

The area of illicit technology diffusion is of the greatest concern to technology owners and suppliers. Legitimate transfers, although not entirely without risks, nevertheless still allow some degree of legal and managerial recourse for the affected company. For instance, the transferring firm could strengthen interfirm control of appropriability in joint-venture and licensing arrangements. The same is true in the case of OEM transfers and mandatory licensing since there is an established relationship upon which redress can be pursued within the context of the contractual agreement. In the case of illegal transmissions, however, the technology owner is almost completely exposed in terms of the loss of appropriability. Exposure to technological risk is intensified particularly in countries that offer inadequate or nonexistent protection for intellectual property rights.

Illicit diffusion of technology consists primarily of product piracy and counterfeiting. *Piracy* refers to a broader process of simulating a product, the packaging, or a trademark without exactly duplicating the patented or protected item. This has been alluded to earlier as unfair competition or imitation that violates legal standards of business behavior. The case of personal computers again offers an illustration of this process. Apple computer lookalikes, for instance, simulate the design, brand name, logo, and packaging of the original with names such as "Pineapple" or "Orange." Imitating the color and logo of a product's packaging is a popular practice worldwide. In this case, the design and color of logo and package are copied without the actual use of the original name itself. Soft-drink makers abroad, for instance, prefer the use of the red color and the lettering style of Coca Cola on their containers without actually using Coke's name itself. Product and design piracy, therefore, borders on the fringe of legality. Although under the law of many host countries this practice is not technically a violation of trademark rights, it has the intended effect of encroaching on the sales of a better-known and recognized product.

Product and trademark counterfeiting is the straightforward and direct attempt to produce forgery or fakes purporting to be the genuine article. In the case of counterfeiting, there is not even the usual pretense of just simulating an existing product or brand as in the case of piracy but instead a direct, clear, and outright attempt to fake a proprietary product or brand name. Product counterfeits affect items ranging from brand-name watches, designer apparels, and audio and video tapes to automobile and even aircraft parts.

Protection Systems and Countermeasures

Assessing and managing technological risks, especially the monitoring and protection of international appropriability, depend to large extent on both the existence and the nature of the protection systems in the host country. In assessing the technology protection system of a specific country, not only the existence of protective laws but also the nature and enforcement of the laws must be taken into consideration. In general, there are four relevant levels in assessing the protection systems for intellectual property rights. The four levels of protection are international conventions, the national protection system in the host country, bilateral agreements between the technology-supplying and recipient nations, and actions taken at the company level.

Most countries belong to one of the several international conventions established to provide guidelines for the registration and protection of intellectual property rights in the form of patents, trademarks, and copyrights in signatory nations. Perhaps the best-known is the International Convention for the Protection of Industrial Property (with revisions at London, Lisbon, and Stockholm), commonly referred to as the Paris Union. The Paris Union, which comprises about eighty member countries, recognizes the rights of protection of trademarks, patents, and other property rights of all member countries. It provides for uniform protection in member countries. Other conventions are regionally based agreements such as the Pan-American Convention, the Madrid Convention, the Trademark Registration Treaty (TRT), the Patent Cooperation Treaty (PCT) of Europe, and the European Patent Convention (EPC).[19]

The Pan-American Convention, which caters to most of the Latin American nations, has provisions similar to those of the Paris Union. The Madrid Convention consists of about twenty-four European member countries and operates the Bureau for International Registration of Trademarks. The TRT runs the World Intellectual Property Organization (WIPO) and provides protection in member countries for trademark registration filed with it. The European-based PCT, comprising twenty-eight member countries, extends assistance in research and facilitates application for registration in the cooperating treaty countries. The EPC has eleven members and provides protection in the member countries through the issue of an European patent. In the area of international copyrights, the principal agreements include the Berne Convention (1886 with amendments), the Universal Copyright Convention (1952 with amendments), and the Rome Convention for the Protection of Performers, Producers of Phonograms and Broadcasting Organizations (1961).[20] Most of the international conventions and treaties provide for uniform and reciprocal protection of property rights in the member countries. Registration with one of the conventions or its affiliated organization is designed to ensure the same protection in other member countries.

One of the major shortcomings of the international conventions is that protective coverage is limited to only the member countries. Many of the important industrializing nations in East Asia are not signatory to some of the more important intellectual and industrial property conventions. Taiwan, South Korea, and Singapore, for instance, are not currently members of the Paris Convention or the Berne Convention. These countries are only recently being prompted by international pressures to strengthen their patent and trademark laws to bring them closer to conformity with the provisions of the international conventions. Thus another level in assessing the protection system of the host country is to examine its national protection system.

The effectiveness of a country's national protection system depends on the nature of its patent and trademark laws, the adequacy of the protective laws, the degree of enforcement, and the complexity of the registration process. Most of the intellectual property protection laws in the Western countries are based on prior use. Under this system, the principle of first-to-use applies. Ownership rights are established through first use of the trademark or invention. Registration serves only to formalize what is already recognized by the common law of the country. National protection systems falling into this category include those in the United States, the United Kingdom, and the other English-speaking countries. In other nations, known as code-law countries, the principle of first-to-register prevails in establishing ownership rights. Countries that adhere to the first-to-register rule include Spain, many of the Latin American countries, Japan, South Korea, Taiwan, and China. Under the first-to-register system, local entities are allowed to undertake preemptive registration of foreign trademarks and patents. In many countries, prior registration can be reversed only through a complicated and costly legal challenge.

In addition to the underlying principle of the patent and trademark laws of the host country, the questions of adequacy of the protective laws and the degree of enforcement are vital dimensions in assessing the efficacy of the country's protection system. Many host countries, particularly the still developing countries, consider infringement of intellectual rights a natural symptom of development. Some nations consider payments for intellectual property rights at best a luxury and at worst a form of extortion that, in their stage of underdevelopment, they can ill afford. In addition, cultural values exert a powerful influence in perceiving intellectual property rights. Some countries lack a comprehension as well as an appreciation of a concept as intangible as that of intellectual property. In certain East Asian cultures, for instance, emulation and copying of well-known art or literary works are not only acceptable but in fact admired traditional qualities. As a result, many of these countries lack economic as well as cultural motivations to formulate and enforce whatever laws they may have in protecting foreign intellectual property rights. The following sections examine the case of two of the most visible and important players in international efforts to improve protection for intellectual property rights.

In the area of enforcement and legal sanctions, two of the most frequently perceived offenders in international product piracy and counterfeiting, Taiwan and Korea, have appeared to make significant progress in their efforts to raise the level of protection and strengthen legal enforcement. In Taiwan the government has set up an Anti-Counterfeiting Committee to strengthen enforcement. Moreover, the government recently promulgated a new trademark law that increases the severity of sanctions and the penalty for infringement. Two additional pieces of legislation, a new patent law and Taiwan's first unfair competition law, are also being prepared for enactment. In addition, the United States is expected to reach a bilateral agreement with Taiwan that will incorporate the substantive provisions of the Paris Convention. Despite such apparent moves, the perceived level of protection and enforcement have still fallen short of desired expectations. Taiwan's existing trademark and patent laws, for instance, have yet to be amended to allow unregistered foreign companies legal standing to file criminal actions against infringers, and police actions appear to be inconsistent and inadequate.

In South Korea, international pressures have also prompted some efforts on the part of the authorities to strengthen and upgrade its intellectual property-protection laws, particularly in the areas of computer software, books, videotapes, chemicals, and pharmaceutical compounds. At present, however, the efforts seem to be stalled at the proposal stage pending further studies on the subject. Foreign patents appear to be adequately protected in Korea within the provisions of the Paris Convention, with the exception of chemicals and pharmaceuticals. Protection of foreign copyrights, however, is virtually nonexistent. Korea's proposals for changes in its protection laws are expected to incorporate clauses providing for more stringent penalties for violators, increased compensation for copyright and trademark holders, and preparations that will pave the way for its joining the Universal Copyrights Convention. The proposed reforms are facing stiff resistance from local industry groups that consider product imitation a necessary aspect of an accelerated industrialization process. However, it is expected that continuing pressures from its huge external debt, its standing as an important emerging member of the international community, and the need to attract foreign capital and technology should eventually lead to stronger protection.

Another dimension important in assessing the national protection system of host countries is the fairness and complexity in the patent and registration procedures. Certain countries have been suspected of using complex registration procedures for patents and trademarks as a form of nontariff barrier. Japan, for instance, is under strong international pressure to bring its intellectual property-protection laws more in line with that of Western industrialized nations. The planned measures include attempts to ease the often stringent and tedious translation procedures and to speed up the processing and approval of trademark and patent applications, which usually takes four to six years. In addition, the Japanese system allows the registration of the same mark in different product categories. This results in the time-consuming process of requiring a foreign company to file multiple applications in the various categories just to protect one mark.

The third level of protection relates to bilateral agreements that may be negotiated between the technology-exchanging countries. This action involves negotiation usually initiated by technology-exporting nations such as the United States that have high stakes in the protection of the technology of their multinationals and exporters. Bilateral negotiations and agreements fill a crucial gap left open by inadequate protection in host countries that are not members of an international convention or that do not have adequate protective laws and enforcement. Recently, for instance, the U.S. government has been stepping up its efforts to increase protection for American intellectual property rights in countries like South Korea and Taiwan by pressuring these countries to strengthen their protective laws. It also announced a program of action that includes efforts to increase negotiation of additional agreements and adopt measures such as possibly denying General System of Preference (GSP) benefits to suspected nations, banning the imports of products that have infringed on U.S. property rights, pushing for a GATT agreement on a code of protection for intellectual property rights, and cooperating with the World Intellectual Property Organization to improve existing international conventions. In addition, the U.S. International Trade Administration and the Patent and Trademark Office have sponsored educational seminars in several Pacific Rim countries to increase awareness of the problem of piracy and counterfeiting.[21]

Finally, the United States is working to ensure that protection of intellectual rights in host countries occurs at the company level. This level of protection would involve adopting measures such as setting up an effective intelligence system to scan, monitor, and police suspected violations of the firm's intellectual rights. In addition to taking the suspected infringers to court, the company could also initiate nonlegal means of negotiating with the infringers. Some companies in Taiwan and Thailand, for instance, have successfully negotiated arrangements with suspected local companies that will appoint them as official licensees with an agreement to defer royalty payments. Although in this case the company may still suffer a financial loss because of nonpayment of royalties, the strategy is that once the suspected infringer is legitimized, it will provide a basis for a more constructive future relationship. In the final analysis, apart from all measures discussed above, the best deterrent against piracy and counterfeiting is to establish and maintain a strong market presence in the host countries.

ECONOMIC AND INTERNATIONAL FINANCIAL RISKS

Apart from the entire spectrum of host-country-dynamics factors that may influence the risk profile for international investment, economic and exchange risks also constitute additional sources of risk. From the standpoint of international business, the bottom-line consideration is the safe and relatively unimpeded repatriation of earnings and capital from the host country. However, companies face a broad array of uncertainties and risks in the repatriation of funds. In addition to deep-seated structural risks arising from poor economic performance, inflationary pressures, and trade and payment imbalances, a company's international flow of funds may be affected by currency fluctuations and the imposition of exchange controls. The following sections briefly examine how these various forces contribute to the broad range of financial risks that confront the international investors, lenders, and traders.

Economic, Transaction, and Translation Exposures

As discussed in Chapter one, international financial risks can be broadly classified into economic, transaction, and translation exposures. *Economic exposure* refers to possible changes in a firm's or project's expected cash flow stemming from an unexpected variation in exchange rates that may result from fundamental changes in the host country's economy. Economic exposures facing the foreign investor in the host country are usually handled as part of the company's long-term business strategy.

Translation exposure usually refers to paper gains or losses arising from translating and then consolidating the foreign earnings and net-worth changes of a subsidiary with the parent company's financial statements. As noted in Chapter one, the effect of the translation on the financial statements of the company depends on the accounting rules and procedures of the home country. The current set of translation rules for U.S.-based multinationals is known as FASB-52 and is issued by the Financial Accounting Standards Board.

Transaction exposure refers to possible changes in short-run and mostly trade-related payments and receivables resulting from possible exchange-rate changes. It therefore includes both potential gains as well as losses arising from settling relatively short-term international financial instruments due to shifts in exchange rates. For instance, if a company has a net-asset position and has outstanding receivables denominated in a foreign currency, a depreciation or devaluation of that currency would result in a foreign exchange loss, whereas an appreciation of the currency would result in a foreign exchange gain. On the other hand, if the company has a net-liability position and has payment obligations denominated in the foreign currency, a depreciation of the currency would lead to a foreign exchange gain, whereas the reverse is true in the case of an appreciation of the foreign currency.

Exchange Controls and Inconvertibility

Host countries impose controls on the free flow of funds in and out of the country for a variety of reasons. Countries that are fiscally conservative, for instance, normally impose strict exchange controls to discourage outflows in an attempt to maintain their balance of payments on the positive side. Exchange controls are also imposed for political reasons. Countries facing political uncertainties are usually compelled to impose strict controls in their attempt to prevent capital flight out of the country. In addition, and on a more serious level, countries are beginning to question their obligations to honor their foreign debts and are considering debt moratoriums and other moves to restructure their payments. All of the above instances reflect the host countries' unwillingness and not their inability to allow the outflow of funds.

In addition, the imposition of foreign exchange controls may result simply from a country's inability to convert local currency funds into hard currency for remittance basically because of a shortage in foreign exchange reserves. Countries with balance-of-payment difficulties, heavy external debt burdens, and serious economic disruptions are likely to impose strict controls in the form of active and passive blockage of funds. *Active blockage* refers to an outright declaration of the refusal to convert local funds for remittance and repatriation. *Passive blockage* refers to the placing of administrative impediments on the processing and approval of applications for remittance without the declaration of an outright ban as in the case of active blockages. Bureaucratic delays and unresponsiveness may be considered a part of the tactics of passive blockage. In many debt-ridden countries, firms have to wait several years for permission to repatriate their cash due to the chronic shortage of foreign exchange reserves. Passive blockages also include tax disincentives such as imposing progressive surcharges on an increasing amount of repatriation. Brazil, for instance, imposes progressive tax surcharges running as high as 40 to 60 percent on repatriation if the amount exceeds 12 percent of originally registered capital. In China, repatriation may be tied to countertrade requirements.

Foreign Exchange Fluctuations

The continuing strength of a currency, such as the U.S. dollar in much of the early and mid-1980s, against the currencies of major trading partners and countries with a tendency toward a chronic balance-of-payments deficit and high debt burden has meant higher translation and transaction risks for U.S firms with foreign operations. Operations in countries with constant currency devaluations and depreciations have resulted in major foreign exchange losses. In terms of transaction exposure, the major losers appear to be exporters and corporations with predominantly sales and leasing subsidiaries abroad because they have sizable receipts and relatively small payment obligations denominated in weakening currencies. Multinationals with manufacturing operations, on the other hand, usually stand to gain from the strong dollar, especially if they are considering acquiring additional foreign currency assets or are expanding their operations. Also, due to the capital-intensive nature of their investments, they may incur substantial foreign currency debt and payment obligations. As the currencies of the host countries weaken, actual dollar outlays needed to pay off the obligations are reduced accordingly.

Foreign exchange exposures are particularly critical in countries with a relatively fixed or "pegged" exchange-rate system. Most of these countries, which tend to suffer from chronic balance-of-payment deficits and huge external debt burdens, are prone to sudden and frequent currency devaluations with the resultant adverse impact on transaction and translation exposures. In a few exceptional cases, however, there are countries with currencies that are pegged to a hard currency like the U.S. dollar, which poses repatriation uncertainties in the opposite direction. These are strong trade-surplus countries like Taiwan, which are frequently compelled to revalue their currencies and hence produce revaluation risks for investors and multinationals in the repatriation and remittance of funds. Foreign exchange losses may be incurred if a company is exposed in a net-liability position in its receipts and payments position when the host country revalues its currency. The actual dollar outlays needed to pay off the obligations are increased accordingly.

Exposures in the fixed-rate countries are exacerbated by difficulty in forecasting the rate changes. Complications in forecasting may stem from the fact that many of these countries tend to adjust their currencies (devaluation/revaluation) as a matter of policy and not strictly to bring their currencies in line with the realities of their balance of payments and economic performance. Usually, the country's exchange authorities tend to hold off a devaluation until its currency is completely out of equilibrium in terms of its balance of payments and hence its value relative to that of its trading partners. In addition to difficulty in forecasting the timing, there is also the difficulty of forecasting the magnitude of adjustment. Because of a tendency to delay adjustment, or the amount of correction needed to restore equilibrium plus an allowance for additional projected depreciation, the required magnitude of adjustment may be as high as 30 to 40 percent. Nevertheless, the forecasting exchange-rate changes of the fixed-rate countries are even more important to international risk assessment precisely because these countries present the greatest risk in the repatriability of funds. Chronic deficit and debt-ridden countries are not only prone to frequent devaluations but also have a greater tendency to restrict profit and capital remittances and impose both active and passive blockages of funds.

Assessing Economic and Foreign Exchange Exposures

The assessment of international financial risks in the form of the various exposures discussed in the preceding sections is vital to risk management in international investment and other foreign ventures. International financial exposures can lead to not only devaluation risks but also currency inconvertibility and exchange restrictions. The discipline of international financial risk assessment, more popularly known as "country-risk" assessment, appears to be relatively more established, better articulated, and better quantified, in terms of its conceptual and methodological formulations, than is political risk analysis. This is partially because the field itself (i.e., country-risk analysis) deals with data of a more quantitative nature and hence is able to lend itself to more objective analysis. The basic approach to the assessment of international financial risks is formulated on the so-called country-ratio analysis. These country or financial ratios are primarily developed from macroeconomic data such as national income and balance-of-payment statistics. These ratios or indices range from measures of a country's total indebtedness and debt-service level to the fundamental capacity of the economy to meet its external obligations.[22]

The framework of analysis is based on developing financial ratios to represent the three fundamental categories of blockage of funds: balance-of-payment block, monetary block, and fiscal block. These three blocks reflect the underlying economic motivations behind the probability of a country seeking to impose restrictions and hence the probability of resulting in a flow-of-funds block.[23] *Balance-of-payment block* is intended to reflect the net effect of capital and trade inflows (imports) relative to the country's official reserves. The *monetary and fiscal blocks* are intended to reflect monetary and fiscal conditions such as money supply and government expenditures relative to national income that may lead to the imposition of flow-of-funds restrictions. The ratios developed to represent the various blocks range from measures of a country's total indebtedness and debt-service ratios to fundamental economic performance. Flow-of-funds-block ratio analysis based on fundamental economic variables therefore allows an assessment of a country's creditworthiness, the repatriability of funds from the standpoint of international business, the potential for default, and the probability of devaluation, all of which constitute critical risks for international investors, lenders, and traders. In short, they provide an indication of a country's ability and willingness to pay foreigners, that is, to meet its external financial obligations to the international business community. Although the flow-of-funds-block approach permits a more in-depth analysis of both the apparent as well as the underlying variables influencing a country's creditworthiness and its fundamental capacity to meet external obligations, most practical country-risk assessment tends to be formulated on the so-called country-risk ratios focusing on a country's external debt and liability situation. Country-risk ratios may be developed to provide a measure of a country's level of total indebtedness, the level of debt-service payment, and the capacity to service external debt.[24] Various country-risk ratios are developed and used by organizations ranging from commercial banks engaged in international lending such as Citicorp and Chase Manhattan to international agencies such as the International Monetary Fund (IMF) and the World Bank.

Some of the most frequently used country-risk ratios include measures of the relative level of total indebtedness, of the relative level of debt-service payments, and of the relative debt-service capacity.

Measures of the Relative Level of Total Indebtedness

Ratio of external debt to GNP or GDP. This ratio usually shows the size of the total external debt, both public and private, relative to a country's gross national product or gross domestic product. It is an indication of the size of a country's debt seen within the broader perspective of its total production of goods and services.

Ratio of total external liabilities to GNP. This ratio measures the total liabilities of a country relative to its gross national product. Total external liabilities include not only a country's loan obligations but also the outstanding amount of foreign-held capital such as direct private investment and foreign government grants. The ratio is intended to provide a more comprehensive measure of a country's total level of indebtedness.

Ratio of total external debt to international reserves. This ratio indicates the total level of external debt relative to a country's total international reserves (foreign exchange, gold, Special Drawing Rights, reserve position with the International Monetary Fund). It is an indication of the country's ability to provide liquid assets to meet its cumulated debt obligations. For instance, if a country has $5 billion outstanding in external debt and $5 billion in total reserves, its net debt position cancels out to zero.

Ratio of external debt to exports. This ratio shows the amount of external debt relative to the country's export earnings and therefore measures a country's foreign exchange earnings against its accumulated foreign indebtedness.

Measures of the Relative Level of Debt-Service Payments

Ratio of debt service to GNP or GDP. This ratio provides a measure of the proportion of a country's total production of goods and services that goes toward debt-service payments. Debt-service payments consist of payments on interest as well as the amortized amount of the loan principal due on an external debt.

Ratio of debt service to international reserves. This ratio shows the level of debt service relative to a country's total international reserves. It is an indication of a country's short-term ability to meet its external obligations from its international reserves. A low reserve position relative to high debt-service payment signifies the possibility of a potential for default.

Other ratios of the level of debt service. In addition to the above ratios, measures of a country's debt-service position can be based on its national savings and public revenues. Such ratios tend to reflect the claims of debt-service payment on the country's savings and government receipts from taxation and other income.

Measures of Relative Debt-Service Capacity

Ratio of debt service to exports. Also known as the current debt-service ratio, this measure provides one of the key indications of a country's ability to service external debt. It is usually expressed as a ratio of debt-service payments on public debt to the export of goods and nonfactor services for a particular year. The ratio may be modified to include private debt as well. The current ratio is therefore a cash-flow concept indicating the proportion of export-generated foreign exchange earnings taken up by debt-service payments. The current debt-service ratio is particularly vital in assessing the debt-servicing capability of countries that are primarily export dependent. The critical level in the current debt ratio has been placed around 20 percent.

Current-investment-service ratio. The numerator of this ratio includes not only debt-service payments but also income payments related to foreign-held capital such as the remittance of profits, dividends, and other fees paid to foreign investors. These total foreign payments are expressed as a percentage of the exports of goods and services. The ratio indicates the proportion of a country's export earnings that may be taken up by foreign income payments as well as debt-service payments. It is thus a more comprehensive indicator of the country's ability to meet all of its total external claims (both debt service and investment income paid to foreigners) from its export earnings.

The preceding ratios include some of the more frequently used and accepted country-risk ratios. Other possible ratios or variants of the above ratios may be developed to provide an indication of specific situations regarding a country's payment capability and relative indebtedness. For instance, the ratio of imports to reserves may be derived to measure a country's ability to finance its short-term trade. Other approaches usually involve refinement of the standard current-debt-service ratio. One example of a modified current-debt ratio involves expressing debt-service payments as a percentage of exports of goods and services less imports plus international reserves. Another useful measure that provides a good indication of the basic strength of a country's export structure is its degree of export diversification. If two countries have the same percentage in their current-debt-service ratio, the one with a more diversified export structure would imply less risk in terms of creditworthiness. Also countries with predominantly manufacturing exports would be less risky than countries with exports dominated by primary commodities because the latter are usually more prone to price fluctuations.

Country-risk ratios are subject to various shortcomings. In the case of the current-debt ratio, for instance, it was noted that it may be difficult to establish a critical level or cut-off point for the ratio. Countries with lower current-debt-service ratios have shown a greater tendency to default than countries with higher percentages of debt-service ratios. Industrialized countries with a stronger and more diversified manufacturing base seem to be able to carry a much higher debt-service burden without defaulting than less-developed countries with a much weaker manufacturing base. In addition, some of the ratios may not be good and accurate predictors of future creditworthiness since the components in the ratios may change. For instance, a country's export earnings may fluctuate, and debt-service payments may vary with maturity, currency fluctuations, and fluctuations in interest rates. Therefore, the ratios by themselves may be inadequate and incomplete indicators of a country's debt position. Other factors such as the prospects for an improved balance of trade, a strengthened economic performance, the country's reserve position, and the availability of alternative financing must all be considered to arrive at a more complete evaluation of a country's external debt situation.

NOTES

1. Raymond Vernon, Sovereignty at Bay: The Multinational Spread of U.S. Enterprises (New York: Basic Books, 1971).

2. Theodore H. Moran, "Multinational Corporations and the Changing Structure of Industries Supplying Industrial Commodities," Journal of

Contemporary Business, Vol. 6, No. 4, Autumn 1977, pp. 121-130.

3. Ibid., pp. 122-125.

4. C. Fred Bergsten, "Coming Investment Wars?" Foreign Affairs, Vol. 53, No. 1, October 1974, pp. 135-152.

5. Wenlee Ting, Business and Technological Dynamics in Newly Industrializing Asia (Westport, Conn.: Quorum Books, 1985), pp. 62-90.

6. Moran, "Multinational Corporations," pp. 122-123.

7. Bergsten, "Coming Investment Wars?" pp. 138-139.

8. Raymond F. Mikesell, "More Third World Cartels Ahead," Challenge, Vol. 17, No. 5, November-December 1974, pp. 24-31.

9. C. Fred Bergsten, "The New Era in World Commodity Markets," Challenge, Vol. 17, No. 4, September-October 1974, pp. 32-34.

10. Chris C. Carvounis, "The LDC Debt Problem: Trends in Country Risk Analysis and Rescheduling Exercises," Columbia Journal of World Business, Spring 1982, pp. 15-26.

11. Ting, Business and Technological Dynamics, pp. 11-18.

12. Raymond Vernon, "The Obsolescing Bargain: A Key Factor in Political Risk," in Mark B. Winchester, ed., The International Essays for Business Decision Makers, Vol. 5. (Houston: The Center for International Business, 1980), pp. 281-286.

13. Wenlee Ting, "New Perspectives on Risk Assessment and Management in the Asia Pacific: A Host Country Dynamics Approach," Proceedings of the Academy of International Business South East Asia Meeting, Taipei, Taiwan, June 1986, pp. 778-795.

14. Eileen Hill, "Protecting U.S. Intellectual Property Rights," Business America, April 14, 1986, pp. 2-6.

15. Stephen P. Magee, "Multinational Corporations, the Industry Technology Cycle, and Development," The Journal of World Trade Law, Vol. 11, No. 4, July-August 1977, pp. 297-312.

16. Ibid., pp. 300-308.

17. Sak Onkvisit and John J. Shaw, "An Examination of the International Product Life Cycle and Its Application within Marketing," Columbia Journal of World Business, Fall 1983, pp. 73-79.

18. Ting, Business and Technological Dynamics, pp. 69-89.

19. Patents throughout the World. Third Edition, Ed., Alan J. Jacobs. (New York: Clark Boardman Company Ltd., 1986).

20. Raymond Maddison, Copyright and Related Rights, Principles, Problems, and Trends (London: Economic Intelligence Unit Limited, 1983).

21. Hill, "Protecting U.S. Intellectual Property Rights," pp. 5-6.

22. H. Robert Heller and Emmanuel Frenkel, "Determinants of LDC Indebtedness," Columbia Journal of World Business, Spring 1982, pp. 28-33; John K. Thompson, "An Index of Economic Risk," in Richard Ensor, ed., Assessing Country Risk (London: Euromoney Publications, 1981), pp. 69-74.

23. Taeho Kim, "Assessment of External Debt Capacity: An Alternative Methodology," Journal of Economic Development, December 1985, pp. 35-52.

24. A. Zuhier Sofia, "Rationalizing Country Risk Ratios," in Richard Ensor, ed., Assessing Country Risk (London: Euromoney Publications, 1981), pp. 49-68.

3

Entry-Management Systems and Market-Entry Strategies

ENTRY-MANAGEMENT SYSTEMS

The series of developments discussed in Chapter two has led to a fundamental transformation in the international investment and business environment, especially in the newly industrializing countries of Asia and Latin America. This transformation is marked particularly by the emergence of microrisks emanating from policy interactions of the multinationals with the host country. This transformation has also brought about a change in the multinational firms' attitude toward the host countries, a shift from one that was previously ethnocentric to one that is primarily polycentric. As a result of the rise of host-country forces, multinationals are compelled to focus more attention on dealing with the specific and peculiar set of active forces each country presents. This stands in stark contrast to the previous era in which multinationals treated host countries as an indistinguishable mass of passive national markets subservient to the global optimization imperatives of the company.

The transformed investment environment also saw a reduction in the relevance of macrorisks arising from ideological shifts in the host country. Although macropolitical risks may still be a probable source of threats in more revolutionary societies, policy risks are now the dominant considerations in many economically and industrially functioning host countries. The major source of microrisk for today's international investors is primarily the broad set of policy risks inherent in the entry-management systems (EMSs) that have been increasingly set up by host countries as a result of their move toward industrialization. Entry-management systems pervade not only the newly industrializing countries but also the industrialized and the less developed countries as well. Even in less industrialized host countries, rudimentary systems are being established to wring more benefits out of the multinational's incoming investment package of technology, training, and export development.[1]

The major implication of the shift from macro to microrisks in the international investment environment encompasses the need for both a perceptual and an institutional change on the part of the Western risk-assessment profession. First, on the perceptual level, there is the need for the risk profession to refocus its orientation from one that is fixated on political instability and violent-prone changes to a more sophisticated analytical perspective attuned to the host country's policy risks. For Western and especially U.S. risk analysts, this may require a fundamental change in the prevailing attitude and perceptions that are currently dominated by the crude notions that developing countries are capable only of violent seizure and infliction of damage on investors' assets. Specifically, the new set of risk-assessment skills must involve the ability to recognize and understand the more organized and rational set of risks stemming from the host country's industrial and investment policies. It should also involve a greater sensitivity to the technocratic mindset of the new generation of host-country decision makers as opposed to previous preoccupation with the political mindset of the host-country politicians. Such a technocratic-oriented mindset is especially prevalent among the newly industrializing countries of East Asia.[2]

Second, on the institutional level, the entire process of defining, identifying, and assessing international risks in corporate and other risk-assessment systems may have to undergo a major reorientation to reflect the emerging importance of microrisks. Specifically, more explicit and systematic identification and definition of micro and project risks should be initiated in existing risk-assessment units. This may involve the formulation of a framework of assessment for micropolicy risks and their probable impact on the company's projects and activities. Such a framework should be capable of capturing the risks stemming from the policy shifts of the host country. The next step would be to integrate this framework appropriately into the firm's overall risk-assessment process. Chapters five and six discuss some suggested approaches on how this should be accomplished. The major requirement is the formulation of a framework for conceptualizing, defining, and assessing the wide spectrum of micro and policy risks faced by the international investors. The rest of this chapter provides suggested approaches for formulating such a framework.

DEFINING THE EMS FRAMEWORK
FOR MICRORISK ASSESSMENT

A conceptually acceptable and practical framework for defining and assessing the role of microrisks and their impact on investment and other international business ventures is to conceptualize an entity appropriately known as the entry-management system. The term *entry management* is more appropriate than something such as *entry controls* because the process involves more than just regulation and placing constraints on foreign investors. It also involves a wide array of facilitating services and benefits offered to the foreign investors. The entry-management system can then be defined as the system, whether or not formalized, consisting of public and semipublic agencies, laws, regulations, and programs established by host-country authorities to both regulate and facilitate the entry and subsequent operations of investment and business ventures of foreign firms. The nature and orientation of an EMS can be defined and described by several dimensions that provide some common criteria for viewing and comparing the different systems over a range of host countries.[3] These dimensions are degree of formalization, dichotomy of the EMS (positive and negative elements), variability of the EMS, and selectivity and flexibility of the EMS.

Degree of Formalization

The definition of the EMS of a host country includes systems that are well formalized and pervasive in focusing on foreign investment to systems that are loosely and informally organized. This implies that host countries' EMSs can range from highly and formally organized agencies and institutions whose special mission is entirely devoted to the management of foreign investment activities to those comprising a loose collection of agencies that are only marginally and peripherally involved with the entry and operations of foreign investors. In the latter case there appears to be no conscious awareness by the host country itself of the EMS as an operational entity. Rather, the investors or the firms themselves will have to visualize and conceive of the existence of such a system by identifying the institutions and agencies affecting the company's entry and operations in a particular host country.

Entry-management systems of host countries fall into three categories. First, countries with aggressive industrialization goals, clearly conceived industrial policies, and high-technology aspirations tend to have specialized and formalized EMSs. This category of countries with institutionalized EMSs mostly includes newly industrializing countries like South Korea, Taiwan, Singapore, and Brazil. For instance, the Economic Development Board (EDB) of Singapore performs all administrative and monitoring functions relating to the attraction and setting up of incoming investments.

In Taiwan and South Korea, the equivalent EMS agencies, known as the Industrial Development and Investment Center (IDIC) and the Economic Planning Board (EPB), respectively, perform similar functions. The IDIC of Taiwan and the Ministry of Economic Affairs deal with all aspects of the investment process from preinvestment feasibility studies to land acquisition, plant construction, and even export promotion. In South Korea, the Bureau of International Finance (BIF) of the Ministry of Finance (MOF) and the Foreign Capital Inducement Deliberation Committee (FCIDC) handle the approval and implementation of foreign investments. These are all examples of highly organized and formal EMS agencies performing strong industrial policy-directed activities in the handling of investment projects.

The second category of countries, particularly those with less ambitious economic goals and poorly defined and inefficiently implemented industrialization objectives, tends to have little or no formally organized EMS. The entry and operation of multinationals in these countries occur on a haphazard and piecemeal basis. There is minimal or no effort consciously to attract or even regulate foreign projects. Most of the developing countries that have yet to take off industrially appear to fall into this category. A third category of host countries, comprising industrialized countries such as the United Kingdom and France, have also set up EMS-type institutions and programs to attempt to revitalize their postindustrial economies and promote high-technology enterprises. In the industrialized countries, the EMSs, like those in the newly industrializing countries, tend to place more emphasis on the positive elements of attracting incoming investment projects and pursue sophisticated and highly structured activities in handling foreign investment.[4]

Dichotomous (Positive and Negative) Elements of an EMS

The entry-management systems established by the host countries are dichotomous. Although the primary objective of these systems is to attract and facilitate the entry of and subsequent operations of the foreign investors, there is also the dimension of control in regulating the activities and behavior of the investing firms. The EMS is in some cases, therefore, a sophisticated mechanism consisting of both positive and negative elements for handling all facets of dealing with the multinational investors. As seen earlier, EMSs vary in degree of formalization among different host countries, ranging from countries with specialized agencies and special legislative codes and programs designed specifically for managing the incoming investment to those countries with informal and uncoordinated units. The latter countries appear to be more preoccupied with the negative or control dimensions of the EMS.

In countries with specialized and organized EMSs, the positive and facilitating dimensions tend to predominate, and the whole thrust appears to focus on paving the way for the smooth entry and operations of the foreign investors. This is particularly the case in countries that have established "one-stop" investment units. With the inception of one-stop investment-processing and approval procedures in many host countries, interministerial units are now set up to administer the EMS and its various incentive and control programs, especially in the newly industrializing countries in Asia and Latin America. Examples of a one-stop agency include the previously mentioned EDB in Singapore, the IDIC in Taiwan, and the BIF in Korea. However, in many host countries with a less organized EMS, there is still a multiple-agency approach in dealing with the foreign investor instead of the centralized one-stop unit.

The EMS, as a facilitating as well as regulating mechanism, thus contains both positive and negative elements impacting on the foreign investment project. Figure 3.1 shows a list of selected positive and negative elements in

FIGURE 3.1
Major Elements of An Entry Management System (EMS)

Positive Elements	Negative Elements
Export Processing Zones	Ownership Restrictions
Tax Incentives	Repatriation Restrictions
Tariffs Concessions	Indigenization
Locational Incentives	Local Contents Requirements
Financial Assistance	Price Controls
Training Assistance	Acquisition Controls
Market Protection	Export Ratio Requirements
Non-Expropriation Guarantees	Lack of Patent and Trademark Protection
Favored Repatriation	Compulsory Licensing
Export Subsidies	Pro-Local Business Bias
On-Stop Approval	Bureaucratic Red-Tape

a typical host country's EMS. The negative elements range from ownership and repatriation restrictions to indigenization, local contents, and export-ratio requirements. On the positive side, facilitating dimensions comprise a whole range of tax and nontax incentives and liberal treatment of repatriation and ownership arrangements. Most notable among the positive elements is the existence of export-processing zones that are essentially tax-free zones provided with a complete spectrum of facilities aimed at maximizing the economic advantages and benefits of locating in the zones.[5]

Many of the EMSs of the newly industrializing countries in East Asia reflect this pattern of negative and positive dimensions in dealing with foreign projects. The entry-management system of South Korea is a case in point and is typical of most EMSs. It consists of a one-stop approval process with selective restrictions as well as incentives for foreign investments. In what is called the "positive" list, about 650 industrial sectors are open to 100 percent foreign equity, whereas in the "negative" list, about 82 industrial sectors are closed to foreign investments. Positive-list projects are accorded the entire range of tax and nontax incentives with no restrictions on repatriation remittance. On the other hand, Korea's EMS also contains a fade-out requirement for joint ventures in which the foreign partner is required to reduce its equity from perhaps 70 to 50 percent or less over a period of about seven years.

Another example is that of Brazil. Brazil's EMS is also established along similar lines although consisting of a stronger preference for joint ventures of less than 50 percent and greater repatriation restrictions. Its EMS restrictions on repatriation include heavy tax surcharges running as high as 40 to 60 percent on dividends remittances paid to foreigners if a remittance exceeds 12 percent of registered capital. In addition, several important sectors such as computers, semiconductors, and fiber optics are designated as "reserved markets" that are closed to foreign investments. The Korean and Brazilian examples illustrate the kinds of risks inherent in the host country's EMS that affect foreign investment projects. The uncertainties stemming from EMS restrictions and the constant policy shifts inherent in an EMS result in a highly risky cash flow being generated by a project. An accurate and comprehensive assessment of project risks must therefore identify such EMS risks and possibly provide a forecast of the impact of such uncertainties emanating from EMS restrictions on, as well as incentives extended to, the project.

Variability of the EMS

The EMS as a policy mechanism and an institutional structure is obviously subject to changes over time. The *variability* of the entry-management system refers to the shifts between liberalness and restrictiveness in its approach and treatment of foreign investors. When a host country proceeds to liberalize its EMS, most of the usual restrictions in terms of ownership, repatriation, local contents, and indigenization are lifted or eased. In the extreme, the liberal treatment may even extend to allowing a favorable exchange rate in profit remittance and providing generous financial assistance to the investors and a whole array of other incentives and benefits. On the other hand, during times of increasing EMS restrictiveness, heavy repatriation and ownership restrictions, in addition to other adverse regulations and operational constraints, are routinely imposed on the foreign investors.

The variability of the EMS may stem from a variety of causes. Macropolitical changes such as a change in the ruling regime or more drastic shifts in political ideology and policies are frequently cited and presumed causes of a negative change in the EMS. The popular scenario is the perception of leftist or socialist host governments resorting to adverse actions and policies toward the international investors. However, recent empirical evidence does not seem to bear out this contention, particularly with the continued welcome of multinationals in revolutionary nations like Nicaragua and Angola. The recent opening up of China to international investment is another case in point. Chinese technocrats, given a free rein by the ruling pragmatist regime, have spurred the rapid emergence of a highly favorable EMS. The whole thrust of the newly emerging Chinese EMS is directed at the energetic enticement of foreign investment through the establishment of special economic zones, broadening the range of incentives, and undertaking the constant revision and updating of its investment laws. Given the variability of Chinese EMS in the past, the major uncertainty facing prospective investors in China is a lack of assurance of how sustained is the latest round of liberalization.[6]

Another major cause of EMS variability is the state of the country's economy. Serious economic difficulties such as a high external debt burden, domestic economic difficulties, and other disruptions occasionally induce the host country's authorities to liberalize and lift restrictions imposed on international investors. Many Latin American nations caught in the throes of economic chaos are reluctantly easing ownership and repatriation restrictions and lowering their local contents and indigenization requirements. However, the pattern of response to economic difficulties appears to be inconsistent. In some instances, the host country may respond to economic difficulties by increasing the restrictions on incoming or existing investment projects and even close off certain of its economic sectors to foreign investment. Countries like Mexico, Brazil, and Venezuela have shown an inconsistent and unpredictable pattern of response to economic difficulties by alternately liberalizing and restricting the role of foreign investment in their domestic economies.

A third major and perhaps more consistent cause of EMS variability is the ascendancy of industrial policies in many of the newly industrializing countries in East Asia. As noted, many countries like South Korea and Taiwan have consciously and deliberately used their EMSs as an instrument of promoting and directing the course of industrialization. Special economic and export-processing zones accompanied with a comprehensive package of incentive programs are routinely provided to investment projects meeting certain policy criteria, particularly in the areas of technology and export contribution. On the other hand, these countries also have been known to use their EMS to deny access for investment projects low on the host country's development priorities. Because the industrial priorities of newly industrializing countries (NICs) are dictated by a constant need to stay competitive in the global markets, market-induced technological and competitive obsolescence can lead to sudden withdrawal of EMS incentives and increased restrictions for a project.[7]

Variability in the host country's EMS is therefore a major source of project risks for multinational investors regardless of whether the swings are toward the positive and liberal end or toward the negative and restrictive end of the spectrum. EMS variability reduces the investors ability to predict and hence formulate effective plans and strategies. Chapter five provides a more detailed analysis of project risks stemming from EMS changes and considers various approaches in dealing with EMS risk assessment.

Selectivity of an EMS

In addition to a pattern of variability, another distinguishing characteristic of an EMS is the selectivity of its impact on specific projects. At any time, a host country's EMS may extend favorable treatment for a certain qualified project while imposing restrictions or even denying entry to another project. This selectivity generally stems from the previously mentioned phenomenon of the host country using the EMS as an instrument of industrialization. However, EMS selectivity may also be motivated by political considerations. An investment project of certain national origin may be discriminated against through more intense restrictions for a variety for political reasons. Exports and business ventures originating from South Africa or Israel may be restricted or even banned, the former particularly in black African countries and the latter by Islamic countries.

In general, technological and competitive obsolescence appears to be the most apparent reason for instigating selective EMS restrictions by the host country. In the context of industrial policy objectives, to stay competitive in the fast-changing global markets, the host country may use its EMS selectively to achieve its industrial policy goals. Projects and other ventures with a continuous edge in technological and export competitiveness are accorded special and privileged treatment, whereas other low-priority projects, if not prohibited altogether, are suffocated by a whole phalanx of restrictions. Chapter five provides more detailed analyses and discussions of the variability and selectivity of the EMS and the resultant risk impact on a project's cash flow.

SELECTED EXAMPLES OF A HOST COUNTRY'S EMS

Figure 3.2 provides a more comprehensive listing of the elements in a host country's EMS. The list also provides a framework for identifying and describing the contents and orientation of the EMS of a particular host country. The framework, in turn, provides a more concrete basis for assessing microinvestment risks. The EMS framework, as depicted in Figure

3.2, has two parts. Part I focuses on the general orientation and underlying policy structure of the EMS, and Part II includes a more detailed listing of

FIGURE 3.2
The Entry Management System: An Analytical Framework

I. General Orientation and Policy Structure of the EMS.

A. General policy on foreign investment: liberal, controlled, restricted.
B. Status of foreign investment: overall level and size, amount in various sectors, FDI/gross domestic investment or capital formation, top foreign investors (company and country) and size.
C. Role of foreign investment in industrial development.
D. General ownership policy: liberal/restrictive, joint venture vs. 100% ownership preference, fade-out requirements.
E. General repatriation policy: capital, dividends, royalties, fees, exchange rate structure.
F. Tax and non-tax incentive policy.
G. Status of the foreign firm: discriminatory/equal/favored treatment.
H. Indigenization: controls and treatment in employment of foreign nationals.
I. Expropriation policy: state intervention, nationalization, creeping expropriation, non-expropriation guarantees.
J. Tax and investment treaties: treaty countries, major provisions.
K. Technology and intellectual property protection: level of protection and enforcement.
L. Business practices: laws, official attitude and practice in bribery and facilitating payments.
M. Others.
O. Brief analysis and implications for company's project.

II. Entry Management Agencies and Programs.

A. Agencies responsible for facilitating and controlling foreign investment: one-stop, uncoordinated units.
B. Specific legislation/laws/regulations/decrees governing and managing foreign investment.
C. Priority category of industries/sectors/products/projects targeted for favored and liberalized treatment.
D. Qualifying and approval criteria for registration as priority investment.
E. Restrictive industries/sectors/products.
F. Incentive programs:
  (i) Export processing or special economic zones, industrial parks.
  (ii) Tax incentives.
  (iii) Tariff and other tax concessions.
  (iv) Locational incentives.
  (v) Capital and financial assistance.
  (vi) Training of nationals.
  (vii) Export promotion incentives.
  (viii) Technology and R&D incentives.
  (ix) Market protection.
  (x) Non-expropriation guarantees and political risk insurance programs.
  (xi) Favorable repatriation programs.
  (xii) Others.

Figure 3.2 contd.

G. EMS restrictions:
   (i) Joint venture pressures and ownership restrictions.
   (ii) Repatriation and remittance: exchange restrictions, application and approval procedures, delays.
   (iii) Local contents requirements.
   (iv) Export ratio requirements.
   (v) Indigenization requirements.
   (vi) Countertrade requirements.
   (vii) Price and other forms of market controls.
   (viii) Anti-trust and fair trade requirements, acquisitions and mergers controls.
   (ix) Environmental controls.
   (x) Patent, trademark and copyright protection: laws and enforcement.
   (xi) Compulsory licensing.
   (xii) Bureaucratic constraints and delays.
   (xiii) Tariff and non-tariff barriers.
   (xiv) Discriminatory taxes.
   (xv) Others.
H. Brief analysis and implications for company's project.

specific EMS agencies and programs. The following sections provide brief illustrations and comparisons of the EMSs of several selected countries in order to delineate certain salient characteristics of the nature and orientation of these entry-management systems.

Venezuela

Venezuela's EMS is in large part shaped by the performance of the country's oil-rich economy. In the late seventies and early eighties, propped by a booming oil-fueled economy and a relatively prolonged period of political stability, Venezuela was able to act very selectively toward foreign investment. It was in a position to impose selective restrictions on the many multinationals eager for a share of the country's economic boom. Thus despite Venezuela's strict adherence to the controversial and influential Decision 24 of the 1970 Andean Pact investment code, the country had no problem in attracting sufficient foreign investment. Decision 24 provides for the imposition of restrictive ownership, repatriation, and indigenization requirements by the Andean Pact countries on foreign investments. The recent economic difficulties brought on by the sharp drop in the price of oil and other economic disruptions, however, has prompted an easing if not a reversal of the restrictive policies associated with the Andean Pact Decision 24. In the newly promulgated "Economic Memorandum," encouragement of foreign investment is now declared a crucial aspect of overall strategy for economic development.[8]

Recent moves to liberalize the EMS restrictions consist essentially of relaxing the interpretation of the provisions of Decision 24, particularly repatriation and ownership restrictions. Instead of the hitherto strict fade-out requirement, which called for the divestment of foreign majority ownership at the end of fifteen years, foreign ownership is now treated with more flexibility. However, there is still a definite preference for foreign minority joint ventures. Companies in Venezuela are classified according to the percentage of foreign ownership into "national" companies (less than 20 percent foreign equity), "mixed" (20 to 49 percent), and "foreign" (over 49 percent). Projects in the agribusiness, tourism, and construction sectors and those exporting more than 80 percent of the output outside of the Andean Pact area are exempted from the fifteen-year fade-out requirement. Since the last round of large-scale nationalization of the oil and other industries in the early seventies, the probability of expropriating foreign investment now appears to be remote.

Restrictions in repatriation of capital and profits have also been eased somewhat. Foreign investors may remit dividends up to 20 percent of the initially registered foreign capital. However, royalties and technical fees may not be remitted by a company that is 49 percent or more foreign owned. In the case of the sale or liquidation of an investment, a foreign firm may repatriate the original amount of his capital plus capital gains, reinvestments, and undistributed profits less losses after payment of the appliable taxes. One interesting feature of the Venezuelan EMS, is the multitiered exchange-rate structure. Certain transactions are permitted to take place on the basis of the preferential rates, whereas others are based on the floating free-market rate.[9]

The major agency having jurisdiction in dealing with foreign investment is known as the Superintendency of Foreign Investment, or its Venezuelan acronym SIEX, an agency of the Ministry of Finance. SIEX has comprehensive responsibility for authorization, registration, and supervision of foreign investment and the supervision of patent and trademark use. Although there are no systematic and specific incentives for encouraging foreign investment in Venezuela, technology development, export promotion, and regional incentives in certain designated areas are available for local and foreign companies. Regional incentives consist of tax reduction, tax holidays, tax credits, and tariff exemptions on essential raw materials, machinery, and capital equipment.

The Venezuelan EMS is typical of the general pattern of behavior of the EMSs in Latin America. Its EMS reflects an underlying nationalistic tendency toward foreign investment and multinationals, a tendency characterized by an ambivalent attitude and treatment of foreign investment. The pattern of EMS variability and selectivity, alternating between liberal and restrictive, is a response to the prevailing economic situation as well as to the ideological orientations of the prevailing power structure. Therefore, the assessment and management of policy risks stemming from this pattern of EMS behavior necessitates a constant review of the underlying policy structure, agencies, and programs in the Venezuelan EMS.

Brazil

Throughout the years, the Brazilian EMS, similar to that of Venezuela, had exhibited a relatively variable and selective pattern in its attitude and receptiveness to foreign investment, fluctuating with the prevailing political ideology, economic difficulties, and industrial priorities. Selective barriers for foreign investment exist in the telecommunications, information, and mining sectors, which come under strong state control. The computer, semiconductor, and aircraft sectors are maintained as "reserved markets" for local Brazilian firms. Major foreign investors, comprised of U.S., West German, Japanese, and Swiss multinationals, and most of the investments are in the manufacturing sector, particularly the automotive, machinery, and pharmaceutical sectors. Despite Brazil's sometimes ambivalent attitude toward foreign investment, a sizable proportion of its manufactured goods are produced by foreign companies. Foreign multinationals have contributed significantly to Brazil's status as a newly industrializing country.

Brazil's ownership policy, although permitting 100 percent foreign equity on paper, shows a clear preference for joint ventures, especially when eligibility for tax incentives, low-cost funds, and other benefits require majority Brazilian ownership. Repatriation is allowed on a restrictive basis. The originally registered foreign investment capital may be repatriated without restrictions or tax surcharges. Remittances of profit, however, are subject to restrictions, and supplementary taxes, ranging from 40 to 60 percent, are imposed on remittances exceeding 12 percent of registered capital. Royalties and other fees paid to foreign companies are subject to a 25 percent withholding tax. Brazil has strict indigenization policy, requiring at least two-thirds of a foreign company's total work force to be Brazilian nationals, although exceptions are permitted in specialized and technical services. Stringent local contents requirements are imposed, particularly on the automotive industry. Bilateral investment and tax treaties are maintained with Argentina, Austria, Belgium, Denmark, France, Portugal, Spain, and Sweden, and repatriation restrictions with treaty countries are more relaxed than they are with nontreaty countries.[10]

The basic Brazilian statutes governing foreign investment are Law 4131 (September 1962) and Law 4390 (August 1964), which regulate the registration and repatriation of foreign capital and profits. Theoretically, they grant foreign investors essentially the same rights and treatment as domestic capital, although in practice there is an increasing movement to favor and protect local Brazilian firms. The Central Bank of Brazil is the chief agency responsible for authorization and registration of foreign investment, profit remittance, and exchange controls. Other agencies such as the interministerial price-control commission, the industrial development council, the national institute of industrial property, and the foreign trade department also deal with the foreign investors in a supervisory and governing capacity in various functional areas. Qualified foreign projects in several high-priority sectors are eligible for numerous incentive programs offered on a federal and state level such as tax concessions and financial assistance. They include locational incentives, sectoral investment incentives, and export-promotion incentives. The various incentives are designed to achieve regional and economic diversification. Regional incentives are particularly attractive in the relatively underdeveloped Northeastern and the Amazonian regions. For instance, companies are eligible for partial income tax exemption and a tax holiday as long as ten years, and they have the options of investing their tax-payable in approved projects.

Mexico

Mexico's attitude toward foreign investment is basically governed by the need to maintain a balance between the urgency of its economic plight and the aspirations for Mexicanization and national independence. In recent decades, the buoyant oil-fueled economy has allowed the country a means of achieving industrialization and improvement in its standard of living without too great a dependence on foreign multinational investors. Its EMS, therefore, was restrictive. Recent economic woes and disruptions brought on by the excessive debt burden and the disastrous 1985 earthquakes coupled with the sharp drop in the price of oil have prompted a drastic change in Mexico's policy toward international investment. The EMS is being selectively liberalized, although on the whole it remains very cautious, tentative, and even ambivalent in its treatment of incoming foreign investment. Mexico sees foreign investment with its capital, technology, and jobs as a means of elevating the country out of its economic misery, but it also is affected by lingering fears and suspicions of foreign economic dominance.[11]

Although no major changes in its 1973 foreign investment law are planned, the Mexican authorities have began to exercise greater flexibility in processing and approval of foreign investment applications. The major agency responsible for processing and authorizing foreign investment is the National Commission of Foreign Investment (FIC). Authorization for investment approval is decided on the basis of a comprehensive spectrum of factors or criteria. These criteria range from factors such as whether the investment will supplement or displace national investment, its balance-of-payment contributions, use of local materials and parts, technological contribution, and training and skills imparted to Mexicans to the development of underdeveloped areas and the preservation of Mexico's social and cultural values.[12]

Major investors include the United States, West Germany, the Netherlands, Japan, and the United Kingdom. Approximately 80 percent of all foreign investment is in the manufacturing sector. Mexico's ownership policy tends to be selective. There is clear preference for joint ventures with minority foreign ownership (limited to 49 percent) in most industries, although majority and even 100 percent foreign ownership are permitted in certain product categories (e.g., industrial machinery, electronics, and pharmaceuticals) and in the Maquiladoras or the so-called in-bond processing plants along the Mexican-U.S. border.[13] The in-bond processing zones offer 100 percent ownership, tariff and duties exemption on materials imported into the zones, and unrestricted repatriation and remittances. Investment incentives are also extended to investors in specially designated zones and could range from tax concessions to access to low-cost loans and other fiscal incentives. On the negative side of the EMS, Mexico imposed a stringent local contents requirement of as much as 55 percent rising to 90 percent, depending on the product category. Price controls are also imposed in product categories such as foodstuffs, medicines, and essential raw materials.

Repatriation and the remittance of funds are complicated by the fact that Mexico operates on a dual exchange-rate system consisting of both a regulated rate and a floating rate. Certain approved transfers are given the more favorable regulated rate, whereas other transfers are remitted on the basis of the floating rates. At least in law, once the foreign investment is registered and authorized, profits and dividends are freely remittable. In practice, however, the investors have to face the prospects of passive blockage and a period of delay arising from the scarcity of foreign exchange.

In brief, the Mexican EMS is the primary instrument for implementing the country's selective investment policies. Like many oil-dependent countries struggling with a depressed oil market and excessive debt payments, Mexico does not offer a blanket liberalization of its industrial sectors to foreign investments. Rather, its EMS remains predominantly restrictive, particularly in terms of ownership, in most industries. The EMS is used to channel investment selectively into the desired high-priority sectors that have the most urgent need for job creation, generation of foreign exchange, and technology development. Selective and cautious liberalization is implemented on a case-by-case basis. The most recent example of this selective policy is the approval given to IBM to establish a wholly owned personal computer (PC) manufacturing plant in Guadalajara. This move constitutes a major departure from Mexico's restrictive ownership policy. As part of the agreement, IBM will export 92 percent of the value of its production and continuously upgrade its microcomputers product line in the Guadalajara plant.[14]

France

The EMS of France is in a state of transition and is fundamentally an expression of a "mixed" economy striving for postindustrial economic expansion and high-technology development. The changing nature of its EMS is mainly reflected in its ownership policy. This ownership policy, overall, has been generally liberal, allowing private industrial ownership although alternating with periods of nationalization and state intervention in key industries. Like the EMSs of many host countries, France's EMS exhibits a pattern of variation that is essentially influenced by the prevailing economic conditions and policy orientations. After the last round of nationalizations by the Socialist government and the economic stagnation and difficulties it brought about, the country is again pursuing policies of privatizations and promotion of market forces in the economy. The recent EMS liberalization resulted in a large part from a worsening balance of payments, high unemployment, and the need for industrial restructuring in the face of intense competition coming from its European Community (EC) partners and particularly the United States and Japan.[15]

France has different EMS requirements for EC and non-EC investors. Investment from individual residents and firms of the community are accorded preferential treatment. EC investors need only to file a "declaration of foreign investment" and automatic approval is usually granted within two months of filing with certain exceptions. Foreign investors are accorded the same rights and extended the same treatment as French firms. Recent official statements have reaffirmed a policy of reducing state intervention, promoting entrepreneurship, and encouraging privatization of industry and market-oriented decisions in the economy, a policy that bodes well for the foreign investors. The major foreign investors are from the United States and the EC.[16]

All foreign investors must file their investment applications or declaration with and receive authorization from the Directorate of Treasury of the Ministry of the Economy. Another major agency responsible for encouraging foreign investment and regional development is the French development agency Delegation a L'Amenagement due Territoire et a L'Action Regionale (DATAR). DATAR is essentially a one-stop agency acting as an intermediary between the foreign investors and the various ministries and departments; it is also responsible for providing assistance to the investors ranging from project feasibility studies to staff recruitment and equipment installation. In addition, DATAR administers the investment incentives programs, which include tax concessions such as tax holidays and accelerated depreciation, financial grants, low-cost loans, and training subsidies, particularly for firms locating in the outlying and high-unemployment regions.[17]

Foreign projects may be granted generous incentives and favorable investment terms if they meet the following criteria: creation and maintenance of jobs, improvement of skills and working conditions, increase in exports outside the European Economic Community (EEC) area, improvement in manufacturing efficiency (e.g., automation), development of new products and processes, energy development, and provisions for high-technology expertise. Investors are also granted a broad range of incentives for locating in the designated special-development areas. There are no restrictions placed on repatriation of capital and the remittance of profits once an investment has been authorized. There are strict controls, however, in the area of monopolistic and anticompetitive business practices.

In sum, the French EMS typifies that of a maturing industrial economy attempting to revamp its economic structure through the attraction and establishment of especially high-technology investment. To attain economic restructuring, the entire industrial environment is placed in the direction of greater liberalization. Specifically, to foster more conducive and positive conditions, privatization of the markets and industries has been given top policy priority. Foreign investment is recognized to play a major role in this industrial strategy, and the country's EMS is therefore positioned accordingly to reflect this orientation. With minimal macropolitical risks to consider, the foreign investors are therefore placed in a position where they need only to focus on optimizing their policy interactions, particularly with the positive elements of the EMS.

Spain

The entry of Spain into the EEC is part of the country's overall objective of achieving accelerated industrialization and bringing its economic and industrial structure into line with that of its EEC partners. The Spanish EMS is therefore shaped accordingly to facilitate the establishment of industries and the encouragement of investment that will assist in its industrial policies. Recent balance-of-payment problems and high structural unemployment also played a part in moving the EMS in a more liberal direction. The official Spanish attitude toward foreign investment is thus one of positive encouragement, and foreign investment is considered a source of capital, technology, and managerial expertise. Despite this overall positive attitude, however, certain restrictive policies and practices imposed on foreign investment continue to persist. Top investors consist mainly of the United States, Switzerland, West Germany, France, and the Netherlands.[18]

In terms of ownership policies, there is a decided preference for joint ventures, particularly for foreign minority ownership, although wholly owned foreign subsidiaries are not entirely prohibited. The major agency responsible for registration and authorization of foreign investment is the Direccion General De Transacciones Exteriores (DGTE) or the Directorate General for External Transactions, a unit of the Ministry of Economy and Commerce. In addition, establishment of new plants requires an industrial permit issued by the Ministry of Industry. For investment of less than 50 percent foreign ownership, no formal approval is required. For investment greater than 50 percent ownership, however, prior authorization is required subject to considerations such as foreign currency and technology contributions, export-ratio requirement, job creation, and a positive foreign exchange contribution. The positive balance-of-payment requirement may be waived if the company exports 50 percent or more in value of its production. Investors are theoretically allowed to repatriate and remit funds once they are registered with the Foreign Exchange Authority. However, in practice, restrictions are sometimes imposed and applications for remittance are subject to strict scrutiny and are examined on a case-by-case basis.[19]

Spain offers a broad range of investment incentives, particularly for specially designated development areas known as *polos, poligonos*, and preferential industrial zones that are located away from overcrowded Madrid and other existing industrial areas. Investment incentives provided include cash subsidies, tax reductions and tax holidays, tariff and duties exemptions, accelerated depreciation, preferential access to low-interest short- and long-term loans, and access to improved infrastructure and amenities. Incentives are divided into four groups categorized by varying degrees of attractiveness. Eligibility for the different incentive groups depends on the extent to which the investment meets established criteria and conforms to the industrial policy objectives noted previously. Incentives for export promotion and technology development are extensive, ranging from cash grants to favorable financing. Spain has strict local contents requirements. Local parts and components must account for as much as 70 percent of all in-factory value in the first year, increasing to 90 percent in subsequent years. Local contents requirements may be waived for highly export-oriented companies. Three free-trade zones have been established at Barcelona, Cadiz, and Vizo.

In sum, the nature and orientation of the Spanish EMS derives mainly from its industrial policy objectives of achieving rapid economic development and industrial expansion. At the same time, however, the EMS exhibits a certain degree of ambivalence toward the foreign investors, especially in the areas of ownership and repatriation. It is a transitional system that has not completely freed itself from the residual need to regulate foreign investment and business strictly. Nevertheless, as Spain gradually integrates its economy and investment policies more in the direction of its EEC partners, the prospects for greater liberalization appear to be good.

South Korea

South Korea is among the most prominent of the successful newly industrializing countries (NICs) in East Asia; other countries and cities are Taiwan, Singapore, and Hong Kong. Its route to industrial and technological success, like that of the other NICs, is essentially based on carving out a highly sophisticated and efficiently planned and implemented industrial policy road map. As in the other Asian NICs, the nature and orientation of its entry-management system is shaped and guided by the industrial policy structure. The primary industrial policy objective of Korea and the NICs is to achieve rapid export-oriented industrialization via an aggressive program of attracting technology and foreign investment in building the industrial base. As an instrument of this policy, the EMS serves to both facilitate and manage incoming foreign investment and technology transfers by means of providing incentives as well as imposing selective controls.[20]

South Korea's fundamental and deliberate policy goal in proactively managing foreign investment and technology is to enable the country to design and fine-tune its industrial and technological structure so as to place it in the forefront of international competitiveness. Reflecting the well-structured nature of its EMS, industries are divided into three major categories for the purpose of managing foreign investments by extending incentives and imposing controls. The industries are classified into Category I, Category II, and a prohibited category. Category I industries of the so-called positive list, comprising about 65 industries at present, are freely open to foreign investment with minimal restrictions. Favored treatment for Category I projects include location in one of Korea's free-export zones, 100 percent foreign ownership, and favorable repatriation conditions. To be eligible for Category I, the investment projects must meet several criteria such as strengthening and contributing to the existing level of technology, contributing to an improved balance of payments, and injecting substantial capital contributions into the Korean economy. Category II industries comprising some 456 industries are open to foreign investment projects only on a joint-venture basis with maximum foreign ownership limited to 50 percent. Negative-list industries such as agriculture, wholesale distribution, and public utilities are closed to foreign investment.

The key agencies with responsibility for approving and managing foreign investment are the Economic Planning Board, the Ministry of Finance, and the Bank of Korea (central bank). Within the Ministry of Finance, the Bureau of International Finance and the Foreign Capital Inducement Deliberation Committee handle the applications and authorization of foreign investment proposals. The approval and operation of foreign investments are governed by the Foreign Capital Inducement Act. The provisions of the act are administered by agencies in the Ministry of Finance. Major foreign investors include Japan, the United States, the

United Kingdom, and West Germany. South Korea's repatriation policy is, in theory, liberal. Capital repatriation is limited to 20 percent of the originally registered capital per year, and approved profits and dividends are freely remittable at the official rate of exchange.[21]

A wide range of incentives are offered to projects operating in the Category I industries. Investment incentives are especially liberal for projects in the automotive, industrial equipment, pharmaceuticals, and electronics sectors. Incentives include tax concessions (tax reduction, credit, and holidays), financing and training assistance, and export-promotion credits and grants. South Korea operates two major Free Export Zones (FEZs) at Masan and at Iri. More than 50 percent of the firms operating in the Masan FEZ are foreign manufacturing subsidiaries, and the others are joint ventures. Apart from the restrictive Category II industries, the negative aspects of South Korea's EMS are its ownership fade-out requirements and its stringent local contents requirements. Foreign investors must adhere to a closely supervised "localization rate" schedule that spells out the amount of local contents requirement over a stipulated period.

In brief, the Korean EMS is a classic example of a well-organized and efficiently managed policy system closely geared to the country's industrial policies. Since its primary mission is to promote industrial and technology development, the Korean EMS is capable of exercising a high degree of flexibility in its treatment of foreign investment. For instance, even in the protected Category II industries, foreign investment projects may be selectively granted exemptions from ownership and other restrictions based on the exceptional merits of the project. In addition, Korea's strict ownership fade-out clause or programmed divestment, which mandates a reduction in the foreign equity share of a joint venture within five to seven years, may occasionally be waived. Johnson & Johnson, G. D. Serle, Eli Lilly, and Schering-Plough are among the U.S. multinationals allowed to maintain a majority share in their joint ventures even after the scheduled fade-out date. To strengthen further the recent move toward EMS liberalization, South Korea may plan on expanding its positive-list industries.

The People's Republic of China

China's opening up to foreign business and its active courting of foreign investment represent perhaps the most dramatic example of a fundamental policy shift ever witnessed among East Asian countries. It went from near isolation toward the late 1970s to becoming a host country with probably the region's most ambitious programs for attracting and encouraging foreign investment and technology transfers. After some thirty years of political isolation and economic disruptions, China is now essentially formulating its economic policies and building its modern investment infrastructure from scratch. The cornerstone of its industrial policy is the Four Modernization programs, an ambitious plan to elevate the country to industrial preeminence. Basically emulating the successful and proven formula that led to the current economic achievements enjoyed by its newly industrializing East Asian neighbors, China is actively pursuing an export-oriented industrialization strategy. It has drastically revamped its outmoded legal structure and has replaced it with a set of new investment laws that attempt to bring the system more in line with that of the rest of the international investment community. Even more fundamental, ideologically, is its attempt to encourage limited free enterprise and private ventures in order to spur the sluggish state-run Chinese economy.[22]

Although uncertainties continue to persist in the minds of many foreign investors and despite being plagued by continuing management and foreign exchange difficulties, the country appears to be well on its way to rapid industrial development. Between 1979 and the present, for instance, China has managed to attract as much as $17 billion in foreign investment. Approved projects range from wholly owned foreign ventures to equity and contractual joint ventures to offshore oil contracts. The top investors are from Hong Kong, the United States, Japan, West Germany, and the United Kingdom. The investment inflow also includes a substantial portion of overseas Chinese capital from Southeast Asia.

Perhaps the most significant piece of investment legislation is the 1979 Joint Venture Law and its subsequent revisions. This set of laws contains provisions for detailed arrangements regarding the approval, the setting up, and the operation of joint ventures. Other relevant legislation deals with the Special Economic Zones (SEZs) and foreign exchange transactions.[23] Since China's entry-management system is still in its formative stages, there is a lack of a clearly defined and efficiently organized set of agencies dealing with foreign investors. The foreign investor usually has to deal with any one of a multitude of agencies ranging from Central and provincial government authorities to one of the many Chinese state corporations. However, the agency with highest overall authority over foreign investment is the Ministry of Foreign Economic Relations and Trade (MOFERT). Investors interested in locating in one of the SEZs have to deal separately with the zone authorities. Perhaps the most influential and visible superagency handling the encouragement of and assisting in the setting up of foreign investment is the China International Trust and Investment Corporation (CITIC), a quasi-independent agency established at the direct order of China's leader Deng Xiaoping. CITIC has set up offices in major cities around the world like New York, London, and Hong Kong and is charged with the responsibility of facilitating, negotiating, setting up, and financing foreign investment projects in China.[24]

The most notable aspects of China's selectively liberalized entry policy are the SEZs located in Guandong and Fujian provinces along China's southern coast. The four SEZs at Shenzhen (near Hong Kong), Zhuhai, Shantou, and Xiamen not only permit wholly owned foreign ventures but also offer a broad range of tax and financial incentives. The SEZs are in fact pockets of free enterprise and private investment in China's vast state-directed economy. In addition, special treatment, including the lifting of restrictions and the offer of incentives, is also granted to foreign projects locating in one of China's inner provinces. Foreign projects are evaluated and approved on the basis of several criteria. The most important criteria for project approval are the transfer of advanced technology, foreign exchange contribution, and contribution to the employment and training of Chinese workers.

Two of the major negative aspects of China's EMS stem from its lack of hard-currency reserves. This lack of foreign exchange has led to a restrictive repatriation policy. Profit remittances are subject to a 10 percent tax, and repatriation of the original investment capital requires special approval from the exchange authorities. Apart from transfer risks, the other shortcoming of the Chinese EMS is the countertrade arrangements required of foreign projects. Contractual joint-venture and coproduction arrangements in which the partners share the output rather than profits are peculiar problems that confront the foreign investor in China. Also, many projects are subject to strict export-ratio requirements in which sometimes as much as 80 percent of a project's output has to be exported. These restrictive requirements, in addition to the problems of bureaucratic efficiency and a clear lack of a supportive investment infrastructure, are the major sources of uncertainties and EMS risks for the foreign investors. However, these problems are not foreseen to be insurmountable, and as the Chinese EMS proceeds to improve in its effectiveness along its learning curve, the resultant industrial performance could well accelerate and smooth its progress toward becoming the next NIC in Asia.

MAJOR MARKET ENTRY STRATEGIES

Increasingly, as the international investment environment shifts toward a predominance of industrial policy and EMS-driven risks, multinational entry decisions have to take into consideration a new and more complex set of entry considerations. The mode of market entry can no longer be based, as was hitherto the case, solely on the firm's optimization and technological objectives without due consideration of the entry conditions and constraints imposed by the host country. Market-entry decisions must now be considered both on a strategic basis as well as on the basis of the imposed parameters of entry set up by the host country. One of the most significant developments on the host country side of the entry equation is the phenomenon known as "unbundling." This *unbundling* process, as the term implies, involves the disaggregation of the various components of the traditional package of wholly owned and controlled direct investment by foreign firms. Unbundling allows the recipient country to partially or totally detach and remove the foreign ownership component from the technology-transfer component. Thus in the joint-venture mode, the recipient can benefit from the technological and management know-how transmitted by the foreign partners through ownership sharing. In licensing, an even more unbundled arrangement, technology transfers may be effected without any foreign ownership whatsoever.

The following sections examine various market-entry modes in light of the changing entry conditions imposed by host countries. Each of the entry options, such as joint venture, licensing, franchising, and various other contractual arrangements, are discussed in relation to the prevailing EMS conditions and constraints. The advantages (and disadvantages) of the wholly owned and controlled direct investment mode of entry has been extensively explored elsewhere in extant literature on the "internalization" theory of the multinational firm and therefore is not repeated here.[25] It may suffice to state briefly that wholly controlled direct investment is the traditionally preferred mode of market entry because of its obvious technological and managerial advantages for the firm's global optimization.

INTERNATIONAL JOINT VENTURES

In a transformed investment environment accompanied by the worldwide trend toward unbundling, joint ventures have emerged as perhaps the dominant and the most popular form of market-entry arrangement among both multinationals and the host countries. Joint ventures, theoretically, may be the most appropriate arrangement that optimally accommodates the needs and objectives of both the foreign investors and the host country.

In practice, however, the investors may encounter a wide array of problems ranging from cross-cultural difficulties with partners, EMS restrictions, and management conflicts to protection of technology, transfer-pricing problems, and the sharing of markets. Since an international joint venture is essentially a contrived "marriage of convenience" between cross-cultural entities, self-exterminating and destabilizing forces may already be operating at the point of inception.

On the positive level, joint ventures offer the foreign investor the advantage of an equity vehicle that effectively deflects nationalistic sentiments regarding foreign ownership while still allocating a significant degree of control. Although it obviously lacks the advantage of a wholly owned and controlled subsidiary, the foreign partner in a joint venture can sometimes enjoy almost total control over operational decisions, particularly when complex management and production technologies are being transmitted to the local counterpart. Joint ventures also offer the foreign investor a vital source of local expertise and connections in structurally and culturally complex markets such as those of Japan and Saudi Arabia. From the perspective of the host country, a joint venture can be equally beneficial. Through maintaining a local ownership position in a joint venture, particularly in projects with a local majority, a host government can substantially diffuse radical political opposition to the investment project and hence reduce potential risks both for the foreign investors and itself. Participation of the local partner in the joint venture's management, production, and marketing activities is usually a valuable source of skills transfers. Therefore, politically, economically, and functionally, joint ventures are perhaps a near-optimal arrangement for the parties involved.

Two general types of joint venture may be distinguished. The more conventional arrangement is that formed between a multinational and local partners of the host country. Increasingly, however, multinational joint ventures involving firms of several nationalities are being formed. Under such an arrangement two or more partners of different nationalities may join forces to undertake projects in a third country. For instance, it is common for three-way joint ventures consisting of Hong Kong and U.S. investors with a Chinese partner to be established in China. Under such arrangement, each of the partners is usually included for a specific purpose. Thus in a typical three-way joint venture, the U.S. partner is primarily responsible for contributing technology, the Hong Kong counterpart provides the funding, and the Chinese side provides the land, factory, and labor. Major construction projects, particularly transportation projects and property development, are usually undertaken by a multinational consortium comprising contractors and engineering firms from several countries. Joint ventures have therefore assumed a special role in fostering an international comparative advantage and in acting as vehicles for international specialization.

Functionally, joint ventures may be formed for a variety of purposes, ranging from manufacturing to marketing joint ventures. Most joint ventures are established for undertaking a particular project based on a specific product or a market. General Motors's manufacturing joint venture with Toyota, for instance, was established to produce a single product, the Nova, for the U.S. market. In other instances, the joint venture may be an umbrella arrangement under which the partners may pursue a combination of projects covering several products and different markets.

EMS Controls

Despite some of its obvious advantages to both the foreign investors and the host country, joint ventures, like other investment vehicles, are perceived ambivalently both by the host countries and by the foreign investors. Although a whole array of incentives are made available to encourage the formation of joint ventures, host countries continue to impose additional constraints on the joint-venture arrangement. In addition to the usual limit of 49 percent foreign ownership, many countries such as Mexico, Argentina, and South Korea impose fade-out requirements, which call for progressive reduction in the foreign equity component over a scheduled period. In the area of repatriation, joint ventures seem to enjoy greater favored treatment than other forms of arrangement. Most foreign minority joint ventures are allowed to remit profits and repatriate capital with less restrictions than are wholly owned subsidiaries. Reduced foreign ownership also entitles the foreign investors to enjoy the right to remit licensing royalties and to qualify for a broad range of selective incentives.

Like other arrangements, joint ventures are usually molded to conform to the host country's industrial and EMS objectives such as contribution to foreign exchange earnings, indigenization, and local contents requirements. In many restrictive EMSs, the extent of foreign ownership, or ownership allowance in a joint venture, is frequently tied to the proposed project's export-ratio contribution. Although there is no strict one-to-one relationship, 100 percent foreign ownership is usually permitted for projects that are 100 percent export oriented, whereas an 80 percent export ratio would perhaps enable the project to qualify for 80 percent ownership. The whole thrust of the EMS's joint-venture strategy, therefore, is to use ownership allowance as an instrument for attaining the host country's industrial objectives. However, overall, since joint ventures are an encouraged form of entry arrangement, they generally suffer less adverse impact from EMS restrictions than from other entry arrangements.

Strategic Considerations in Joint Ventures

From the standpoint of the multinational investor, joint ventures are relatively more effective in diffusing potential risks stemming from adverse nationalistic sentiments toward foreign business. Joint venture through ownership sharing with the local nationals is one of the most widely accepted integrative risk-management strategies practiced by multi-nationals. Since it involves greater direct interactions on a functional as well as a managerial level and is hence more integrated into the business fabric of the host country, a joint-venture arrangement tends to reinforce the positive perceptions of the local nationals. At the same time, because it involves equity participation, control of technology and managerial prerogatives need not be sacrificed. Significant if not near total control can still be exercised by the foreign partner even in minority joint ventures.

International joint venture as an appropriate mode of market entry can also be viewed within the context of the international product cycle. When the international product cycle has been firmly implanted in a recipient country in terms of product introduction and market growth, greater strategic and operational effectiveness would require deeper and more intensive localization of marketing and production activities. Joint ventures are perhaps the more appropriate vehicles for production and marketing localization since locally shared management and control are more superior in terms of local product and market expertise than a wholly foreign controlled subsidiary. In addition to the production and marketing economics inherent within the product cycle, other market dimensions may render joint ventures as superior entry vehicles. This is particularly the case in markets that are highly complex, structurally and culturally, such as those of many developing countries. Many multinationals lack expertise in markets that are still functioning at more primitive stages of marketing development. The local market expertise provided by the joint-venture counterparts could also be vital in markets characterized by highly fragmented and complex channels of distribution. This partially explains why most consumer marketing efforts in a culturally complex market like that of Japan are almost always operated on a joint-venture basis with local partners.[26]

A more immediate benefit of joint venture as an entry vehicle is assured and instant access to a lucrative and frequently government-controlled market. Increasingly, more and more joint ventures are formed between a multinational firm and local partners who are usually major users or consumers in a given product market. The joint venture therefore sells primarily to buyers who are in reality also the joint-venture partners. Such partner-buyer joint ventures are usually established with official agencies of the host country, state-owned and -supported companies, and public-sector corporations. Recently, for instance, manufacturing joint ventures between several U.S. multinationals such as AT&T and GTE were formed with the state-owned Taiwan Bank of Communications and a state-owned communications company to manufacture and sell communications equipment to the Taiwan government. The U.S. companies contributed technology and manufacturing know-how and received in return access to the state-controlled communication products market.

Conflicts in Joint Ventures

Although international joint ventures are fast becoming the dominant market-entry vehicle with many built-in positive features, they also fall prey to built-in negative features as well. As seen earlier, joint ventures are subject to both external as well as internal stresses. The cross-cultural nature of the joint-venture arrangement is a ready source of potential conflict at the personnel and management levels. Although joint ventures, even within a single culture, are at best a difficult proposition among domestic firms, the potential for difficulties are multiplied several times on an international level. Potential clashes may develop not only in terms of management culture, management objectives, and managerial styles but also in terms of operational issues. A mismatch in management objectives is the most apparent source of stress between international joint-venture partners. A joint venture between a U.S. partner with priority objectives of short-run profit maximization and a Japanese firm with long-run market-growth objectives would result in highly destabilizing tensions that would very likely lead to a breakup of the joint venture.

At the operational level, issues such as technology contribution, production sharing, and transfer pricing may all be sources of potential conflict. Some production arrangements are resolved with relative ease, especially if the situation is dictated by the special needs and circumstances of the moment. The GM-Toyota joint venture for the production of the Chevrolet Nova in Fremont, California, settled for an arrangement where-by GM would contribute an idle plant in Fremont while Toyota would contribute the basic product and manufacturing technology. Although it appears that Toyota has gained the better part of the arrangement due to greater value added, since most of the major components will be imported from Japan, GM stands to gain from maintaining a vital stake in the U.S. small-car market. In other cases, the issue of production sharing may not be as easily resolved as each partner attempts to vie for a greater share of the manufacturing value added.

Transfer pricing, or pricing of technology, equipment, components, and parts supplied by either partner to the joint venture, may also develop as a potential problem. Differences in estimates of technology contribution and the price of component and parts frequently lead to disagreement on the valuation of the items between the partners. Most multinationals tend to overestimate the value of their technology contribution and charge higher transfer prices than are warranted by the market. Overvaluation is usually used as a means of siphoning off extra cash flows from high-risk and high tax-rate countries. In addition, if the joint ventures sell primarily to government buyers, the pricing of the finished products is another area of contention. As the host country imposes stricter vigilance on the technology-transfer process, transfer prices and technology valuation proposed by the foreign partners are frequently disallowed. Intense negotiations on the pricing of inputs and outputs have therefore become perhaps one of the most intractable problems associated with international joint ventures.

Other areas of potential conflict may arise from strategic issues such as new-product development by the joint venture and future market expansion. Questions about who should have the rights to future product development and innovations and responsibility for expansion into new markets may have to be resolved. If, for instance, GM-Toyota decides to export to the Asian and the European markets, will GM's overseas subsidiaries or Toyota's representatives be given the responsibility of marketing the Nova? Similarly, if product improvements or even innovations are to emanate from the joint venture, who should have the primary rights to the new product or process? Similar issues may arise in the areas of financing, marketing, personnel, and distribution.

In sum, all of these potential problem areas point to the need for a well-designed control and decision-making system to be agreed to by the partners in the initial negotiations. The areas of authority and responsibility for both strategic and operational decisions should be delineated and clearly spelled out. At the operational level, for instance, when designing the initial organizational chart of the joint venture, an agreement should be reached concerning who should have primary responsibility for the various functional areas. In addition, guidelines for decisions about and implementation of strategic issues by the board of directors should also be laid down. Most importantly, the joint-venture agreement should contain a mechanism for problem resolution such as laying out provisions for possible arbitration and mediation and setting up channels for legal resolution. The agreement should provide an agreed-upon mechanism for divestment to ensure a nondisruptive termination of the arrangement. As noted, despite shared ownership, most foreign investors tend to retain significant control in the joint venture, particularly over operational issues, because of their dominant position as the transmitter of the technology. In addition, local ownership could be arranged so as to diffuse the influence of the local partners by choosing either friendly or inactive local partners. On balance, therefore, ultimate control of a joint venture depends not so much on the percentage of ownership as on the relative dominance of the partners in technology, marketing, and management.

INTERNATIONAL LICENSING

The nature and orientation of licensing may be examined from both a legal and an economic/technological standpoint. From the legal standpoint, *licensing* may be defined as the granting of the rights of use and enjoyment of a proprietary and patented product or an industrial process to a recipient. From a business standpoint, the scope of licensing activities is varied and extensive. It could range from the transmittal of manufacturing procedures in the forms of blueprints and designs and know-how in setting up and operating a manufacturing system for the production of parts, accessories, semifinished, and finished products to the installation of equipment and sometimes complete factories. In addition, most licensing arrangements include provisions for technical assistance, quality control, supply of parts and raw materials, and instructions and training of the licensee's personnel. In its most complete form, licensing may incorporate the transfers of not only production skills but also management and marketing skills.[27] In this configuration, licensing assumes the scale of a "turnkey" project in which a complete technological and business system, fully set up and immediately operational, is turned over to the recipient. In the following sections, discussions are confined to licensing in the conventional sense, that is, the imparting of production skills and know-how.

EMS Controls

International licensing as a market-entry mode is viewed with mixed perceptions and involves conflict of objectives among the parties involved. This is reflected in the host country's ambivalent attitude toward licensing. On the one hand, it is a preferred mode of technology transfer for many host countries sensitive to foreign ownership. As an unbundled arrangement, licensing offers the recipient country a means of quick access to foreign technology without the attendant stigma of foreign ownership and hence foreign economic dominance. On the other hand, it may be viewed with suspicion by the host-country decision makers as a possible channel, in the case of parent-subsidiary licensing, for siphoning off excess local profits and as a means for foreign firms to dump old technology of dubious value onto the local recipients. In fact, the royalty payment from licensing is the remittance outflow most regulated and controlled by host countries. In many host countries, a maximum royalty payment of around 5 percent of gross sales is frequently imposed. In addition, in countries with a parallel exchange-rate system, royalty payments are converted at the nonpriority rate and are subject to a more stringent tax surcharge than other types of outflow.[28]

International licensing may be classified in two major categories: internal licensing and independent licensing. The former arrangement refers to a licensing relationship created between the parent company (usually the licensor) and its subsidiary in the host country (usually the licensee). The latter arrangement involves a licensing agreement between two independent companies and represents the more popular notion of licensing. At best and from a more favorable standpoint as far as the host country is concerned, an internal licensing agreement may be viewed as the formalization of an actual process of information transmittal from the parent multinational to the foreign subsidiary. The internal license arrangement is set up for no reason other than to provide for actual technology transfers of value to the subsidiary. At worst, many internal licensing arrangements are viewed by the host country as suspected vehicles for siphoning profits from the subsidiary by the parent firm. In fact, as a safeguard against such a siphoning function of licensing, some host countries have imposed restrictions on royalty payments by local subsidiaries of foreign multinationals. For instance, Brazil forbids the payment of royalties by a majority-owned subsidiary to its foreign multinational parent.[29]

Conflicts in International Licensing

Multinational companies and a host country tend to enter into licensing for motives that are mutually at conflict. Most companies see licensing as a way of penetrating the local markets of the host country with a product or technology at the standardized stage of the product cycle. This reduces the risk of "appropriability" of a still innovative technology by the recipient. The dominant focus is therefore on capturing returns from the domestic markets of the host country through transmitting a standardized product. This is essentially a market-extension strategy for a product already fully exploited in the home market. Advanced country licensors, for understandable reasons, normally shy away from licensing cutting-edge and innovative technologies that still command a sizable potential return in the home as well as in the open export markets. The innovating firm has a greater tendency to want to maintain the appropriability of its product innovation at earlier stages of the product cycle. There are too few safeguards in the foreign markets to ensure the protection of the still innovative technology.

On the other hand, many host countries, especially the newly industrializing ones, consider technology transfers through licensing as a contributory component of their overall industrial and technological policies. From the recipient country's perspective, the desirability of licensing is evaluated on the basis of its net contribution to the country's industrial development, particularly the promotion of export-oriented industrialization. Thus the most desirable forms of licensing are those with up-to-date and leading-edge technologies producing products aimed at exports to the global markets. China, for instance, has written into its joint-venture laws the requirement that the transmitted technology be current and up to date. Such an EMS requirement is completely at odds with the licensing strategies of most advanced-country licensors, which is basically one of capturing worldwide returns with a relatively standardized and hence low-risk technology aimed primarily at the local markets of the recipient country.

From the company's standpoint, therefore, licensing especially of still innovative technology has traditionally been castigated as a high-risk arrangement involving possible loss of control on a proprietary product/technology, creating a potential competitor out of the licensee and at worst falling prey to international piracy arising from illegal leakage of the technology or know-how. On the other hand, even in the face of such entrenched negative perceptions of international licensing, it nevertheless constitutes a substantial part of international business flows. Despite some of its perceived shortcomings, international licensing offers many advantages as a means of market entry compared to other entry modes.

These advantages include conditions relating to the product, the firm, and the target country.

Strategic Considerations in International Licensing

On a product level, licensing offers a traditional means of generating international profits from a product or technology at the maturing or standardized stages of the product cycle in the domestic market. Traditionally, products that are considered obsolete and declining in the home markets are usually prime candidates for licensing. However, in today's technological environment of rapid worldwide diffusion, product obsolescence no longer suffices as a reason for international licensing. Instead, in an era of rapid technological turnover and widespread global proliferation of technology and innovation, international licensing may have taken on a new and different strategic role. It could serve, for instance, as a profit-generating activity in and of itself, a process in which the innovating firm "sells" the innovations and the associated know-how directly to the market.[30] Internationally, it could serve as a strategy to preempt the rapid rise of local competition by establishing an international network of closely supervised and affiliated licensees.

Licensing in the face of rapid technological turnover also allows the firm to capture at least some returns before the product's life expires. This partially explains the fact that in electronics, particularly in devices such as microprocessors and memory chips, licensing is a standard industry practice. Even the latest product technologies, such as video-cassette recorders and audio compact disc players, are widely licensed internationally to maximize worldwide returns while still at the innovative stage of the product cycle. Another product-related reason for licensing relates to the nature of the industrial production process itself. Given the complex and interchangeable nature of the industrial production process and the expensive undertaking of R&D, it may be more economical for competing firms to exchange technology for certain products and parts. This mutual exchange of product technology, known as cross-licensing, offers the parties involved the advantage of mutual safeguards and tremendous savings in avoiding research duplication. Cross-licensing is particularly popular among international pharmaceutical and industrial equipment companies.

On the firm level, licensing offers a relatively inexpensive means of penetrating a foreign market. Many small-to-medium-sized firms have turned to licensing because of a lack of the managerial or financial resources needed to engage in direct investment. In the case of large, multiproduct, R&D-intensive firms, licensing offers a convenient and profitable means of disposing of technologies that do not have an appropriate fit with the company's existing product line or market-mix configuration. Thus instead of developing the product in-house, a firm may decide to license the non-mainstream technology to an outside firm. Many large multinational, R&D-intensive firms like General Electric have in fact begun to treat licensing as a stand-alone profit center for the wide range of surplus technologies that its R&D division produces.

Still another strategic reason favoring licensing is the dependency relationship that could be created between the licensor and the licensee. The strong technical and organizational linkage that could sometimes be established through the licensing relationship allows the licensor a certain degree of control in an otherwise foreign and distant market. In addition, the licensing linkage usually leads to supplementary flows of parts and material to the licensee arising from the original licensing arrangement. Sales of supplementary parts and components provide the licensor with a substantial amount of additionally generated licensing revenues. More importantly, a licensing relationship can set the stage for future expansion if the licensor firm decides to venture into direct investment. An exisiting foreign licensee would be a ready, willing, and technically proficient prospective joint-venture partner.

Conditions in the host country may also favor licensing. For instance, licensing may be the only available means of entering the market of a country with high tariff and nontariff barriers against imported products or one that restricts direct investment. Moreover, because it involves minimal investment exposure, since no major plant and equipment investment are made, licensing would be suitable in entering countries with a high degree of macrorisks facing direct investment such as expropriation and nationalization. In such an event, the only risk for the licensor would be the cash-flow loss instead of the loss of expensive assets like plant and equipment. Moreover, in countries where direct investment cannot be justified by the marginal attractiveness of the local market, licensing provides a relatively inexpensive and low-risk-entry alternative. However, in countries with dominant EMS-based risks, licensing may be more risky than direct investment because it is usually subject to greater restrictions by the host country.

Pricing and Operational Considerations

Since licensing royalties are subject to strict vigilance by the host country, the licensor must pay careful attention to the pricing decision in international licensing agreements. The pricing decision therefore has to take into consideration both market forces (supply and demand) and host-country EMS constraints. The licensing pricing structure usually consists of three major components: (1) royalties payments stemming directly from the use of the licensed technology or know-how, (2) lump-sum payments paid up front and usually known as the "disclosure fee," and (3) revenues generated from ancilliary and supplementary flows of parts and components to the licensee. This trilevel structure offers a certain degree of pricing flexibility in the face of host-country restrictions. For instance, if direct royalty payments are limited to a restrictive level, the licensor may compensate for this by increasing the proportion of the up-front payment. In fact, in a high-risk arrangement, the up-front payment is priced at a level that would allow the licensor to recoup his costs plus profits even with little or no royalty payments. Pricing the supplementary parts and components to recoup cost plus margin is another way of offsetting the restrictions on royalty payments. In any event, given the intense competition and hence efficiency in the international technology and licensing market, negotiated payments for licensing often tend to approach the long-run market value of the licensed technology.

INTERNATIONAL FRANCHISING

International franchising is a market-entry vehicle of growing importance. It can be distinguished from joint ventures and wholly owned subsidiaries not in terms of the extent of ownership but in terms of its concept and operations. This is because international franchising may be undertaken as a joint venture or as a wholly owned operation. Strictly from a legal perspective, franchising may be considered similar to licensing since it involves assigning the rights of use or enjoyment of a product, a trademark, or certain proprietary know-how to the recipient. Both in concept and in practice, however, franchising has sufficient special features of its own to merit its distinction from licensing. It differs from licensing on several dimensions.

First, *franchising,* at least in terms of its conventional usage, refers to a transfer process that is broader than straight licensing. Licensing is normally limited to a narrower scope of activities, involving the transmission of mainly production know-how and occasionally the product's trademark. Franchising, on the other hand, usually encompasses the transfer of the entire business system including production, marketing, and management know-how to the franchisee. Second, licensing applies to a broader range of products and processes, both industrial and consumer. Franchising, in contrast, refers mainly to the transmission of consumer-oriented products and services, particularly in the fast-food and personal-service fields. Third, the responsibility and technical involvement required of the recipient in licensing transfers are more demanding. The licensee is required to provide not only money but also a requisite level of skills and technical know-how to make the licensing process a success. In comparison, all that is required of the franchisee, normally, is the investment of cash. The franchisor provides a complete system consisting of the product, the trademark, the functional know-how, and the training to operate the franchise.

Strategic Considerations

International franchising as an entry vehicle is suitable for most types of convenience consumer products and services such as fast food, printing, convenient food stores, photo finishing, and beauty care services. Because of its more integrated and complete transmission of almost all facets of a business, franchising allows the franchisor to pursue a one-product and one-company image worldwide. International food and beverage franchising such as that of McDonald's and Coca Cola has developed an integrated global image among international consumers in terms of brand recognition and loyalty, product quality, service, and operations. More importantly, because it involves the complete transmission of a standardized and integrated system, franchising allows the franchisor company to develop its own independent distribution channels almost from scratch and reach the local consumers directly. This instant and direct access to local consumers enables the franchisor to create and maintain customer recognition, acceptance, and loyalty without having to depend on the complicated local channels. In the case of other nonfranchised consumer products, the marketer frequently loses control of the product and its marketing activities once it enters the often convoluted, complex, and fragmented local channels of distribution.

Just as in the case of licensing, the primary franchising process can generate additional sources of revenues through the supply of materials, management counseling, and training to the franchisee. In addition, if the franchising is set up under a joint-venture arrangement with host-country nationals, the franchise operation may be subject to fewer EMS restrictions. However, some restrictions may apply to the remittance of franchise profits and imports of franchise materials. This is because franchising tends to be considered by the host country to be in the luxury-oriented consumer-product area and therefore usually does not qualify as a high-priority project eligible for incentives and the lifting of restrictions.

From the standpoint of the franchisee, an international franchise offers the advantage of an almost instantaneous start of business. After the initial investment of cash, the franchisee is handed a complete and ready-to-go system capable of generating cash flows from the start. For instance, the opening of the McDonald's franchised outlets in Taiwan resulted in perhaps the largest single first-day sale ever generated in the company's history. Unlike the setting up of other nonfranchised businesses, startup problems, errors, delays, and the resultant costs can be avoided. In addition, cost savings can be gained from the efficiency of standardized and volume operations normally found in franchising. Most importantly for the franchisee, since most well-known franchises, especially in fast food, have established prior brand recognition and consumer acceptance, the product is presold. The synergistic benefits from joint advertising and promotion is another important advantage of franchising.

Constraints in Franchising

Despite its many positive features, franchising still faces several shortcomings, particularly in the international markets. Franchising, as a relatively advanced marketing system, may require a well-developed marketing infrastructure and a potential market of relatively affluent middle-class consumers. Although the distribution channel can be self-established with relative ease, other elements of the marketing infrastructure may be lacking in many countries. For instance, adequate mass advertising capability essential to maintaining a customer base for the franchise chain may be lacking. Moreover, additional market, official, and cultural constraints may prevail in other areas. Franchising projects for consumer products and services usually involve luxury items and hence may face both official and social resistance in the recipient country.

More serious in terms of erosion of market potential are cultural resistance and adverse nationalistic sentiments facing the international franchisor. Fast-food franchising, for instance, is often identified with U.S. life-styles and cultural values. Therefore, the often high-profile nature of franchising, which involves active promotion of foreign cultural values and standards, may be a source of political risk that may include special targeting by local radical groups. Apart from ideologically inspired radicalism, the franchising may be impeded by traditional consumer values that frequently restrict quick adoption. The appropriate market segments most ideal for franchising—relatively young, upwardly mobile, middle-class consumers—usually occupy a very narrow base in most recipient markets. From the standpoint of the foreign franchisees, some of the drawbacks of entering into the franchise include the loss of the identity, tied-in purchases of franchise materials and supplies, and lack of freedom to develop and expand business.

In addition, problems may arise from resistance from tradition-oriented competitors fearful of the innovative and more dynamic marketing methods introduced by franchising. Other risks associated with franchising relate to problems stemming from product and operational adaptation. Although international franchisees may remain faithful to the original standardized franchise format, cultural imperatives usually necessitate some degree of adaptation. The menu of many U.S.-based fast-food franchises in foreign markets, for instance, have to include local product offerings in addition to the standard items. The degree of adaptation depends to a large extent on the specific franchise in question. McDonald's demands strict uniformity of its foreign franchisees in order to maintain its crucial integrated one-product image worldwide. Other franchisors are more flexible because of the more varied nature of their business. The franchised outlets of 7-11 stores in the Far East markets have undergone almost total adaptation in terms of store layout, product-line offerings, and business hours. Countries like Japan, which imposes strict regulations on closing time for business, have made the original twenty-four-hour format impossible. At the same time, store offerings have to be adapted to the localized products and product lines.

COUNTERTRADE AND OTHER
CONTRACTUAL ARRANGEMENTS

Background

Countertrade is a generic term covering a broad range of "nonmonetized" transactions usually involving payments in goods and services rather than cash. This form of exchange is not a recent development and can be traced back to barters in premonetized economies. Recent variants of nonmonetized exchanges arose from a combination of forces that have emerged in the global trading and financial systems in the last couple of decades. Toward the middle and late sixties and the early seventies, increased import needs of many developing nations coupled with their lack of ability to generate sufficient foreign exchange earnings meant that some means had to be found to maintain viable international trade flows. For a while, this need was met by the surplus liquidity generated by the recycling of petrodollars in the late seventies, and huge loans were extended to the needy developing countries to finance their import and development expenditures. Toward the late seventies and the early eighties, the resultant heavy debt burden together with a worldwide inflationary environment, falling commodity prices, and other economic disruptions finally began to undermine the continued viability of the international trade payments systems.

The liquidity crunch caused by a massive shortage of hard currency was further exacerbated by an emerging oil glut and near defaults of especially the Latin American debtor countries. As a result, to conserve depleted hard-currency reserves, many of the afflicted countries began to turn to countertrade as a means of maintaining continued international flows in technology transfers and trade. Countertrade can therefore be viewed as a problem-solving mechanism to overcome both temporary and sustained economic obstacles to market-oriented cash-based international trade. Countries that have built elaborate countertrade systems into their international trade structure include Indonesia, China, Poland, and many of the debt-ridden Latin American countries. Such economically struggling developing countries are thus using countertrade as the major strategy to maintain some degree of viability in the global trading system.

Countertrade, however, is not the exclusive preserve of the debt-ridden or struggling developing countries. Occasionally, transactions between industrialized countries may also involve countertrade arrangements. This usually occurs in major large-expenditure transactions involving government purchases. General Electric, for instance, arranged for the purchase of F-18 jet fighters equipped with GE engines by the Canadian government using a compensation arrangement. In return for the purchase, GE agreed to set up an aircraft plant in Quebec and made commitments to purchase Canadian aircraft parts and components and various Canadian exports by GE's worldwide affiliates. Other developed countries like Belgium and the Netherlands similarly require countertrade offsets when making major armaments purchases.

Forms of Countertrade

Countertrade arrangements are as varied and diverse as the specific needs and situations of the parties involved. The kind of countertrade deals that can be arranged are limited perhaps only by the imagination of the deal makers, and it has been noted that no two countertrade arrangements are the same. In addition, countertrade arrangements can be melded with other kinds of more conventional arrangements such as licensing and joint ventures. However, a basic pattern of countertrade appears to have emerged in terms of the regional countertrade flows. Essentially, countertrade arrangements, also known as "offset," usually involve the exchange of technology and industrial goods supplied by a multinational corporation (MNC) from an industrialized country for related or unrelated goods supplied by the technology-recipient country, usually a lesser developed country (North-South flows). Other countertrade arrangements involve exchanges between the Eastern Bloc and Western industrialized countries (East-West flows) and between the less developed countries (LDCs) themselves (South-South flows). In the latter case, a wide array of goods ranging from raw materials to manufactured goods may be exchanged, usually on a barter basis.

Countertrade can be set up under a variety of forms, but the most common arrangement is *counterpurchase*. Under this arrangement, the company supplying the technology or equipment agrees to accept payment in goods unrelated to the transmitted technology or unrelated to its product line. Thus, for instance, a U.S. supplier of electric turbines to a Polish buyer may agree to accept Polish agricultural products in return. In another example, McDonnell-Douglas accepted canned ham as partial payment for supplying aircraft components to Rumania. Counterpurchase usually entails a much greater degree of risk when it comes to disposing and marketing the products accepted as payment. As a result, some companies agree to accept only partial counterpurchase commitments.

Compensation trade, or *buy-backs,* refers to an arrangement whereby the seller or technology supplier agrees to accept as payment products related to the transmitted know-how and technology or related to its main product line. Levi Strauss, for example, transmitted jeans manufacturing know-how and licensing to Eastern Bloc countries such as Rumania in return for finished blue jeans, which it then marketed in the West. In another example, one West German firm supplied woodworking machinery to Bulgaria in exchange for processed wood products. One of the most successful compensation arrangements concluded in China involved the establishment of a container-manufacturing plant by U.S.-based Containers Transport International (CTI). CTI supplied the needed equipment and technology and agreed to accept the manufactured containers as payment. Compensation arrangements may sometimes merge into counterpurchase. The firm supplying the technology may accept outputs produced by the technology or other related products as partial payment together with other unrelated products. Compensation arrangements tend to entail lower risks of unmarketable or low-quality products.[31]

Other, more complex countertrade deals include contractual joint ventures and switching arrangements. Under contractual joint ventures, an arrangement commonly found in China, the partners enter into a contract with one side (usually the foreign partner) contributing the technology and know-how and the other side (usually the Chinese partner) contributing land and labor. Both sides then agree to share in the output. The Chinese are also noted for processing arrangements, whereby the foreign firm supplies know-how and raw materials for the Chinese to manufacture products according to the company's design and specifications. Switching or clearing arrangements are more complex and are usually stage managed by a middleman expert in the field. The success of such clearing arrangements depends to a great extent on the middleman's existing network of international trade contacts and an information system geared toward the matching of diverse needs of international sellers and buyers. Under such arrangements, the switch trader, normally an European trading house or bank, assumes the risk of accepting and marketing the goods provided by an Eastern Bloc or LDC buyer and in turn guarantees cash payments to the Western technology supplier. The switch trader has managed, therefore, to facilitate the implementation of a difficult transaction by acting as deal maker, financier, and marketer.

Strategic Considerations

Although it may appear that the developing countries have the most to gain from countertrade, MNCs and Western technology suppliers may also reap certain countertrade benefits from a strategic standpoint. In many instances, countertrade may be the only available means of market penetration for especially big ticket items such as aircraft, industrial plants, military goods, and armaments. The arms and aerospace sectors may account for the largest share of the global countertrade volume. Oil, minerals, and agricultural products are routinely traded for aircraft, jet fighters, and military hardware. This also partially explains the fact that major MNCs in the armaments and aerospace industries like GE, General Motors, McDonnell-Douglas, and Boeing have been the most instrumental and innovative in setting up sophisticated in-house countertrade units.

Many companies consider countertrade as an instrument of long-term market development. Many of the companies eyeing the vast potential of the Chinese market, for instance, have entered into so-called goodwill countertrade deals, although there are no immediate prospects for profits. Moreover, existence of a countertrade trading arm allows a company greater leverage in successfully negotiating other forms of market entry. A host country with strict countertrade requirements, for instance, tends to prefer joint-venture and licensing arrangements with a company that could provide countertrade facilities for its products. MNCs willing to enter into countertrade arrangements are usually viewed more favorably by the host country in terms of complying with its EMS requirements and providing it with access to the company's export channels.

An additional consideration is that countertrade arrangements can be used to gain liberalized treatment from the host country such as being allowed to repatriate blocked funds that would normally be restricted by the host country. In general, countertrade has been increasingly used as a leverage to gain other benefits from the host country including obtaining an import license, securing the right to submit bids for large government projects, and receiving other tax and financial incentives. More importantly, the decision to engage in countertrade and the setting up of a centralized in-house unit to coordinate countertrade and other trading activities would provide a company with an organizational and hence a competitive advantage. Many companies and major banks like Bank of America, Security Pacific Bank, and First National Bank of Boston all have set up countertrade facilities as part of their export trading companies (ETCs) to provide overall strategic coherance and guidance for a vital aspect of their business.[32]

EMS and Implications for Risks

Apart from using it as an expedient way of overcoming the shortage of hard currency, countertrade also offers the recipient country additional advantages. Many countries, for example, consider countertrade an excellent means of gaining access to the world markets particularly for their difficult-to-market traditional products such as local arts and crafts. It also serves as a means of disposing of and sometimes dumping surplus goods on the world markets. In addition, countertrade contributes to the host country's export performance and helps to reinforce a bilateral trade balance on a country-by-country basis. As a result of these clear advantages, many countries have legislated countertrade obligations into their EMS. Indonesia, for instance, has incorporated countertrade as an official trade policy requiring varying percentages of counterpurchase for most imports, and Mexico is expected to follow suit. Other countries have also begun to link countertrade to the degree of priority of their purchases and technology needs. Countertrade requirements are particularly mandated for low-priority imports. Conversely, countertrade requirements are usually waived for high-priority imports. China, for instance, pays hard currency for high-priority purchases in areas such as energy, transportation, and electronics.[33]

From the perspective of the seller, countertrade is a major source of microrisks not only because of the complicated nature of most countertrade arrangements but also because of the acceptance of the goods themselves. As noted, most countertrade items are either difficult-to-market traditional products or goods of inferior quality. Some firms have attempted to reduce product risks by accepting related and familiar products for which they have a better degree of expertise. Other companies have contracted for outside clearing arrangements to dispose of particularly unrelated products. Another approach involves limiting countertrade to goods that could be used in house. Still other companies have seized upon countertrade as a profit opportunity and have set up their own specialized countertrade units. Ultimately, most MNCs will have to come to terms with the countertrade phenomenon, particularly in view of the fact that it now accounts for as much as 20 to 30 percent of total world trade according to some estimates. International companies should approach countertrade just as they would other business challenges by designing appropriate strategies to maximize the gains and minimize the risks.[34]

NOTES

1. John K. King, "Political Risk Assessment for Food Company Foreign Operations," Food Systems Update, December 1984, pp. 10-17; J. Alex Murray and Lawrence Leduc, "Public Attitudes and Foreign Investment Screens: The Canadian Case," paper presented at the Academy of International Business Annual Meeting, Cleveland, 1984.

2. Wenlee Ting, Business and Technological Dynamics in Newly Industrializing Asia (Westport, Conn.: Quorum Books, 1985), pp. 18-31, 51-61.

3. Wenlee Ting, "New Perspectives on Risk Assessment and Management in the Asia-Pacific: A Host Country Dynamics Approach," paper presented at the proceedings of the Academy of International Business South East Asia Meeting, Taipei, Taiwan, June 1986, pp. 778-795.

4. C. T. Crawford, R. M. Hammer, and G. Simonetti, Investment Regulations around the World (New York: Wiley, 1981).

5. Ting, "New Perspectives," pp. 786-789.

6. John Frankenstein, "Trends in Chinese Business—Changes in the Beijing Wind," California Management Review, Fall 1986, pp. 148-60.

7. Ting, Business and Technological Dynamics, pp. 18-26.

8. "Andean Countries Liberalize Foreign Investment Policies," Business America, August 5, 1985, pp. 23-25.

9. Price Waterhouse, Doing Business in Venezuela, Price Waterhouse Information Guide, 1985.

10. Business International, Investing, Licensing, and Trading Conditions Abroad—Brazil (New York, January 1985).

11. Robert E. Looney, Development Alternatives of Mexico (New York: Praeger, 1982).

12. Price Waterhouse, Doing Business in Mexico, Price Waterhouse Information Guide, 1984.

13. "Maquiladoras: Profit for Production Sharing," The Wall Street Journal, September 24, 1984.

14. "IBM Is Cleared by Mexico to Build a 100% Owned Plant," The Wall Street Journal, July 24, 1985.

15. Price Waterhouse, Doing Business in France, Price Waterhouse Information Guide, 1985.

16. Business International, Investing, Licensing, and Trading Conditions Abroad—France (New York, February 1985).

17. Foreign Investment in France, DATAR, Paris, 1984.

18. Business International, Investing, Licensing, and Trading Conditions Abroad—Spain (New York, January 1985).

19. Price Waterhouse, Doing Business in Spain, Price Waterhouse Information Guide, 1982.

20. Business International, Investing, Licensing, and Trading Conditions Abroad—Korea (New York, June 1983).

21. Investment Guide to Korea, Ministry of Finance, Republic of Korea, 1983; A Guide to Investment in Korea, The Korean Chamber of Commerce and Industry, 1983-84.

22. S. P. Ho and R. W. Huenemann, China's Open Door Policy: The Quest for Foreign Technology and Capital (Vancouver, B.C.: The University of British Columbia Press, 1984).

23. "China's Trade and Investment Laws," The China Business Review, November-December 1985, pp. 40-45.

24. "China's Economic Bureaucracy," The China Business Review, May-June 1982, p. 22.

25. A. Louis Calvet, "A Synthesis of Foreign Direct Investment Theories and Theories of the Multinational Firm," Journal of International Business Studies, Spring-Summer 1981, pp. 43-59.

26. Ting, Business and Technological Dynamics, pp. 62-89; Duane Hall, International Joint Ventures (New York: Praeger, 1985).

27. Dieter Pfaff, "International Licensing Contracts, Transfer of Technology, and Transnational Law," in Norbert Horn and Clive M. Schmitthoff, eds., The

Transnational Law of International Commercial Transactions (Antwerp, the Netherlands: Kluwer/Deventer, 1982), pp. 199-209.

28. L. Mytelka, "Licensing and Technological Dependence in the Andean Group," World Development, June 1978, pp. 447-459; Tom Arnold and J. T. McCarthy, Domestic and International Licensing of Technology (New York: Practicing Law Institute, 1980).

29. Wolfgang Fikentscher, "The Typology of International Licensing Agreements," in Horn and Schmitthoff, Transnational Law, pp. 211-222.

30. David Ford and Chris Ryan, "Taking Technology to Market," Harvard Business Review, March-April 1981, pp. 117-126.

31. Stephen Markscheid, "Compensation Trade: The China Perspective," The China Business Review, January-February 1982, pp. 50-52.

32. Carol S. Goldsmith, "Countertrade, Inc.," The China Business Review, January-February 1982, pp. 48-50.

33. Cathleen Maynard, Indonesia's Countertrade Experience, American-Indonesian Chamber of Commerce, November 1983.

34. Business International, Threats and Opportunities of Global Countertrade: Marketing, Financing, and Organizational Implications (New York, 1984); idem, 101 Checklists for Coping with Worldwide Countertrade Problems (Geneva, Business International S.A., 1985).

4

International Investment-Risk Analysis

DISCOUNTED-CASH-FLOW ANALYSES

Capital-budgeting procedures consisting of discounted-cash-flow analyses such as net present value (NPV), internal rate of return (IRR), cost-benefit, and profitability-index techniques are established methods for investigating the economic feasibility of investment projects. Although not originally designed for risk assessment, capital-budgeting-type procedures offer a flexible method of incorporating risk analysis into the decision-making process. The general procedure in integrating risk analysis into project evaluation is accomplished by modifying and adjusting the cash flows in the NPV or IRR analyses.

The process of evaluating international projects differs from that of evaluating domestic projects because of substantial variation in the operating and risk environment across a broad spectrum of host countries. The difference in approach lies in the contents but not in the technique of analysis. The environmental variation stems primarily from the consequences and implications of multinational firms operating in multiple currencies and multiple entry-management systems. For example, most multinational firms face a bewildering array of macropolitical risks such as possibilities of wars, revolutions, and expropriation; micro-EMS risks such as repatriation and ownership restrictions; and exchange risks arising from currency fluctuations and differential inflation rates. All of these risks have to be factored into the project-evaluation process.

The various discounted-cash-flow procedures offer a convenient way of integrating international risks into the decision-making process. A wide spectrum of decisions ranging from host-country location, entry modes, and arrangements to the actual configuration of the specific investment package may be based on discounted-cash-flow procedures of project evaluation. In host-country-screening decisions, for instance, discounted-cash-flow analysis leads to an acceptance or rejection of a particular country on the basis of the computed net present value that has incorporated, for example, the probability of expropriation. In the entry-mode decision, the discounted-cash-flow analysis could take into consideration the different levels of ownership, repatriation, and export orientation to determine whether a joint venture with high export orientation would be more appropriate than some other form of entry for a given host country. Likewise, in the case of exchange risks, the project's estimated cash flow can also incorporate the probabilities of currency fluctuations in computing the net present value or internal rate of return.

The major decisional process in a country-specific project-level evaluation, therefore, is to determine the risk-adjusted NPV or IRR for the various project options under consideration. In the case of the NPV approach, the decision is to accept the project if its NPV is greater than zero. In the case of IRR analysis, the decision is to accept projects whose IRRs are greater than the firm's cost of capital. Then, following conventional capital-budgeting criteria, projects with the highest positive risk-adjusted NPVs or with positive NPVs above a certain predetermined cutoff point will be selected. For instance, in the case of the entry-mode decision, the risk-adjusted NPVs for perhaps a joint venture, a licensing arrangement, or a wholly owned subsidiary would be computed, and the options with the most favorable risk-adjusted NPVs would be selected. Alternatively, the group of projects with risk-adjusted NPVs above a certain cutoff point would be selected subject to a given level of budgetary constraint.[1]

Determining the Risk-Adjusted Net Present Value

Although there are several discounted-cash-flow procedures available to the risk analyst, the most commonly used is the net present value method. Sometimes the internal rate of return may also be computed to allow comparison with the firm's cost of capital or some other benchmark rate. The following sections present the salient features of the NPV and the IRR methods, and the various techniques of incorporating risk into the analysis are also examined. The usual procedure is to compute the after-tax NPV of the project given by the formula:

$$NPV = -I + \sum_{i=1}^{n} \frac{R(t) - C(t)}{(1 + r)^i},$$

where

I = Investment expenditure at time 0.

$R(t)$ = Project's estimated revenues at time t.

$C(t)$ = Project's estimated costs at time t.

r = Discount rate.

In international project evaluation, the basic NPV method is adjusted for risk. As noted in Chapter one, various methods have been suggested for adjusting the NPV analysis to reflect these risks. Some of more commonly suggested approaches include:

1. Adjusting the discount rate by adding an "arbitrary" risk premium to the cost of capital, the hurdle rate, or the required rate of return. This method involves adding certain percentage points to r. For instance, if the unadjusted hurdle rate is 10 percent, r can be raised to 15 percent to reflect the additional risks. The unadjusted rate of 10 percent is known as the riskless rate, whereas the incremental 5 percent represents the risk premium. The risk premium is frequently a subjectively derived quantity but is nevertheless supposed to be based on some risk/return function of the decision maker. The risk premium therefore corresponds to the risk/return function or market indifference curve along which the investor is indifferent between various risk/return combinations.

2. Accelerating the cash flow by assuming a shorter payback or investment period. For example, if a project has an expected economic life of eight years, a higher degree of risk can be factored in by reducing the project's life to five years.[2]

3. Adjusting the estimated cash flow of the project itself according to specific information generated by risk assessment. This usually involves assigning probabilistic values or some coefficient to the project's estimated cash flow. A higher level of risk can be incorporated into the NPV analysis either by reducing the period's estimated revenues or by increasing its estimated costs.

Each of these approaches has advantages and disadvantages. Adjusting the discount rate is perhaps the method that is the easiest to use since it involves only the adjustment of the discount rate. Adjusting the project's estimated cash flow is theoretically more acceptable because it allows a more specific and therefore more exact consideration of the probable impact of risks on the different period's cash flow but in practice is more difficult to implement. Since, presumably, the adjustment is based on detailed and well-researched risk information for each of the project periods, this method is more accurate and reflective of the specific risk impact. The major shortcoming of the cash-flow approach is the difficulty and high cost of obtaining accurate and reliable risk information to perform an acceptable adjustment on the cash flow.

Although easier to implement, discount-rate adjustment does not discriminate between the different degree or level of risk that may prevail in each period of the project's life. It discounts all periods' cash flows equally with the same level of risk premium. Hence the discount-rate-adjustment method does not adequately consider the differential risk impact on each period's cash flow. Since it does not take into account the time pattern of the risk impact and since cash flow in the more distant future is more risky, the method tends to penalize the earlier cash flow more severely. The same criticism can be raised against shortening the project's payback period. Arbitrarily shortening the payback period also does not take into consideration the differential impact of risk over the economic life of the project.

Nevertheless, discount-rate adjustment and payback-period adjustment are employed frequently by companies to incorporate international risk. This is because they are easy to use and also because adequate and accurate information necessary to adjust a project's cash flow is often a luxury as far as foreign investment projects are concerned. Many companies lack the time, money, expertise, or even inclination to undertake expensive in-depth risk assessment needed for generating accurate risk forecasts. Thus in the absence of or with the lack of specific and reliable information required for precise adjustment of the project's cash flow, discount-rate and payback-period adjustment appears to be the next-to-best approach in incorporating international risks. In addition, the discount-rate-adjustment approach is presumably based on informed managerial judgment and experience. The risk premiums merely reflect the different levels of risk at which the investor will discount future cash flows to obtain a desired level of return. It is the incremental discount level that will allow the investor to remain indifferent between the various net present values. In other words, an investor is indifferent between net present values derived from discounting at perhaps a riskless rate of 10 percent or a risk-adjusted rate of 15 percent. Discount-rate adjustment is part of the general process of determining strategic hurdle rates for capital investment.[3]

Adjusting the Project's Cash Flows

The general discounted-cash-flow procedures are flexible enough to accommodate several approaches to cash-flow adjustment. These approaches range from naive and straightforward techniques of adjusting the cash flow by multiplying each period's cash by some subjective probability of risk to more sophisticated techniques that involve consideration of the timing of the risks, compensation payments, and terminal values.

In the first example, the estimated cash flow of a project will be adjusted on the basis of possible expropriation stemming from political instability. The project has an estimated life of six years, and it is assumed that the probability of expropriation by the host country is 80 percent in the fifth year of the project. The risk-adjusted cash flow is then the sum of the net cash flows for the first four years plus the fifth-year cash flow weighted by 1.00 minus 0.80 and any anticipated compensation from the host government. The resulting adjusted expected cash flow is then discounted by the firm's hurdle rate to arrive at an expropriation risk-adjusted NPV. The project is expected to generate the following estimated cash flows in the absence of any expropriation:

Investment Period (Years)	Cash Flows ($ million)
Initial investment outlay	−8.50
1	1.50
2	2.45
3	1.15
4	3.65
5	2.50
6	4.25

Table 4.1 illustrates the mechanics of the computation. The computed net present value discounted at 15 percent is $0.58 million in the absence of expropriation. If the expropriation takes place, the adjusted fifth-year cash

TABLE 4.1
Risk-Adjusted NPV for Investment Project

Period (Years)	Cash Flow (Million $)	PV Factor @ 15%	Present Value
0	−8.50	0	−8.50
1	1.50	0.870	1.305
2	2.45	0.756	1.852
3	1.15	0.658	0.757
4	3.65	0.572	2.088
5	2.50	0.497	1.243
6	4.25	0.432	1.836
Unadjusted NPV			0.581

Present Value discounted at 15%
Internal rate of return—17.12%

Expropriation in Year 5

(1) Expected cash flow in Year 5	— 2.50 × 0.497 (1-0.8) =	$0.2486
(2) Expected compensation	— 3.0 × 0.497 (0.8) =	$1.1928
(3) Net cash flows from Years 1-4	— 6.002 − 8.50 =	−$2.4980
Risk-adjusted NPV		−$1.057
Risk-adjusted internal rate of return	—10.18%	

flow is expected to be $248,600. This is derived by multiplying the original $2.5 million by the present value (PV) factor, 0.497, and then weighting the result by 0.2 (1.00 minus the probability of expropriation). If compensation of $3.0 million is paid by the host government, the expected value of the compensation is $1.19 million ($3.0 million multiplied by the PV factor, 0.497, and weighted by 0.8 or the probability of expropriation). The risk-adjusted expected NPV of − $1.057 million is obtained by adding the cumulative net cash flows until the year of expropriation to the expected fifth-year cash flow and the expected value of the anticipated compensation. Thus as a result of incorporating the possibility of expropriation into the cash-flow analysis, the computed NPV of the project was lowered from a positive amount to a negative NPV. This has the effect of rendering an originally acceptable proposed project unattractive. Since the decision criterion calls for rejecting a project if its net present value is negative, the possibility of expropriation has clearly rendered the project unacceptable.

In addition to the net present value analysis, the internal rate of return may also be computed to allow the company to evaluate a project without having to decide on an appropriate rate of discount. In the net present value analysis, the firm is required to arrive at an appropriate discount rate with which to discount the adjusted cash flow. Using the IRR approach, the derived internal rate of return can be compared to a benchmark or hurdle rate to judge the attractiveness of the proposed project. The *internal rate of return* is defined as the rate of discount that causes the sum of the present value of the cash flows to just equal the net investment outlay. In other words, the IRR is the discount rate that sets the NPV or sum of discounted cash flows of an investment project equal to zero. Referring to Table 4.1, the computed IRR for the project in the absence of expropriation is equal to 17.12 percent. The risk-adjusted IRR is 10.18 percent. Thus incorporating the possibility of expropriation into the analysis has reduced the attractiveness of the project by lowering the internal rate of return.[4]

When the risk-adjusted IRR exceeds the firm's cost of capital, the project is deemed acceptable. In addition, the risk-adjusted IRR can be used to determine the risk premiums associated with investment projects. The difference between the risk-adjusted IRR and the original unadjusted IRR may be considered an approximation of the magnitude of risk or a "risk rate" associated with the expropriation event. In fact, theoretically, if a series of risk-adjusted IRRs are computed for a range of projects that have incorporated anticipated political risks, the resultant "risk rates" could thus provide an average measure of the specific political risks for the projects. Furthermore, if the risk rate is country-specific, that is, reflecting the overall risk in a given host country, it may be used as the risk premium for adjusting the discount rate in evaluating projects in that country. For instance, in the example shown in Table 4.1, the expropriation risk rate is equal to 6.94 percent (17.12 − 10.18). The risk rate of 6.94 could then be added to the firm's cost of capital as a risk premium to arrive at the required rate of return for computing a project's discounted cash flows.

Break-Even Probability Analysis

Another alternative approach in incorporating risk information into discounted-cash-flow procedures is the break-even probability analysis suggested by Alan C. Shapiro.[5] The approach suggested is one that considers the impact of expropriation on the project's net present value. The approach focuses on the use of a break-even probability that will produce a positive expected NPV if that probability exceeds the probability of expropriation. Essentially, this method involves dividing the expected net discounted cash flows in the absence of an expropriation by the discounted cash flows that would have been lost to expropriation plus the expected value of any anticipated compensation. This is given by the formula:

$$P* = \frac{\text{Expected Net Present Value without Expropriation}}{\text{Expropriated Cash Flow} - \text{Expected Compensation}}.$$

In the expression, $P*$ represents the break-even probability. If $P*$ is greater than the probability of expropriation, the project will have a positive net present value. In other words, the investment project should be undertaken if the anticipated probability of expropriation is less than $P*$. The decision rule based on the break-even probability formula appears to be intuitively appealing and is easier to use since it does not require knowledge of a precise level of the probability of expropriation. For instance, if $P*$ is determined to be 0.4, any anticipated expropriation with probabilities exceeding 0.4 will cause the project to be rejected. In addition, the procedure has the advantage of allowing a simulation of various expropriation dates and compensation amounts that will result in a break-even probability of a positive NPV.

To illustrate, assuming that an anticipated expropriation will occur early in the project's life, this would result in the loss of a greater amount of cash flow that could be realized had there been no expropriation. Under this circumstance, a lower break-even probability would result, and only a probability of expropriation lower than $P*$ would cause the investment to be accepted. Similarly, the greater the amount of anticipated compensation, the higher would be the break-even probability. Hence there is a greater likelihood of accepting the investment project when given a moderate probability of expropriation. In general, the lower the value of $P*$ (earlier expropriation and lower compensation), the less likely the investment will be undertaken because a lower expropriation probability is required for the net present value to break even. On the other hand, the higher the value of $P*$ (later expropriation and higher compensation), the more likely the investment will be undertaken since a less stringent level of expropriation probability would be required for the project to break even.

This can be illustrated by the previous example presented in Table 4.1. If the anticipated expropriation occurs in Year 5 of the project, the lost cash flows in Years 5 and 6 that could have been realized had there been no expropriation is equal to $3.079 million (1.243 + 1.836). The discounted value of an anticipated $3.0 million compensation is $1.497 million (3.0 × 0.497). The break-even probability is then equal to 0.37 (0.581/3.079 − 1.497). This suggests that the project should be rejected if the forecasted probability of expropriation is greater than 0.37. If the anticipated expropriation occurs even earlier, for example, in the fourth year of the project, and the compensation is expected to be only $2.5 million, the computed break-even probability is equal to 0.155. Thus for the project to be accepted, the required probability of expropriation should be less than 15.5 percent. With earlier expropriation and lower compensation and hence a lower break-even probability, only a very slim chance of expropriation would render a project acceptable.

In short, the break-even probability approach requires only the knowledge of a "less or greater than" chance of expropriation when compared to the break-even probability in order to arrive at an accept or reject decision with respect to a project. Shapiro also suggested that a firm could potentially affect the chances of expropriation. For instance, a company can have an influence on the probability of expropriation by designing a risk-management program that will reduce this probability. Such risk-management strategies could include switching from a wholly owned subsidiary to a joint venture or restructuring the project to increase its perceived benefits for the local economy.

The major shortcoming of the break-even probability approach based on expropriation is its lack of relevance to today's international investment environment in which host countries, as seen in Chapter two, have developed industrial dynamics that are far removed from the expropriation mindset of an earlier era. In a transformed international investment environment, the scenario is more of one in which subtle changes in the host country's EMS and other policy risks are more likely to affect a firm's investment than extreme actions such as expropriation.

In view of the importance of microinvestment risks, the same break-even probability technique can also be extended to the analysis of more EMS-oriented kinds of risk such as blocked funds and exchange restrictions. In a similar approach, the break-even probabilities derived from incorporating these risk events into cash-flow analyses can be compared with the forecasted probabilities for each of these occurrences to arrive at a yes or no decision. In adjusting for exchange risks, Shapiro suggested analyzing the actual impact of an exchange-rate change on the project's revenues, costs, and depreciation. This would allow a more precise adjustment of each period's cash flow according to the specific risk impact of that period.

Additional Cash-Flow-Adjustment Approaches

An additional approach in adjusting cash flow to incorporate risk is the use of the certainty-equivalent method.[6] The adjustment approach entails multiplying the project's cash flows by a certainty equivalent coefficient as shown in the following equation:

$$NPV = -I + \sum_{i=1}^{n} \frac{q \times E(t)}{(1 + r)^i},$$

where $0 < q < 1$.

In the equation, q is the certainty coefficient and $E(t)$ represents the net cash flow in period t discounted by the a risk-free rate r. The coefficient q is the certainty equivalent factor and is obtained by dividing the "certain" or risk-free cash flow by the risky cash flow, that is, q = certainty cash flow/risky cash flow. The q coefficient is therefore inversely related to the degree of anticipated risk. When q equals 1, risk is negligible and the project's estimated cash flow is almost certain to be realized. On the other hand, if q approaches zero, or the lower its value is, the greater is the uncertainty associated with the project's cash flow. By specifying a certainty-equivalent cash flow based on the same subjective perceptions of risks, this procedure allows a measure of the decision maker's risk/return-preference function to be incorporated into the risk-adjustment process. In addition, the approach also takes into consideration the timing of the differential impact of the risk estimates on each period's cash flow. In other words, it allows each period's cash flow to be adjusted according to that period's anticipated political risks estimates.

Another suggested approach is to adjust the project's cash flows by charging to each period's cash flow the cost of political risk insurance or other costs of risk management. For exchange-risk adjustments, Arthur Stonehill and Leonard Nathanson suggested a similar procedure of charging the costs of hedging for exchange risks against the project's cash flows. Specifically, this calls for multiplying the project's cash flow in local currency by the forecasted rate of exchange.[7]

The foregoing discussions show the range of possible variations in discounted-cash-flow techniques available to the risk analyst. The advent of the microcomputer further enhances the potential of experimenting with the different techniques to arrive at the optimal package appropriate to a company's risk-assessment process. The use of computers has also opened up the possibility of simulations with each of the discounted-cash-flow techniques. Regardless of the approach, the analyst can simulate the effect of the impact of a broad range of risks on the risk-adjusted NPV or IRR.

Selection of Discount Rates

Although there are drawbacks associated with the discount-rate-adjustment approach, it is nevertheless widely used and easy to implement. The short-comings of employing this method could be minimized by carefully selecting the base rate and an appropriate risk premium for discounting the cash flows. When the discount-rate-adjustment method is used, the selection of the discount rate should incorporate both the required rate of return or the base rate plus a risk premium to reflect the political risk estimates. The selected rate should therefore not only reflect market forces specific to the type and nature of the investment project in question, it must also reflect the specific market forces and risk dimensions in the target host country. The use of host-country-oriented rates could potentially contribute to an effective and well-designed risk-reduction or risk-management program.[8]

Some rule-of-thumb choices in selecting the base rate that may better reflect the economics of the project as well as the market dynamics of the target host country in which the project is to be located include: (1) the long-term bond rate of the host country, which reflects the rate of expected inflation in the host country; (2) the long-term interest rates in international capital markets such as the London Interbank Offered Rate (LIBOR), which reflects the market-determined perceptions of risks and returns associated with long-term financing of international projects; (3) the "shadow rate" of interest, or the rate that reflects the host country's opportunity cost of capital; normally, the shadow rate is derived as a weighted average of the host country's cost of funds from various sources; and (4) the company's cost of funds in the home country.

The choice of the actual rate will depend on factors such as corporate objectives with respect to marketing and investment goals, terms and degree of commitment to a project in a host country, and other short- and long-run considerations. In addition, the company has to consider whether the use of single or multiple rates for different projects and different host countries would be more appropriate. Because of the segmented nature of international capital markets and hence variations in the cost of funds between different countries, the use of a single rate for all projects and countries may be problematical. This is because a rate based on one particular market may not reflect the risk/return configurations of markets in other countries. In particular, firms that select a discount rate based on the home country's cost of capital may understate the true cost of utilization of funds in a capital-poor country. Therefore, a multiple-rate approach appears to be more appropriate. This approach would require the use of different rates for different projects in different countries. However, if domestic and international investment alternatives are considered homogenous and if firm-specific budgeting considerations are overriding concerns, the company may decide on the use of a single discount rate based on the firm's usual cost of capital in the home country.

Adjusting for Exchange Risks

The foregoing sections have focused on the impact of expropriation and other political risks on a project's cash flows. In addition, multinationals must consider the uncertainty of exchange-rate fluctuations on a project's cash flow, particularly from the standpoint of repatriation of funds. To incorporate exchange risks into discounted-cash-flow analysis, it is necessary to select approaches that will enable exchange-risk-adjusted NPVs and IRRs for the investment projects to be derived. Essentially, risk analysts have the option of using either the home country's currency or the host country's currency as the base currency in the discounted-cash-flow analysis. Most analyses are normally conducted using local currency cash flows. The use of local currency cash flows in the NPV or IRR analyses has the advantage of avoiding the need to decide on some rate of exchange for converting the cash flows into the home currency. On the other hand, such an approach would have ignored the impact of exchange risks on the project's cash flow. Furthermore, since repatriation of foreign earnings is the bottom-line objective of most firms, converting the local currency cash flows into home-currency cash flows may be appropriate in terms of corporate goals. There are several alternative rates of exchange available for use in conversion.

The use of the official rate of exchange appears to be most obvious. However, the use of this option is complicated by the fact that some countries have a multiple-rate system with several official rates. In addition, for many countries with weakening currencies, the use of the prevailing rate tends to ignore the very real possibility of currency devaluation. Just as in the case of financial statement translation under the new FASB-52, mentioned in Chapter one, a possible approach in converting the foreign cash flows may involve the use of an average rate of exchange, that is, averaging the host country's fluctuating rate of exchange over an appropriate period.

Alternatively, the analyst could select an appropriate forward rate of exchange for converting the local currency cash flows. Ideally, the choice of a conversion rate must be long-range oriented so that the selected rate will reflect the long-run trend in the host country's external equilibrium or its balance of payments. Since for many currencies long-term forward rates are not available, short-term forward rates must be used, and such rates are appropriate only with short-term projects. Many forward markets do not extend beyond a year, and the use of a short-term forward rate would reflect only the short-run equilibrium in the host country's balance-of-payments position. Moreover, even in the case of short-term forward rates, for many pegged currencies, there is frequently a lack of an existing forward market. Hence the use of forward market rates would be precluded for these currencies, and some other proxy market rates, for example, four- or five-year rates, even if they are available, they tend to be poor predictors of future exchange rates due to long-term structural uncertainties in the currency markets.

For countries with pegged currencies and strict foreign exchange restrictions, the official rate of exchange is frequently not reflective of the true market value of the currency. Instead, the official rate is usually an overvaluation of the local currency, particularly for countries with balance-of-trade deficits, and an undervaluation for countries with a balance-of-trade surplus. This happens because currency adjustments through devaluations or revaluations normally entail a time lag behind the market. Under such circumstances, the use of a proxy market rate such as a "shadow" rate of exchange may be appropriate. A shadow rate of exchange is a hypothetical rate computed on the assumption that the currency is "freely" traded on the open markets and is not subject to any exchange restrictions. It is usually computed as a trade-weighted average that is supposed to reflect the actual balance-of-payments impact on the rate of exchange and is not used as a transaction rate. As an economic rate of exchange, the shadow rate tends to be a more accurate measure of the true opportunity cost of currency exchange for a project when compared to officially mandated rates that are often artificially maintained.

Alternatively, in countries with pegged currencies and stringent exchange restrictions, proxy market rates that can be used in converting local currency cash flows include the black market rate. This alternative, however, should be approached with caution not only because of the legal implications but also because of possible conceptual shortcomings. Stripped of its legal connotations, however, the black market is fundamentally an unrestricted market for a country's currency where exchange rates are essentially determined by market forces of supply and demand. In addition, in countries with political uncertainties, the black market rate also incorporates a political risk premium. It reflects the perceptions of the local nationals concerning their economic as well as political confidence in their country's currency and is therefore essentially an economic and political risk-adjusted rate of exchange.

Typically, in a developing country with a pegged currency, balance-of-payment deficits, strict exchange restrictions, and political uncertainties, the following relationship between its official, shadow, and black market rates of exchange holds true:

$$R \text{ (official)} > R \text{ (shadow)} > R \text{ (black market)},$$

where R represents the exchange rate per unit of local currency.

The impact of this relative-rate relationship on conversion from the local into a foreign currency can be illustrated by a simple example. Assume that the official rate of exchange is 35 paritas (local currency) per unit of foreign currency (e.g., the dollar), the shadow rate is 55 paritas per dollar, and the black market rate is 70 paritas per dollar. Furthermore, assuming that an investment project is expected to generate a net cash inflow of 250 million paritas in the first year, the converted equivalent amount in dollars would be $7.14 million using the official rate, $4.55 million using the shadow rate, and $3.57 million using the black market rate. The $3.57 million dollar equivalent based on the black market rate represents the risk-adjusted cash flow incorporating both economic and political risks. Since the black market is frequently an expression of the economic and political confidence in a country's currency, the converted foreign currency equivalent essentially reflects the ''certainty value'' of the local currency. If a project's cash flows are converted using the black market rate, a risk-adjusted NPV may then be derived.

Computer Simulations

Given the numerous possibilities available in approaching political risk assessment through discounted-cash-flow analyses, the analyst is confronted with difficult choices. The possible approaches, as seen in the above-mentioned sections, range from various techniques in adjusting cash flows and discount rates to alternative options in base-rate selection and exchange-risk adjustment. The choice of an optimal approach would probably consist of not just one approach but perhaps a combination of the various approaches. A combined approach is now increasingly made possible by the widespread availability of micro and personal computers. Today's relatively inexpensive computing power has in a sense made ''number crunching'' more easily accessible and affordable. In addition, versatile computer software such as financial spreadsheet programs makes possible a multiplicity of combinations and variations in standard financial analysis techniques. Within the discounted-cash-flow analysis, the analyst could simulate a range of values for factors such as the timing and extent of expropriation, foreign exchange restrictions, multiple exchange rates, base discount rates, and risk premiums to see the resultant impact on the risk-adjusted discounted cash flows.

ASSESSING ENTRY-MANAGEMENT-SYSTEM RISKS

Sources of EMS Risks

The foregoing sections have mainly focused on adjusting for macropolitical risks like expropriation and exchange risks. In addition, microrisks must also be incorporated into discounted-cash-flow analysis. As was seen in Chapter three, the host country's entry-management system (EMS) is a major source of microrisks. A project's cash flows therefore have to be adjusted for the EMS risks. Specifically, each period's estimated cash flow will have to be adjusted for the impact of the different elements in the host country's entry-management system. This can be done by monitoring the effects of the various EMS elements on each period's revenues and costs. Apart from the EMS, the impact of microrisks stemming from project obsolescence must also be taken into consideration.

A few examples will illustrate how both the positive and negative elements in the EMS affect a project's revenues and costs. Local contents requirements, a major negative EMS element, tends to raise the sourcing costs of raw materials and intermediate inputs whereas price controls tend to depress project revenues. Taken in combination, price controls and local contents requirements act as a squeeze on profit because the former places an upper limit on revenues, whereas the latter raises the cost of inputs. In the case of ownership restrictions, fade-out requirements tend to disrupt the potential for future profit because of the management and control uncertainty they impose on the investment project. Hence the project's estimated revenues and costs will have to factor in the effects of ownership and control uncertainties. On the positive side, selective incentives extended to a high-priority project also must be accounted for in cash-flow adjustment. Most incentives have the effect of raising project revenues and lowering costs. For instance, the location of the project in the host country's special economic zones will entitle it to a broad array of special incentives like tax holidays, tariff concessions, and favored and unrestricted repatriation as well as a full range of financial subsidies.

The riskiness of the host country's EMS stems mainly from the fact that its incentives and restrictions are variable and selective over time. More-over, the whole tenor of the EMS has the tendency of moving between restrictiveness and relative liberalness. The variability and selectiveness of the entry-management system therefore impose a dimension of uncertainty on the cash flows of an investment project. Since the adoption of the EMS approach by many host countries in their drive for industrialization, the liberalness and restrictiveness of the EMS have not always remained constant over time and between projects. The variation of the general overall direction of an EMS in terms of its moving between liberal and restrictive entry requirements is a source of project risks that tends to be overshadowed by the more visible and easy to identify macrorisks. Further-more, it is difficult to pinpoint the specific position of the EMS even at a particular time because of its selective nature toward different projects. At any time, the EMS may be selectively restrictive toward a nonpriority project while showering incentives on another project such as a high-technology export-intensive venture, which ranks high on the country's priority list.[9]

Figure 4.1 shows the selected aspects of the variability in a host country's EMS along a liberalized-restrictive continuum. When the EMS swings toward the restrictive end of the continuum, most of the negative elements, such as ownership and repatriation restrictions and stricter local contents requirements, are invoked against the project. On the other hand, when the EMS moves toward the liberal end, benefits such as favored repatriation, unrestricted ownership, and tax concessions begin to accrue to the project.

FIGURE 4.1

Variability in a Host Country's Entry Management system (EMS)

LIBERALIZED   **RESTRICTIVE**

←— — — — — — — — — — — — — — — —→

Selected Elements	**Selected Elements**
Free and Favored Repatriation	Controlled Repatriation
Liberalized Ownership	Restricted Ownership
Tax Advantages and Incentives	Strict Local Content Requirements
Export Subsidies and Grants	Strict Export Ratio Requirements
Efficient One-Stop Approval	Bureaucratic Delays and Barriers
Market Protection	High Import Barriers

The variability in the EMS may stem from a variety of causes ranging from economic difficulties and rising economic nationalism to a fundamental shift in political direction. Generally, economic difficulties such as persistent balance-of-payment deficits, a heavy external debt burden, and economic sluggishness in conjunction with the policies of a probusiness regime may induce the host country to liberalize the EMS. Positive elements like liberal ownership arrangements, favorable tax treatment, and other forms of incentives are extended to attract a greater inflow of foreign investments. Mexico, China, and South Korea are recent examples of a liberalizing EMS with relaxed ownership rules and the provision of additional incentives. Mexico and South Korea liberalized their EMSs probably because of their need for economic recovery and an accelerated rate of industrial development. In the case of China, the opening up of a liberalized EMS stems mainly from a fundamental shift in the country's ideological direction.

Conversely, the EMS can become more restrictive as a result of various economic and political factors. For instance, economic restructuring implemented under a host country's industrial policy may close off certain high-priority sectors or industries in which the country is aspiring to achieve a national competitive advantage in the global export markets. In addition, import-substitution programs can also have similar restrictive effects when only local firms are given the exclusive rights to develop certain product areas. Economic nationalism can also induce ambitious local business firms to exert pressures on the government to appropriate ownership and control of existing foreign projects for themselves or perhaps exclude foreign participation altogether. Thus industries such as airlines, telecommunications, and computers are basically off-limits to foreign investors in Brazil, and in Australia natural resource and broadcasting are similarly reserved for domestic companies only. The shutting off of the EMS could also be ideologically motivated. In the extreme, a country may partially or completely remove itself from the international trading and investment system such as we have seen in Iran and other revolutionary regimes.

A major feature of a host country's EMS is its selectiveness with respect to different projects. It is selectively restrictive in certain sectors and markets reserved for nationals and liberal in some priority areas that require foreign participation at the same time. Although petrochemical investments are on the wane in many host countries with multinationals divesting at substantial losses from these projects, high-technology investments have been beneficiaries of red-carpet treatment from many host countries' entry-management systems. In addition to the type of industry, other project and firm-specific factors may trigger selective EMS restrictions. As seen in earlier chapters, rapid project obsolescence tends to trigger greater EMS restrictions. Sometimes perceptions of the firm's image from the standpoint of the host country may also precipitate increased EMS restrictions. Later sections in this chapter examine in greater detail the effects of these factors on the risk profile of a project.

A selective "tightening" of the EMS against a project may involve increased restrictions in the negative elements or an elimination of positive elements in the EMS. The resultant impact on an investment project can translate into increased risk exposure. In terms of the negative EMS elements, risk exposure can increase in the areas of ownership, indigenization, and local contents requirements. In ownership, for example, greater pressures can be exerted by the EMS on the foreign investors to "fade out" an equity position faster than the originally agreed-upon schedule.

Moreover, the host country may intensify its demands for more rapid indigenization, and such demands could lead to unexpected training and additonal personnel costs to prepare the nationals for management responsibility. Similarly, pressures on the foreign project to increase its local contents requirements will directly raise sourcing costs and reduce the multinational's ability to control material and product quality, which it otherwise could have done if it sourced from the open markets. In terms of the positive EMS elements, risk exposure could increase from the removal of previously granted tax and tariff concessions and financial subsidies. Thus whether it is increased restrictions or the abrogation of incentives, a tightening EMS has the net effect of imposing greater risk on a project's cash flows.

EMS Risks and Discounted Cash-Flow Analysis

Since an EMS is variable and selective with respect to an investment project, discounted-cash-flow procedures must be able to incorporate such risks into the analysis. This could be accomplished either by directly adjusting each period's cash flow based on anticipated changes in the EMS or using the expected NPV method. The latter involves the assumption of variable EMS scenarios and is perhaps a more appropriate approach precisely because it reflects the variability of and hence risks emanating from the EMS.

The expected NPV approach can be illustrated by a simple example. Table 4.2 shows the anticipated NPVs (V) of two projects and the associated subjective probabilities (P) under different EMS scenarios. For Project A, the expected NPV under a very restrictive EMS is $2.65 million with an outcome probability of 0.25. The corresponding NPVs under a moderately restrictive and a liberal EMS are $5.30 million and $8.45 million, respectively. The respective outcome probabilities are 0.50 and 0.25. This example shows that under the very favorable circumstances of a liberal EMS, which has a 25 percent chance of being realized, the firm can expect the project to generate $8.45 million. However, a moderately restrictive EMS generating a possible $5.30 million appears to be more likely at 50 percent probability. The expected value of the NPV for Project A is computed as shown in Table 4.2 and is equal to $5.425 million. Table 4.3 shows the standard deviations and coefficients of variation for Projects A and B.

In the case of Project B, the EMS outlook appears to be more variable than that of Project A. There is a 10 percent chance of a very restrictive EMS, which could cause the project to generate a negative NPV of $-\$2.75$ million. However, there is also a 25 percent chance that a liberal EMS will occur, and this could lead the project to generate an anticipated NPV of $15.65 million. Again, the most likely outcome, at 65 percent probability, would be a moderately restrictive EMS with an expected NPV of $6.20 million. The expected value of the NPV is computed and is equal to $7.67 million.

Comparing the expected values of the NPVs for Projects A and B would lead one to the conclusion that Project B is preferable to A since it has a higher expected NPV. However, it is still necessary to determine the variability in the expected returns and hence the riskiness of the two projects. This is usually accomplished by computing the standard deviation and then the coefficient of variation of the distribution. The standard deviation of

TABLE 4.2
Expected Values of NPVs for Projects A and B

	Project A		
	V_i (Million $)	P_i	$V_i \cdot P_i$
Very restrictive EMS	2.65	0.25	0.6625
Moderately restrictive EMS	5.30	0.50	2.6500
Liberal EMS	8.45	0.25	2.1125
Expected Value (NPV) $\bar{V}_A = \sum\limits_{i=1}^{3} V_i \cdot P_i$			5.4250

	Project B		
	V_i (Million $)	P_i	$V_i \cdot P_i$
Very restrictive EMS	-2.75	0.10	-0.2750
Moderately restrictive EMS	6.20	0.65	4.0300
Liberal EMS	15.65	0.25	3.9125
Expected Value (NPV) $\bar{V}_B = \sum\limits_{i=1}^{3} V_i \cdot P_i$			7.6700

TABLE 4.3
Calculation of Standard Deviations and Coefficients of Variation for Projects A and B

	Project A				
V_i	$\bar{V}$	$V_i - \bar{V}$	$(V_i - \bar{V})^2$	P_i	$(V_i - \bar{V})^2 \cdot P_i$
2.65	5.425	-2.775	7.70	0.25	1.925
5.30	5.425	-0.125	0.016	0.50	0.008
8.45	5.425	3.025	9.151	0.25	2.288
					4.221
Standard deviation			$\sigma = \sqrt{4.221}$	$=$	2.05
Coefficient of variation			$\dfrac{\sigma}{V} =$	$\dfrac{2.05}{5.425} =$	0.38

	Project B				
V_i	$\bar{V}$	$V_i - \bar{V}$	$(V_i - \bar{V})^2$	P_i	$(V_i - \bar{V})^2 \cdot P_i$
-2.75	7.67	-10.42	108.58	0.10	10.86
6.20	7.67	-1.47	2.16	0.65	1.40
15.65	7.67	7.98	63.68	0.25	15.92
					28.18
Standard deviation			$\sigma = \sqrt{28.18}$	$=$	5.30
Coefficient of variation			$\dfrac{\sigma}{V} =$	$\dfrac{5.30}{7.67} =$	0.69

the distribution of the returns or the NPVs is given by the following formula:

$$\sigma = \sum_{i=1}^{n} (V_i - \overline{V}) P_i,$$

where

V_i = NPV for ith EMS.
$\overline{V}$ = Expected NPV.
P_i = Probability of outcome of ith EMS.

Table 4.3 shows the calculations for determining the standard deviations of the NPVs for Projects A and B. The computed standard deviations for the two projects are 2.05 and 5.3, respectively. Although Project B has a higher standard deviation than Project A, it is still not safe to conclude that it is more risky than A. To compare the riskiness of the two projects, their coefficients of variation must be calculated. The coefficient of variation is computed by dividing the standard deviation e by the expected value of the NPV (V). As seen in Table 4.3, the coefficients of variation for Projects A and B are 0.38 and 0.69, respectively. Since the higher the coefficient of variation, the more risky the project, it is safe to conclude that Project B, although having a higher expected NPV, is more risky than Project A. The final choice of the projects would depend on the risk/return preference of the decision maker. A more conservative decision would lead to the choice of Project A over Project B, assuming that only one project is to be selected. On the other hand, a risk/return function that is more risk prone would tend to cause Project B to be selected over Project A.

Selective restrictions and variability in a host country's EMS are major sources of microrisks for international investors. A comprehensive risk assessment must also consider other microrisk dimensions that have a significant impact on an investment project. Sections in Chapters one and two have discussed the effects of project obsolescence on risk exposure. Rapid obsolescence of a project, particularly technological obsolescence, tends to trigger selective restrictions against the project. In addition, perceptions from the standpoint of the host country regarding the image of a company may also significantly affect the risk profile of an investment project. The following sections examine the risk dimensions of a firm's corporate image.

The Firm's Corporate Image

A major source of microrisk for investment projects that has frequently been overlooked and ignored in risk assessment is the firm's international corporate image. A corporate image is the sum of all perceptions, from the standpoint of the host country, regarding a company's reputation, past activities, performance, degree of social responsibility, and compliance with the host country's EMS. The level of favorableness in perceiving a firm's corporate image is a major determinant of the risk exposure the company may face in the host country. A more favorable image is normally associated with a relatively nonconflictual relationship with the host country. On the other hand, an unfavorable image implies a potential for negative interactions with the host country and hence a higher probability of provoking negative measures against the firm. With the traditional focus and emphasis on macropolitical risks, risk analysts have tended to disregard the fact that the way a multinational is perceived by the host country is a source of risk. Corporate image is therefore one of the major missing links in political and country-risk assessment. Comprehensive risk assessment should consider the importance of corporate image in influencing its prospects for success or lack thereof in the host country.[10]

Unfavorable or negative perceptions of a company stem from the so-called image baggage that multinationals, knowingly or unknowingly, have to carry with them as a result of past activities. For instance, companies involved in political activism in Latin America in the 1970s would presumably be perceived in a somewhat more ambivalent light by other host countries and hence might encounter a greater degree of vigilance by the local nationals. On the other hand, the EMS of a host country may be more favorable toward a multinational whose track record in other countries has been exemplary in terms of its more cooperative and contributory interactions with the country. In view of the differential perceptions of multinationals, any risk analysis should take into consideration the potential of the multinational in question in provoking a more retaliatory and restrictive stance by the EMS of a host country. The fact that the company itself has some impact on risk exposure also implies that it could have a certain degree of control on its own destiny as far as risk reduction and risk management are concerned. By pursuing more integrative strategies such as continuous technological upgrading and compliance with the EMS requirements, the multinational may place itself in a position where it can perhaps reduce the degree of risk exposure for its investment project and in the process further reinforce its image.

Following an approach similar to that of incorporating EMS risk in discounted-cash-flow analysis, an expected distribution of project NPVs may be developed by assuming different corporate-image scenarios. A very favorable and positive corporate image can be expected to generate a higher anticipated NPV, whereas a less favorable image would be expected to generate a lower NPV. Using the expected NPV approach, the expected value of NPVs under different levels of corporate image may then be computed. Such an analysis would allow the firm to evaluate the impact of different corporate-image options on the project's cash flows.

A MODEL FOR INVESTMENT-PROJECT-RISK ANALYSIS

Given the various dimensions that could affect the risk profile for a project, a political risk model at the project level must be able to incorporate the impact of these factors on a project's cash flows. *Political risks* at the project level can be defined as the uncertainty regarding the impact of a combination of risk dimensions on the revenues and costs of a project. These risk dimensions include structural transformation in the project's markets resulting from the expanding role of local firms in the same industry, normal as well as rapid project obsolescence, and the corporate image of the company in the host country. Adverse or unfavorable developments in any or all three of these dimensions would tend to trigger an increase in the selective restrictions of the entry-management system against the investment project in question and cause the project's cash flows to be exposed to greater risks.

The project political risk model, as shown in Figure 4.2, depicts the rela-

FIGURE 4.2
Strategic Planning, Project Risk Assessment and Host Country Dynamics

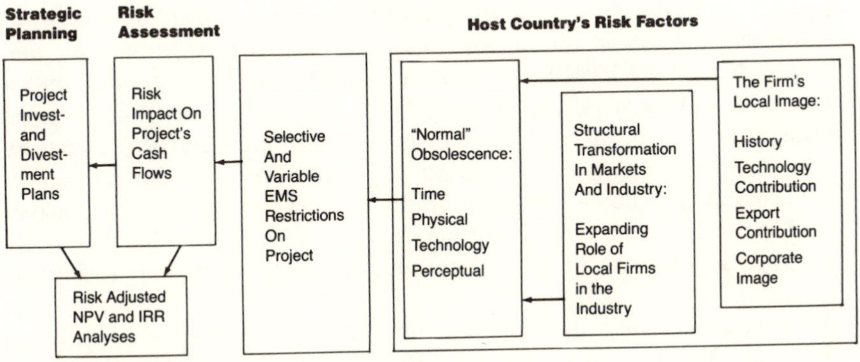

Note: NPV—Net Present Value
IRR—Internal Rate of Return

tionships between the key risk variables, the EMS, and strategic planning for the project. The figure shows the combined effect of the risk dimensions on the "worth" of a project that, in turn, may cause selective variability in the EMS and hence increase restrictions against the project. The worth of a project as perceived by the host country is shown to be affected by the normal rate of time and physical and technological obsolescence, as discussed in Chapter two. Higher than normal or rapid obsolescence of the project can also be precipitated by structural changes in the markets and industry in which the project operates as well as the company's corporate image (dotted lines).

The entire set of risk dimensions can also be viewed as a lessening in the "demand" for an investment project as seen from the perspective of the host country. The project's declining worth leads to a reduced demand for the project, and this, in turn, results in higher risk exposure. The strategic implication of the obsolescing demand phenomenon affecting a project is the need for the multinational to recognize and anticipate the inevitability of such a decline in the project's perceived value. It also implies the resultant need for possible planned strategic divestment. Ignoring the obsolescing demand phenomenon and hence rising risk exposure would leave the firm unprepared and without a strategic plan to deal with the ensuing risks. A lack of divestment planning, for instance, could result in million dollar losses for a multinational, especially when decreasing "demand" for its project could induce the host country to intensify its EMS restrictions against the project.[11]

Figure 4.3 is a graphical representation of the project-risk model. The perceived worth of the investment project is represented by the downward sloping obsolescing curve. The obsolescing curve reflects the declining "demand" for a specific investment project as seen from the perspective of the host country. This is shown in Graph I of Figure 4.3. Curve $C(a)$ represents some normal rate of decay of the demand curve for a project, perhaps stemming from time and physical and technological obsolescence. Structural changes in the markets resulting from the expanding role and importance of the local firms operating in the same industry may spur a faster than normal decline in the obsolescing curve. Structural market changes can also be brought about by more intense competition provided by other technology suppliers in the industry. Moreover, a negative image of the firm may also accelerate the decline in the curve. All of these risk factors tend to produce a faster than normal decline in the curve, which then shifts to $C(b)$. They may also trigger greater selective EMS restrictions against the project.

Conversely, a more liberal EMS directed at the project may cause the curve to shift upward to $C(d)$, reflecting a more favorable and positive demand for the project. Additionally, the multinational itself may also slow the decline in the project's worth by adopting more integrative risk-management strategies. Such strategies, which could potentially maintain the project demand curve, include the continuous injection of upgraded and more desirable technology into the project, expanding the project's export contribution, or reinforcing the positive aspects of its corporate image. Such actions may raise the curve to $C(d)$, essentially reflecting a more positive demand for the project.

A planned divestment strategy by the multinational based on the risk and demand dynamics in the project-risk model may help it to avoid major losses resulting from unplanned divestment. A planned divestment strategy is an important part of a defensive risk-management or risk-avoidance strategy. The planned divestment strategy requires the multinational

FIGURE 4.3
Obsolescing Demand And Risk Exposure Models

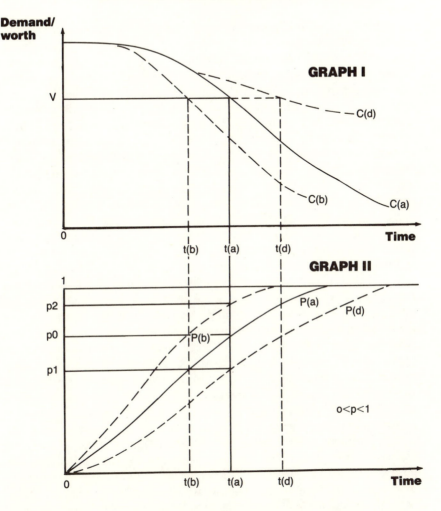

planners to set a predetermined level in the project's worth that will trigger a voluntary and orderly withdrawal after negotiation with the host country. This trigger level can be viewed as that level of the project's worth that will spur the host country to expropriatory actions against the project. In other words, it is that stage of obsolescence in the project's worth that would lead the host country to invoke selective restrictions against the project. If V is such a trigger level, the project should be divested at time $t(a)$, assuming a normal obsolescence rate. However, if the demand curve drops to $C(b)$ because of greater project risks and a more restrictive EMS, the project will have to be divested sooner at time $t(b)$. On the other hand, the multinational can afford to extend or delay the divestment time to *t(d)* if the demand curve shifts upward to *C(d)* as a result of the company adopting a mo$_{NPV}$. integrative risk-management strategy and a more favorable EMS facing the project.

Graph II of Figure 4.3 shows the corresponding risk-exposure curves that are derived directly from the project demand curves. Risk-exposure curves *P(a)*, *P(b)*, and *P(d)* correspond to demand curves *C(a)*, *C(b)*, and *C(d)*, respectively. Thus a more rapidly falling *C(b)* results in higher rate of risk exposure as depicted by curve *P(b)*. Similarly, a slower declining *C(d)* leads to a slower rising *P(d)* and hence shows a lower rate of risk exposure, possibly because of a more favorable perception of the project by the host country. Divestment at points *t(b)*, *t(a)*, and *t(d)* are vertically projected from Graph I, assuming "trigger" worth level *V*. The derived risk-exposure curves also allow the multinational planner to determine various risk probabilities for the project at any time in the project's life. At time *t(a)*, for example, the risk-exposure curve, *P(a)*, would entail a risk probability level at *p*(0). Similarly, a faster rising *P(b)* curve would increase the project's risk probability to *p*(2), whereas a slower rising *P(d)* curve would lower the probability of risk to *p*(1) at time *t(a)*.

The earlier sections in this chapter on discounted-cash-flow procedures have examined techniques that incorporate probabilities of risk events in the risk-adjusted expected net present value analysis. These probabilities were alluded to as subjective probabilities. However, if more objective probability estimates are desirable, these estimates can be based on those derived from the project-risk model. For instance, assuming that *V* is the level of project worth that will trigger intensified EMS restrictions against the project, the corresponding probabilities associated with the obsolescence curves may be used as the probability values in the discounted-cash-flow procedures.

In addition, investment and risk assessment at the preentry stage can include sensitivity analysis using the NPV and IRR procedures by assuming different risk-exposure levels in the project-risk model. Likewise, at the postentry stages, the project can be monitored and evaluated continuously by assuming different rates of risk exposure corresponding to the different rates of demand obsolescence of the project. The company's in-house risk-assessment unit can set up a monitoring system that can track the rate of obsolescence of its various overseas investment projects. Such a monitoring system will essentially act as the firm's early-warning sensors, which will focus on changes and developments in the set of risk dimensions such as structural changes in the markets, the company's image, and the rate of project obsolescence.

The project-risk-model approach to risk assessment and management based on the obsolescing demand model permits a more precise anticipation of the host-country risks that may impact on specific investment projects and ventures. The project-risk model could also provide the risk analysts with more relevant project-specific risk dimensions on which to focus. Most importantly, it provides a basis for divestment planning by monitoring the critical level at which the rate of obsolescence and risk exposure would activate selective EMS restrictions against the project. In an era when international investors and host countries no longer countervail each other with hostile postures and radical actions, the project-specific risk model is more appropriate to the current investment environment in which both sides pursue carefully calibrated policies and actions aimed at maximizing mutual economic benefit.

With host countries holding sway, national industrial ambitions, widely diffused technology, and more sophisticated EMSs have become potent and immediate concerns with which the multinational has to deal. Another important implication of the project-risk model is that the multinational has a certain degree of control over the risk exposure of its project by virtue of its actions and operations in the host country. This control can be exercised through the adoption of a set of integrative risk-management strategies that can influence the rate of the project obsolescence. A multinational's risk strategies within the context of today's international business dynamics is therefore primarily a strategy of fine tuning the policy and EMS interactions between itself and the host country in the investment process.

NOTES

1. Harold Bierman, Jr., and Seymour Smidt, The Capital Budgeting Decision, 3d ed. (New York: Macmillan, 1971).

2. Wilbur G. Lewellen, H. P. Lenser, and J. J. McConnell, "Payback Substitutes for Discounted Cash Flow," Financial Management, Summer 1973, pp. 17-25.

3. Gordon Donaldson, "Strategic Hurdle Rates for Capital Investment," Harvard Business Review, March-April 1972, pp. 50-58.

4. James C. T. Mao, "The Internal Rate of Return as a Ranking Criterion," Engineering Economist, Winter 1966, pp. 1-13.

5. Alan C. Shapiro, "Capital Budgeting for Multinational Corporations," Financial Management, Spring 1978, pp. 7-16.

6. Alexander A. Robichek and Stewart C. Myers, Optimal Financing Decisions (Englewood Cliffs, N.J.: Prentice-Hall, 1965).

7. Arthur Stonehill and Leonard Nathanson, "Capital Budgeting and the Multinational Corporation," California Management Review, Summer 1968, pp. 39-54.

8. Donaldson, "Strategic Hurdle Rates."

9. Wenlee Ting, "New Perspectives on Risk Assessment and Management in the Asia Pacific: A Host Country Dynamics Approach," Proceedings of the Academy of International Business South East Asia Meeting, Taipei, Taiwan, June 1986, pp. 778-795.

10. Ibid., pp. 782.

11. Ibid., pp. 782-792.

5

Corporate-Risk Assessment

DIMENSIONS OF CORPORATE-RISK ASSESSMENT

The increasing awareness of the enormous impact that political developments can have on international business, marked especially by the epoch-making Iranian Revolution, has stimulated an upsurge in interest in political assessment and analysis among the multinationals. The emerging pattern of risk assessment ranges across a wide spectrum of orientation, approaches, methodologies, and systems. Regardless of the different approaches that the multinationals may adopt, there is an underlying recognition by management that political risk analysis is now going to be firmly established as one of the essential international business functions.[1]

A comprehensive perspective of the nature and process of political risk assessment in multinational companies would require a consideration of several dimensions. Corporate-assessment systems can be examined from the standpoint of five major dimensions:

1. Overall nature and orientation of risk facing the company
2. Corporate strategies, objectives, and risk/return orientation
3. Organization of the risk-assessment and management function
4. Analytical approaches and formulation
5. Integration with decision making

Overall Nature and Orientation of Company Risk

The nature and methodology of the risk-assessment process depends to a great extent on the type of multinational business in which the firm is engaged. Various multinationals face a wide array of political risks ranging from exposures to the probability of expropriation and damage from political conflicts to policy risks such as inconvertibility of local currency earnings. Some firms face predominantly asset-exposure risks, whereas others are more affected by cash-flow-exposure risks. In general, the nature of the risks and therefore the risk-assessment process can be delineated according to the following categories of firms engaging in international business: manufacturing-based multinational corporations (MNCs), banks or international lenders, exporters and international traders, and nonbank service firms such as international fast-food franchising. Although it is possible to make a rough distinction between the predominant types of risk, there are overlaps, and some of the political risks are common to a firm whether it is mainly a lender or a manufacturer.

Manufacturing-based MNCs are exposed to perhaps the most comprehensive spectrum of risks since the nature of their operations requires an almost complete integration into the economic as well as the sociopolitical fabric of the host country. Accordingly, they demand probably the most complex and comprehensive kind of risk assessment. Manufacturing activities involve considerable investment expenditures and a costly transfer of technology to the foreign operating environment. In addition, the firm has to deal with conditions relating to marketing, personnel, and financial operations. The range of risks facing the multinational manufacturer therefore extends from uncertainties regarding production and technology to uncertainties in marketing and finance. Manufacturing multinationals are exposed to assets as well as cash-flow risks. The need to consider a wider range of risk dimensions accordingly increases the complexity and scope of the risk-assessment process. Relatively, therefore, the risk-assessment process for firms engaging in international manufacturing is least amenable to precise and narrow quantitative analysis. Because of the high stakes involved, there is greater justification, and hence it is more cost-effective for companies with manufacturing exposure, especially those with extensive multinational coverage, to set up an in-house risk-assessment unit.

In the context of risk assessment, international banks are essentially a one-product firm dealing with one commodity, money. In the absence of any concerns regarding production or technology decisions, the international lenders can concentrate on the uncertainties surrounding the flows of its single commodity. The risk-assessment process is therefore more narrowly, precisely, and clearly defined. Risk assessment focuses on one major key variable: the loan-repayment willingness and capability or the default potential of the borrowing country. Apart from perhaps office investment in the host country, there is no substantial fixed-asset exposure, and banks face mostly cash-flow and movable-assets exposures. During times of political uncertainties, therefore, risks would appear more in the form of freezing or the seizure of their monetary assets. However, in normal political times, with the exception of willful repudiation of debt, most of the uncertainties underlying a country's debt-servicing capacity stem directly or indirectly from economic conditions. Even if the underlying reason for the uncertainties is political, the effects on debt repayment are felt via economic indicators, such as the deterioration in the balance of payments and the external debt situation resulting from continuing political turmoil in South Africa and the Philippines.

Because of the nature of their country exposure, banks are in a position to use more "quantitative" economic indicators such as GNP, inflation rate, balance of payments (BOP), and debt-related statistics in the risk-assessment process. The availability of such numerical data permits the use of more sophisticated econometric models. In the context of decision making, moreover, the analytic process is also well defined. The major focus of country risk-assessment in banks is to determine country-exposure limits and the quality of the loan portfolio. Thus the numerical nature of the data and the more narrowly defined decisional focus put the lenders in a position to set up more structured and formal risk-assessment systems. Evidence appears to suggest that even before the debt crises of the 1980s, most banks had already established some form of formalized risk-assessment system.[2] In a survey conducted by the U.S. Export-Import Bank before the 1980s debt crises, it was found that at least 85 percent of the respondents reported the use of a systematic approach to risk assessment. The systems used range from fully qualitative, structured qualitative, and "quantitative" checklists to fully quantitative methods.[3] Such evidence and the rash of problematic loans of the 1970s raise certain questions regarding the soundness of the assessment methods or perhaps the possible existence of an "implementation gap" between the assessment and the actual lending practices.

In the period following the 1980s debt crises, U.S. banks have had additional reasons for setting up a more structured and formal risk-assessment system and a closer policing of their international loans. The free-wheeling lending practices toward the late 1970s and the resulting debt crises led to the imposition of a stricter regulatory environment on banks by federal and state agencies such as the Federal Reserve and the Comptroller of Currency. Wall Street also sent its own signals by spurring a drastic decline in the stock prices of most of the major money-center banks that have the large exposures in high-risk foreign loans. This has provided strong motivations for the banks to set up as well as reinforce mandatory formalized and systematic evaluation procedures and perhaps to adopt stricter implementation of the risk-assessment results regarding country-exposure limits.

Exporters and traders are more similar to the banks in their foreign exposures. Again, apart from perhaps minimal distribution investment, exporters have no fixed-assets exposures but are predominantly subject to cash-flow and movable-assets exposures. During more normal political times, the traders are exposed to a narrower and more defined range of concerns such as delayed or nonpayment, transshipment risks, market restrictions, and other common commercial risks. Most of these commercial risks are already inherently absorbed into the existing structure of international trade financing and insurance through, for instance, the issuance of letters of credit and shipping-insurance programs. Contract frustrations and repudiation, adminstrative impediments, import restrictions, and restrictive market penetration are some of the major concerns. Therefore, typically, export and other trading firms place greater emphasis on market research and market-potential studies. Risk assessment in the form of environmental scanning is usually factored in as part of the marketing studies. Although exchange-rate fluctuations are critical to the profitability of trading firms, most of them lack any in-house expertise, nor do they have the resources to engage in exchange-rate assessment but rather must rely on outside information suppliers.

Among the many types of international business, nonbank service firms have the most "positive" type of risk exposures. Unlike manufacturers, banks, and even the exporters, service-oriented firms have no substantial amount of products to sell or money to lend. These firms are mainly in the business of selling know-how and expertise. As such, they face predominantly cash-flow-exposure risks. Service firms operate mostly on a contractual basis with little or no equity involvement overseas. Their main business consists of providing technological, management, and marketing know-how via licensing, franchising, and management-contract operations. Apart from construction projects, in which the contractors may have expensive equipment exposure, the major uncertainties for the service firms are payment capability, contract performance, and product piracy in the host countries in which they operate. International service firms range from large multinational franchising chains in the fast-food business to international licensors and management-contract firms in the health care, construction, and hotel businesses. The service firms are likely to conduct formalized risk assessment according to the nature and extent of their foreign involvement.

Corporate Strategies and Risk/Return Orientation

Another major dimension influencing the nature, direction, and scope of the risk-assessment and management function is the perception of risk by the firm itself. The manner in which a company perceives and analyzes political risks basically determines how systematic and sophisticated is its risk assessment. The risk/return-preference curve is known to vary across companies depending on a wide range of firm-specific factors. Within the same company, the risk/return preference may also vary between the firm's domestic and international operations. Thus a firm that is a high-risk taker in the home market may at the same time be a risk avoider in the international markets. The risk-avoidance orientation of a firm in the context of its international operations depends first on its strategy and objectives and second on economic-efficiency considerations.

On a strategy level, some firms are inclined to adopt a more aggressive stance vis-à-vis their international exposures for reasons of history and experience. In general, companies with a longer record of extensive and deep overseas involvement have a willingness to absorb a greater level of risk than companies without comparable involvement. Their established scanning capability and the ability to marshall greater resources to assess, analyze, and absorb the foreign risks contribute to a higher risk-taking orientation. In addition, companies with a strategic advantage in some areas of their operations such as a superior technology and production capability also tend to be more willing to bear the additional risk of international operations. Finally, the management philosophy, objectives, and managerial style of the firm's managers determine to a large extent how risk oriented the company is with respect to its overseas operations. Hence firms whose management has adopted aggressive assets growth and market-expansion strategies are inclined to overlook near-term risks in order to position themselves for subsequent projected improvement in the market share of high-risk countries. Size, experience, strategic advantage, and management philosophy of the firm are therefore major variables in determining the company's international risk orientation.

In short, large multinationals with extensive operations overseas would be more inclined to spend more time and resources to set up efficient and well-organized risk-assessment systems. Such firms also tend to have better organized risk-management and absorption programs for their operations abroad. Empirical evidence seems to be provided by multinationals that have not only entered but have expansion plans for countries with undisputedly high-risk-operating environments. Thus major multinationals like IBM and Ford have recently set up investment projects in Mexico and other Latin American countries despite the immense restrictions and repatriation risks prevailing in these countries.

On the economic-efficiency level, some firms by virtue of their production process tend to view international operations as essential to their strategic and operational efficiency. Oil firms, for instance, are among the first multinationals to venture overseas because of their need to achieve vertical integration in their operations. Given the indivisible factors of production of the oil firms, that is, the enormous fixed investment in capital and equipment, economic efficiency dictates that upstream (exploration) and downstream (marketing) activities be integrated with production. Thus major oil companies took to the international markets naturally in order to attain the efficiency of vertical integration. This could partially explain the presence of Gulf Oil in Angola despite the political risks of operating in that host environment. In addition, firms operating in an oligopolistic market structure often consider expanding overseas as a natural extension of the strategy to preserve their oligopolistic advantages. Oligopolistic multinationals are under constant pressures to maintain their market share both domestically and internationally by resorting to nonprice competitive strategies like product differentiation and niche marketing.

The existence of market imperfections in the factors market and the market for intermediate inputs also necessitated the internationalizing of production and marketing. By establishing a global network of subsidiaries, a multinational can derive certain efficiencies from internalizing the market for intermediate inputs like technology, capital, and managerial expertise. The development of such an intrafirm market for capital, technology, marketing, and managerial resources helps the firm to maximize the appropriability of its technological advantages, to allocate worldwide resources, and to preserve marketing control. All of these strategic advantages contribute to the firm's ability to attain global optimization. In the face of such dictates of the markets, therefore, risk absorption is merely a by-product of the internationalization process. The perception of international risks, both political or otherwise, have therefore to be viewed in the context of the economic demands on firms to enter into foreign markets.

Organizing the Risk-Assessment Function

Another major dimension in viewing the risk-assessment process by multinationals is the pattern of actually organizing the risk-assessment function. This pattern appears to vary across a wide variety of approaches ranging from ad hoc intermittent assessment to well-organized formal risk-assessment systems. In surveys conducted before the Iranian and Nicaraguan revolutions, various observers have noted a lack of systematic and sophisticated approaches to risk assessment even among large multinationals. One study noted that multinational companies attempt to factor in political risk by investing in subjectively perceived "safe" countries.[4] In another survey, it was found that the firm management's subjectively derived perceptions of relative risks were shaped and influenced by general news sources and advice from banks. Less than a quarter had any formalized in-house risk-assessment unit, and about 10 percent reported using outside consultants.[5] Although such observations date from the pre-Iran era, they nevertheless provide some measure of the level of sophistication in corporate-risk assessment.

In general, the pattern of setting up and organizing formalized risk-assessment systems tends to vary widely among major manufacturing-based multinationals and money center-banks. The systems could range from those composed primarily of specialist staff units working independently or together with line managers to those comprising only line personnel. The organization of the risk-assessment unit can be line centered, staff centered, or a combination of both. In the line-centered approach the political risk-assessment function is usually organized within the corporate operating product divisions, which are then closely supported by country managers, product-planning units, and other staff specialists. The initiative for risk assessment therefore originates from the line managers, and the process is highly integrated into product and market decisions.

In staff-centered approaches, the responsibility for risk assessment is predominantly vested in the hands of staff specialists, and the assessment process is frequently an integral part of overall corporate strategic planning. Line personnel in this case play a supporting role. The approach that is most appropriate for accurate and unbiased risk assessment appears to be the two-tiered or parallel risk-assessment system. In this approach, both line and staff personnel generate their own assessment independent of each other, and subsequently the assessments are coordinated and combined into a well-tested consensus. The parallel-systems approach enables the firms to build a checks and balance mechanism into their risk-assessment systems and help to avoid any possibility of product, market, or personal biases.

In banks, approaches to country-risk analysis can also be either line centered or staff centered. In the staff-centered approach, the risk-assessment process is carried out mainly by economists, political analysts, and other staff specialists at corporate headquarters. The line personnel or the lending officers then integrate the output of the assessment into their country-lending decisions, Similarly, in the line-centered approach, the main responsibility of country-risk assessment is vested with the actual lending officers and their supervisors. In general, a possible shortcoming of the line-centered approach could be that the built-in operating biases of the lending officers may adversely affect the objectivity of the assessment process. Problems of validity and objectivity could also arise from the line personnel's lack of a conceptual frame of reference, which normally can be better provided by full-time staff specialists in the different disciplines of economics and political analysis. Finally, operating officers simply lack sufficient time for in-depth and dedicated assessment of country risks. To further systematize and improve the output quality of the risk-assessment process, banks are increasingly turning to the parallel-assessment system involving concurrent but independent analyses and evaluation by both the line and staff personnel. The parallel system has the advantage of retaining risk assessment as an intrinsic part of lending decisions while providing the rigor and analytical power of a multidisciplinary framework of analysis. For the majority of U.S. banks, the need for compliance with Federal Reserve regulations necessitates the setting up of formalized country-limit or country-exposure committees to conduct systematic country-risk assessment and to decide on country-risk exposure.

The pattern of organizing the risk-assessment function seems to be inconsistent and varies widely among the different companies engaging in international business. The pattern varies in terms of the degree of formalization of the risk-assessment structure and the importance of the assessment function. As mentioned earlier, the size and the scope of a company's international operations appears to be a major force shaping the type of risk-assessment process carried out by firms. Generally, smaller to medium-sized firms that are mainly traders and exporters tend to have a less formal and organized approach to political risk assessment. Systematic risk assessment among these firms is minimal to almost nonexistent. Most conduct little or no in-house risk assessment themselves and instead rely on information supplied by external risk-forecasting services. For those that perform some degree of in-house assessment, an ad hoc assessment process ranging from guesswork and hunches to simple rule-of-thumb procedures are used. In other firms, the risk-assessment process is mostly incorporated into market-research studies. For larger multinationals with more extensive international scanning capability, formalized staff- or line-centered structures or a parallel structure are usually the prevailing practice. Strictly from the standpoint of functional specialization, the political risk assessment should be a part of overall strategic planning. Thus the political risk-assessment units, whether they are staff- or line-centered or parallel, would be more appropriately integrated with the corporate strategic-planning structure, especially since risk-assessment forecasts have now become a routine part of corporate planning.[6]

Analytical Approaches and Formulations

The actual analytical process of risk assessment follows mainly from how the assessment process is organized, although it could also be influenced by other organizational and functional factors. Staff-centered risk assessment normally tends to rely more on conceptually based frameworks and models of analysis since the analysts are mostly specialists in their respective disciplines. These models and frameworks of analysis also tend to be more "quantitative." The actual analytical formulation used depends on the background and discipline of the staff analyst. Thus economists would have a preference for econometric models, and political analysts would tend to employ political science-based analytical formulations. In line-centered assessment, on the other hand, the analysis tends to reflect the more operational perspectives of the line managers. Risk assessment would therefore be focused on market-penetration strategies, production considerations, and other functional decisions. The analysis here tends to be more qualitative. In addition, risk analysis could range from subjective to objective methods depending on the nature of the data analyzed. It should be noted here that a "quantitative" approach does not necessarily suggest whether the analysis is objective or subjective. Even subjective data such as opinions and perceptions, as will be seen later, can be quantified with the help of ordinal scaling techniques and thus rendered amenable to numerical analysis. The two sets of descriptors, quantitative-qualitative and objective-subjective, therefore, would be more appropriately treated as distinct dimensions.

Many studies have attempted a classification of analytical techniques or approaches used in company-risk assessment. R. J. Rummel and D. A. Heenan, for instance, identified four major types of approaches to risk analysis among U.S. companies: grand tours, old hands, Delphi techniques, and quantitative methods. Stephen Goodman similarly distinguished between three major approaches to country-risk assessment: fully qualitative, checklist, and quantitative. These authors also suggested the use of a combined approach comprising the above methods. Stephen Kobrin in a survey of corporate-risk-assessment practices also found a mixture of methodologies ranging from Delphi approaches to quantitative indicators of economic and sociopolitical risks.[7]

The following sections provide a discussion of the various analytical approaches using Rummel and Heenan's classification.

Grand tours. This is essentially a qualitative approach in analyzing country risks. The grand-tour method consists of obtaining firsthand information on the target country by traveling to the actual location. The most obvious advantage of this approach is the ability of the decision maker to get an intimate and intuitive feel for a range of factors in the actual operating environment. However, on the negative side, a brief visit could provide only a narrow and perhaps biased impressionistic view of the host country. Observers tend to focus on the more visible aspects of the country without having an opportunity for a more in-depth analysis. Also, the expense of sending an investigative team to several candidate countries may be prohibitive and may not be justified by the amount and quality of information collected. Nevertheless, when combined with other more rigorous methods of assessment, an actual tour of a location could "flesh out" certain dimensions that have been identified as significant and then subject these factors to closer scrutiny.

Old hands. As the term implies, the old-hands approach is based on the acquisition of and obtaining an access to expert information from persons who have been intensely and intimately involved with a specific host country or a specific region. Such information involves the experts' judgment and opinions regarding the sociopolitical conditions in the host country. The acquisition of old-hands information could be accomplished by retaining outside consultants who have the requisite expertise. Such experts could range from former diplomats and officers of international agencies to journalists and academics. Again, by itself, the old-hands approach has the potential shortcoming of being subject to biased and obsolete information because of the constant and rapid changes in the host country. On the other hand, in combination with the other assessment methods, the old-hands approach can provide insightful information on impending changes in a host country. Most major multinationals have at least some form of old-hands information input. For those who cannot afford the retainer fees for high-level consultants like former Secretary of State Henry Kissinger, there are private consultant units like Probe International. Operated by ex-foreign service officers, the company provides analysis on political and economic developments in a target host country for multinationals on a contractual basis. The service is essentially built around contacts with and special accessibility to foreign politicians, bureaucrats, and other decision makers. Thus for large multinationals to smaller and medium-size firms, the old-hands approach can provide a valuable source of risk information on macropolitical risks, which would contribute to reinforcing other risk-assessment approaches. Both the old-hands and the grand-tour approaches can be considered qualitative risk-analysis methods.

Delphi techniques. The Delphi technique is essentially a more systematic and comprehensive version of the old-hands or expert-knowledge method. It is a set of techniques traditionally used by social scientists and futurists for prediction of discrete events and for projecting scenarios in the socio-political environment. This approach is appropriate to the forecasting of discrete events such as socioeconomic and political occurrences that do not lend themselves to continuous trend analysis. Instead of individualized and unstructured advice as in the case of the old-hands method, this approach consists of a systematic generation and quantification of expert knowledge. A panel of experts is convened to generate and rank a set of independent or causal factors that are believed to affect dependent sociopolitical variables such as the political stability of a regime. If done rigorously, the process of generating and ranking the factors consists of successive stages of feedback and screening among the panel members in order to arrive at what is, by consensus, the final set of the most critical and significant factors. Alternatively, the same process could also be used directly to forecast sociopolitical scenarios. This latter process is likely to be costly because the panel would have to be retained on a continuous basis and convened each time a forecast is required.

The generating and selection of the risk indicators, appropriately weighted, is more cost-effective. Once the set of risk dimensions has been determined and formulated into a measuring instrument, it can be used on a regular basis to rank potential target countries, either by a panel of experts or a trained team of analysts. In a typical example of a Delphi-derived country-rating system, the panel of raters are required to rank the country on a set of predetermined dimensions, such as changes in political leadership, economic stability, policy restrictions, and cultural complexity, seen as having a significant impact on the investment climate in that country. Figure 5.1 depicts a simplified country-rating procedure. Each of the eight

FIGURE 5.1
Weighted Country Rating System

1. Political Stability (2–18)

a. Very stable long-term	18
b. Stable over long-term	12
c. Active factional tensions	8
d. Continuing and worsening turmoil	4
e. High probability of regime change	2

2. Economic Stability (0–16)

a. Stable and high growth	16
b. Moderate and stable growth	14
c. Low growth and some inflation	10
d. Economic stagnancy with high inflation	6
e. Severe economic disruptions	0

3. Currency/Exchange Stability (2–14)

a. Freely convertible stable currency	14
b. Freely convertible and moderately stable currency	12
c. Weakening currency	8
d. Inminent depreciation expected	6
e. Hyperinflation and successive devaluation	2

4. Capital/Profit Repatriation (2–12)

a. Free remittance with no approval needed	12
b. Free remittance with approval	10
c. Limited remittance allowed but with delays	8
d. Strong exchange controls	6
e. Active blockage of transfers	2

5. Technology Protection (2–10)

a. Strictly enforced patent and trademark protection	10
b. Well-enforced but ambiguous patent laws	8
c. Protection but mandatory licensing required	6
d. Protection system poorly enforced	4
e. No protection system	2

6. Attitude Toward Foreign Investment (0–10)

a. Very positive and pro free-market policies	10
b. Positive policies with incentives	8
c. Investment not actively encouraged	6
d. Selective investment allowed	4
e. Completely hostile to foreign investment	0

7. EMS Incentives/Restrictions (2-12)

a. Very liberal and positive EMS requirements	12
b. EMS selectively positive	10
c. EMS selectively restrictive	6
d. Severe ownership and repatriation restrictions	4
e. EMS completely restrictive	2

8. Cultural Interactions (0–8)

a. Open and receptive cultural environment, geocentric	8
b. Moderately receptive cultural environment	6
c. Culturally sensitive and selective	4
d. Complex interactions required; culturally ethnocentric	2
e. Hostile toward foreign influence	0

TOTAL SCORE (10–100)

Source: Reproduced with permission of Transource Service Corp., 1986

major dimensions is identified, selected, and weighted during the Delphi screening process. Ideally, the selection of the risk dimensions should be both conceptually and empirically substantiated. In addition, the assigning of relative weights should be both conceptually and empirically valid. However, in most cases, the determination of the weighting system is mainly subjective. In Figure 5.1, for instance, the political stability dimension has been assigned a greater weight (2-18) than the cultural interactions dimension (0-8) perhaps because the panel that formulated the rating system may have perceived political risk as being more critical in its impact on business than cultural interactions. This particular set of weights obviously has not allowed for the fact that cultural interactions may in fact be a more critical factor than political stability in a country like Japan.

A country is rated by a team of analysts, and the individual weighted scores for each of the risk factors are then aggregated horizontally to produce a weighted average score for each risk dimension. Next, the averaged weighted scores are added vertically to arrive at an overall index of risk for the country in question. The country-rating procedure is therefore a method of "quantifying" what are essentially subjective data, that is, the perceptions and opinions of selected observers. Most of the syndicated risk-forecasting services employ a modified Delphi-type approach in generating country-risk measures on a range of risk dimensions. As will be discussed later, the procedures used by some of the risk-rating services are not strictly valid Delphi procedures since they are not normally based on a rigorous process of multiple screenings and the use of expert-derived output.

Quantitative approaches. This category of approaches would include any analytical procedures that are based on data that can theoretically lend themselves to statistical or mathematical operations. Thus the range of available analytical methods could potentially be very extensive, ranging from marketing-research methodologies to operations-research and econometric models. For instance, analytical procedures including multivariate techniques such as multiple regression and factor analyses, multidimensional scaling and discriminant analyses, linear programming, and other optimization models can potentially be applied to political risk assessment. In most of the cases, multiple regression (for continuous numerical data) and discriminant analysis (for categorical variables) can be used to relate a dependent risk variable such as the probability of rescheduling, expropriation, or repatriation with a set of determining or independent variables. The derived regression or discriminant function is then used as a forecasting device by entering projected or current data on the independent variables into the model. Thus besides analyzing economic variables, sophisticated multivariate methods can even be applied in analyzing subjective data, especially sociopolitical variables, provided that these variables can be coded or measured along some sort of nonparametric or ordinal scales.

Simple country-rating procedures, shown in Figure 5.1, belong to the category of approaches called "naive" quantitative methods, which consist simply of ranking a country on a factor or a series of factors coded or measured along a Likert-type ordinal scale. Sophisticated or "true" quantitative methods consist of the multivariate methods mentioned above, including both parametric and nonparametric statistical procedures. Since even quantitative methods such as multiple discriminant analysis can be easily applied to political risk data, these procedures offer a potentially powerful tool for risk forecasting. The regression or discriminant function offers the analyst an empirically derived model describing the underlying relationships between the independent variables and the dependent or criterion risk variable. Once the parameters of the system relationship, that is, the structural coefficients, have been determined, the derived model can be conveniently used to simulate a wide range of "if-then" scenarios in the sociopolitical environment of the host country. The major shortcoming of the more sophisticated quantitative approaches, however, is the difficulty for the average manager fully to understand the underlying complex statistics and mathematics involved, in addition to the difficulty in interpreting the output. Nevertheless, this is not an insurmountable problem. With the recent proliferation of personal computers and the availability of user-friendly software, most managers may find it easier to enter at the user level. This may well increase the attractiveness of the multivariate analysis option.

The wide variety of analytical options available to the corporate-risk analyst suggest a very promising potential for creativity in designing analytical formulations in the risk-assessment process. The final package of analytical formulations selected by the firm should not only reflect the corporate-risk orientation and organization of the assessment function but also the cost-effectiveness of these procedures and their potential integration with decision making.

The range of analytical formulations in actual use by companies includes both objective and subjective methods and a combination of quantitative and qualitative approaches. The general trend in analytical approaches appears to be one of progression from nonsystematic and unstructured analysis to systematic and structured analysis as firms expand their scope and increase the depth of their international operations. In the companies that are adopting a more systematic and structured approach to risk assessment, there is no indication that the use of subjective and qualitative methods is precluded as long as the analytical and the assessment processes are carried out in a structured and organized manner. In many instances, strictly quantitative approaches may in fact be suboptimum because many of the risk data do not lend themselves to easy quantification. The forced use of quantitative methods in this case may defeat any meaningful analysis and assessment and would seriously undermine the validity of the risk forecast. Perhaps in recognition of this pitfall, some companies that had initially adopted a strictly quantitative approach have abandoned it in favor of a combined quantitative and qualitative approach.

For companies that lean heavily in the direction of quantitative approaches, the analytical formulation, that is, the measuring instrument, could range from simple country-rating methods to those that have installed sophisticated quantitative models. The use of checklist and simple ranking methods are frequently used in initial screening of candidate countries. When a company has to evaluate as many as fifty to one hundred target host countries, the countries are ranked on an overall risk scale, usually on a scale of zero to one hundred, with the highest score being the least risky. The rating or measuring instrument discussed in earlier sections essentially consists of adding up the weighted scores on several risk dimensions for a specific country. The weighted scores on all combined risk dimensions are usually designed to add up to a total score of one hundred. Simple country-rating procedures represent one of the easiest quantitative methods to use.

For companies and banks that deal with risk data in basically numerical form, such as financial and economic variables like balance of payments, debt-service ratios, and inflation rate, the use of quantitative methods seems to hold more promise. Several U.S. and non-U.S. banks have developed elaborate and sophisticated econometric models to analyze lending risks such as potential default and other debt-repayment difficulties. A broad spectrum of quantitative techniques can readily be incorporated into country-risk assessment.[8] Even among banks, a strictly quantitative approach is sometimes considered inadequate because of the inherent inability of such techniques in handling qualitative sociopolitical risks data. To improve on the effectiveness of the risk-assessment process, corporate-risk analysts have found it advisable to employ a structured qualitative approach or an approach that combines quantitative and qualitative methods.

Integration with Decision Making

The most challenging and probably the most difficult part of the entire corporate-risk-assessment process is the integration of the output of the assessment process into both strategic and operational decision making. The degree and effectiveness of the integration depends on a variety of considerations ranging from the type of decision to be made, the type of risk facing the firm, the risk orientation of the firm, and the type of analysis used in the assessment process.

In terms of the type of decision and the type of risk facing the firm, the integration of risk analysis with decision making seems to be relatively more straightforward for international lenders. Banks are mainly concerned with debt-servicing and repayment risks of the borrowing countries, and the major decisional focus is the minimization of exposure to these risks in the bank's lending activities. The entire risk-assessment process is aimed at the decision of determining country-exposure limits and the maintenance of the quality of the international loan portfolio. Assessment of economic, political, and policy risks are all directed to this end. For exporters and international traders, the assessment of exchange and transshipment risks leads directly to the decision to export and to the type and amount of the insurance coverage required. In the case of manufacturers, however, the use of the risk-assessment output appears to be more complex and involved. Risk assessment theoretically can be useful in a broad range of "what, how, and when" decisions surrounding an investment project. For instance, at the preentry stage, the various decisions for direct investment projects are the selection of the target host country (what?), the mode of market entry (how?), and the estimated life span of the project (when?). At the postentry stage, risk-assessment information can be potentially helpful in market/ product decisions such as whether to expand, what products and markets to plan for, and whether to divest or withdraw wholly or partially from a host country. Risk-assessment data are also useful for designing risk-management strategies and programs.

The extent of integrating risk-assessment output effectively into decision making also depends on how project-specific the risk analysis is and on the type of analytical formulation used. The use of a naive "quantitative" method such as simple country rating would be appropriate for screening countries on a yes or no basis for entry decisions. The acceptance decison could be based on some predetermined cutoff point in terms of the country's overall score or on a predetermined number of countries for acceptance, such as the top four or five ranked countries. However, when it comes to a decision on the mode of entry and other project-level decisions, country-rating techniques are unable to provide any guidelines. Similarly, the use of more macrolevel analytical formulations like the Political System Stability Index (PSSI) or Delphi-based country-rating techniques would also stop short of providing any specific recommendations for project-level decisions like mode of entry and the strategic design of the project. The major drawback in using macrolevel analytical formulations, as seen in Chapter one, is their inability to differentiate between the riskiness of different projects. They are therefore suitable primarily for preentry-country-screening decisions and also perhaps provide a basis for defensive risk management. Also, it may be possible to use the country-risk scores to determine the hurdle rate of return in net present value (NPV) and other capital-budgeting analyses. But, as noted in the earlier chapters, adjusting the discount or hurdle rate to include a risk premium may not be conceptually acceptable because the differential impact of risks over the life of the project is not taken into account.

For project-level decisions, the project-demand model described earlier appears to offer more definite guidelines.[9] The model could be a basis for making both strategic and operational decisions. Such decisions could include the mode of entry, the percentage makeup of a joint-venture arrangement, the project's export-ratio requirement, strategies for anticipating and managing other dimensions of the host country's EMS, technology strategies, and a basis for integrative risk management and an early-warning system for divestment. The project-demand model could be easily integrated into capital-budgeting procedures such as NPV and internal rate of return (IRR) analyses by using the predicted risk estimates to adjust the project's cash flow. The project-demand model therefore offers a promising potential for aiding a wide spectrum of project-level decisions, especially those relating to microrisks and those relating to policy interactions with the host government. Other studies also emphasized the importance of project-level risk assessment. Two of the studies suggested the use of project-specific risk assessment as a basis for entry decision as well as for postentry monitoring of project risk. Both suggested that risk assessment should start with a particular investment project and be done in the context of the project's benefit-cost interactions with the host country. Such project-level assessment could also be a basis for risk reduction and strategic planning.[10]

In more sophisticated quantitative analyses, techniques like system simulation can be used to generate sociopolitical scenarios and their associated probabilities. These probability estimates can then be incorporated into capital-budgeting procedures such as a NPV or an IRR analysis, particularly through cash-flow adjustment. In qualitative or written risk analysis, the managerial judgmental process is required to produce explicit recommendations on the whole range of investment decisions. Since political risk assessment remains essentially an art and is heavily dependent on human judgment, one possible direction in developing future analytical techniques could be the use of artificial intelligence (AI). Just as in AI applications in medical diagnosis and other professional decision-making systems, areas of prediction and judgment that are akin to political risk analysis, AI application through simulating the expert judgment and decision processes of political risk analysts is a distinct possibility.

Figure 5.2 summarizes the relationships of a few selected analytical formulations with the type of risk facing the firm, the type of decision, the type of risk-management strategy for which the analytical formulation is suitable, and a brief description of the nature of the methodology and data used. The form of decisional output for each of the various analytical formulations is also shown. For instance, the use of country rating is appropriate for screening potential target countries based on a yes or no type of decision. The level of risk indicated by country rating may also be used as a basis for adjusting the hurdle rate in discounted-cash-flow analysis and deciding on the kind and amount of political risk insurance coverage for the

FIGURE 5.2

Analytical Formulation, Risk Management and Integration with Decision Making

Selected Analytical Formulations	Type of Methods	Type of Data	Relevance to Type of Risks	Decision Type	Decision Output	Risk Management
Country Rating (Checklist)	Naive or Quasi-Quantitative	Subjective (Opinions, Judgement)	Macro	Country Screening	• Yes/No • Adjust Hurdle Rate of Return	Mainly Defensive (Political Risk Insurance)
Country Exposure Limit Assessment	Quantitative and Structured Qualitative	Objective (economic variables) and Subjective (Socio-political variables)	Mainly Macro	Lending Level	Loan Amount Committment	Mainly Defensive (Minimize Lending Exposure)
Socio-Political Models (PSSI, Propensity to Expropiate)	Quasi-Quantitative	Coded Subjective (Socio-Political Variables)	Mainly Macro	Country Screening	• Yes/No • Adjust Hurdle Rate of Return	Mainly Defensive (Political Risk Insurance)
Project Demand Model	Quantitative and Structured Qualitative	Objective (Level of EMS Restrictions)	Mainly Micro	• Project Implementation • Technology Decisions	• Yes/No and Scope • Adjust Cash Flow in NPV Analysis	Mainly Integrative (EMS Interactions)
Multiple Regression and Discriminant Analyses	Fully Quantitative	Objective Numerical and Coded Subjective	Macro and Micro	• Country Screening • Project Decisions	• Yes/No • Adjust Cash Flow in NPV Analysis	Defensive or Integrative

Source: Reproduced with permission Transource Services Corp., 1986

different host countries. Likewise, sociopolitical models are useful in assessing macrorisks and hence would be appropriate for country screening and adjusting hurdle rates of return. Both country ratings and sociopolitical assessments are appropriate to risk-avoidance strategies. The output of multivariate analyses may be applied to a range of possible uses, such as using the derived probabilistic estimates for cash-flow adjustment. The project-demand model would be appropriate if answers to more specific questions were needed. The model provides specific guidelines on decisions relating to entry mode, entry negotiations, project implementation, integrative risk management, and an array of other decisions relating to policy interactions with the host government.

ILLUSTRATIVE CASES

The following sections examine the risk-assessment process of a major multinational automaker and a group of major money-center banks. The cases are intended to illustrate some of the key dimensions in the orientation, methodologies, and systems of the corporate-risk-assessment process. The illustrative cases are therefore generally presented along the lines of the major dimensions discussed in the preceding sections: organization of the risk-assessment function, analytical approaches, data bases, and integration with decision making.

A Major Multinational Auto Manufacturer

Organizing the risk-assessment function. International Motors Corporation (IMC) is a major auto maker with extensive multinational manufacturing and marketing coverage.[11] It has established a formal and well-organized in-house risk-assessment system. The risk-assessment function is organized primarily according to a parallel type of line and staff system. The assessment function is therefore performed by various line and staff units independently at the country and the corporate level for the respective market/product areas, and the independently arrived assessments are coordinated later. IMC has developed three major parallel sources of risk assessment:

1. Field reports from foreign subsidiaries in the form of medium-term and long-term business plans that incorporate assessments of economic and political developments that may affect its operations in the various national markets.

2. Reports from the corporate headquarters staff that constitute a part of the overall corporate product and business-development planning. The reports assess the political, economic, and business conditions that may influence global activities of the company. Staff specialists on government affairs and the car industry also contribute reports that examine relevant developments in these areas that could potentially impact on company's activities.

3. Reports produced by a special country-risk-assessment staff unit that provides in-house analysis and forecasts of economic, political, and business risks for the company as a whole.

Analytical approaches and data base. The major analytical vehicle is in the form of written reports and analyses, and the process can be characterized as primarily a qualitative assessment of industry-specific risks. Although the assessment includes the use of quantitative economic and ranked political data, the assessment output is predominantly oriented to a judgment-based process of decision making in the areas of strategic planning, investment decisions, and interactions with host governments. The risk-assessment output is also intended to serve as a kind of early-warning system for risks that are relevant to the company's operations and activities.

The primary sources of information for the written analyses include consultations with knowledgeable public officials, diplomats, academics, journalists, corporate and industry risk analysts, and other business specialists both in the United States and in the target host country. Additional information sources include economic and political data from secondary published sources and visits to the country locations. Although the assessment process is mainly qualitative, quantitative forecasts of macroeconomic trends such as exchange rates, inflation, and growth rates are also developed to reinforce the entire risk-assessment process. Projections of scenarios in the political, economic, and regulatory environments are developed from the written analyses and are then combined and integrated into an auto industry-specific risk forecast. Another output of the assessment process is in the form of a risk index ranking some sixty-four major countries. The risk index is based on fifteen weighted factors, which rank the countries into four major risk categories of low, medium low, medium high, and high.

In short, IMC's risk-assessment process involves extensive and comprehensive analyses of a broad spectrum of macro and microrisk data. Information on economic, political, and business conditions such as GNP and economic growth, balance of payments, external debts, political stability for the host country overall, and industry data such as regulations and policy restrictions specific to the auto industry are all combined to produce an integrated risk forecast for the company in its international operations. The overall and ultimate objective of IMC's risk assessment is to arrive at predictions on the anticipated impact of the broad range of macro and microrisks on the company's profitability in the respective host countries and on the probability of profit and capital repatriation.

Analysis of host country's EMS. IMC's assessment process pays equal if not more attention to micro or industry-level risks. This specific focus requires a more in-depth look at the factors in the host country's operating environment that are relevant to the auto industry. This would essentially entail a careful analysis of the EMS of the country, especially in terms of how it impacts, particularly on the auto industry. For instance, specific issues that need to be considered would include auto-industry regulations, energy problems, export-development and import-substitution policies, government-industrialization programs in the auto industry, price controls, local contents requirements, and local ownership and management participation. This project-specific analysis will enable the company to evaluate the impact of the EMS policies on the profitability of a specific project and will also provide guidelines for managing its policy interactions with the host country.

In this context, therefore, IMC appears to be highly attuned to the recent shift in host-country and multinational firm interactions to that of the host-country-demand (HCD) model and the resultant risk scenarios. An observer commented on IMC's risk orientation: "What the company faces in Latin America and elsewhere is an increasingly subtle and complicated regulatory environment. The strident anti-multinational rhetoric of the 1970s . . . and threats of sweeping measures such as expropriation or nationalization is giving way to carefully structured measures that enable governments to control foreign investor activity without sacrificing the benefits of a continued role for the multinationals.''[12] Thus the company recognized that an understanding of the complexity and subtlety of the host country's regulatory environment is more relevant in today's political risk milieu than focusing on political instability. Other studies also confirm the importance of micropolicy and market risks in the host country. A historical survey of investment in the auto industry showed that the expansion of motor-vehicle production is not significantly affected by political instability but rather by market and development risks.[13]

Integration with decision making. The entire risk-assessment process including the analyses of macropolitical and economic risks and the analysis of the host country's EMS relating to a specific project in the auto industry are all integrated into a qualitative forecast of the projected risk scenario for both the short and long term. The risk forecasts generated by the assessment process are then used as a basis for decisions on matters such as new investment, the expansion of existing investment, negotiation with the host country, mode of entry options, and the operational and financing structure of the investment project. In addition, specific EMS dimensions such as local contents requirements, repatriation restrictions, and labor and employment practices are all analyzed in relation to the project in question. In short, the company's risk-assessment process enables it to plan for and anticipate events that will affect its objective of maximum profit repatriation, and it also aids in management of interactions with the host government.

Major International Banks

The following sections provide a composite picture of the risk-assessment process in several major banks. Major banks with substantial participation in international lending are compelled, both by law and by competitive pressures, to accord critical importance to country-risk analysis. The risk-assessment objectives, functions, and organization of international lenders differ slightly from the risk-assessment orientation of multinationals engaged mainly in manufacturing and production activities abroad. The difference in approach stems mainly from the nature of their business. The former tends to favor a more macro or broad national perspective in risk assessment since borrowers may range across industries and sectors in the host country. Multinational manufacturers, on the other hand, are literally tied into a specific industry or sector of the host country and would be exposed to more specific industry-level risks.

International banks deal essentially with the end product (i.e., money) of the entire business or productive processes of their borrowers and have themselves no equity exposure in business operations in the host country apart from perhaps office investments. There is a greater concern, therefore, with the debt-servicing capability of the host-country lenders and with the quality of their loan portfolios. Since the array of risks facing the lenders are of a more aggregated nature, in terms of covering a broad spectrum of the sectors of the host-country economy, the assessment and analysis are likewise more aggregated, comprehensive, and perhaps amenable to quantitative analysis than a similar assessment by manufacturing-based firms. The banks are less likely directly to encounter microlevel EMS risks aimed at specific industries, although they may be affected indirectly through debtor firms in the affected industry. An additional source of risk for banks, especially with the recent spate of rescheduling for troubled debtors, is the availability of funds to refinance the rescheduled loans or existing exposures.[14]

The major decisional outputs of the risk-assessment process for international lenders are the country-exposure limits, the rejection or acceptance of specific loan proposals, and the maintenance of the quality of the loan portfolio for the various borrowing countries. Country-exposure limits set the maximum amount the bank is willing to lend to a particular country. This exposure limit is a function of the market potential of the country, the bank's equity and availability of funds, and the debt-servicing capacity of the country in question. The quality of a loan portfolio is determined by the terms of the loan (maturity and spread), the type of borrower such as a public- versus a private-sector loan, and the purpose for which the loan is made. The setting of exposure limits should also take the quality of the loan portfolio into account. In general, on a scale of relative riskiness, a private-sector business-working-capital loan is superior to a public-sector loan extended to finance development projects. An infrastructural development loan in turn is considered a better risk than a balance-of-payment or government budgetary loan for financing day-to-day government operations of the host country. The bottom-line consideration is whether the purpose for which the loan is applied will generate sufficient cash flow to finance the debt-servicing capability of the borrowing units.[15]

Organizing the risk-assessment function. With the recent series of crises in the international financial system arising from the deteriorating debt situation and the near default of many overstrained developing economies, the gravity of the situation began to hit home on the major money-center banks. Before the crises and the resultant loss of confidence in the international banking system, very few of the major banks were prepared for or anticipated the near disasters that would result from their lending practices. In fact, many observers have attributed the surge of high-risk loans to less developed countries (LDCs) in the late seventies to poor screening and evaluation by overeager lenders flushed with surpluses of petrodollars. This occurred despite the fact that most banks have better and more formally organized risk-assessment practices than other kinds of international business. In the postcrisis period, the awareness of the banks of international lending risks had obviously undergone a dramatic reawakening.[16]

Country-risk assessment is now a top priority in most major international banks, and many of them have instituted and strengthened the process of setting up sophisticated and elaborate risk-assessment systems. Unlike manufacturing-based multinationals, which still have an inconsistent pattern of formalized risk assessment, banks to a large extent have established formalized in-house risk-assessment systems.

In most of the in-house systems, the responsibility for the risk assessment function is vested in either the line or staff personnel or frequently in a parallel system combining the two. When an integrated parallel team approach is used, the difference in the assessment approaches between the banks lies in the role of the staff risk analysts relative to that of the lending officers. Some are more staff centered, and others are line centered. Most banks, however, are increasingly encouraging the setting up of a parallel but independently generated assessment in order to maximize the advantage of a broader consensus of views and judgments. A typical assessment unit would consist of the lending officers of the country concerned who are expected to provide direct operating inputs concerning the loan or loan proposal and staff specialists such as economists and political analysts who are expected to provide broader conceptual and referential inputs. The inputs from both sides are then integrated to arrive at a consensus forecast and assessment.[17]

One major international bank set up a country-review system comprising the principal lending officers involved with a specific country on the one hand and a staff economist and political analyst on the other hand. Each member of the team is expected to generate an independent written assessment of the policy and sociopolitical and economic environments of the target host country. Regular review meetings are then scheduled to examine the analysis of the respective team members and the rationale behind the assessment. The purpose of the country-review meetings is to decide on either maintaining or increasing the exposure limits of the respective countries that were reviewed. To generate objective and more accurate risk-assessment data some banks have deliberately built in an adversarial relationship among the various analysts of the assessment team so that no individual judgments will escape the critical scrutiny of others in the team. This system of formalized checks and balances built into the bank's internal assessment system is aimed at producing a relatively unbiased, objective, and accurate evaluation of the lending risks.[18]

Analytical approaches. The spectrum of analytical approaches and formulations in political and country-risk-assessment systems of international banks varies from highly quantitative approaches to those based mainly on structured qualitative judgments. Some of the major banks have reservations concerning a strictly quantitative approach to risk analysis. They have reservations about whether such strictly quantitative approaches would be able to deal with what essentially are unquantifiable sociopolitical data. Also, even if some form of quantitation is possible for such data, the scoring and weighting process, that is, the construction of an appropriate measuring instrument, remains essentially subjective. Nevertheless, several well-known banks have opted for a predominantly quantitative approach through developing sophisticated econometric models especially for analyzing more amenable economic data. The majority appears to have adopted a combination of quantitative and qualitative approaches, whereas others have instituted predominantly qualitative but structured and systematic approaches to risk analysis.[19]

In general, since banks deal with a broader array of direct and indirect risk variables on a very aggregated level, their analytical methodology essentially reflects the comprehensive nature of the risk-assessment process. Data, either quantitative or qualitative, are generated at both the country and at the headquarters level for each of the three major areas of risks relevant to the payment ability and willingness underlying the country's debt-servicing capacity.

The three main areas of risk assessment are economic risks, political risks, and policy risks. Economic-related risks such as balance-of-payment difficulties and domestic economic problems affect the ability of the country to generate sufficient foreign exchange to meet external debt obligations. Sociopolitical risks involving political instability, social upheavals, and disruptions affect the country's willingness to meet its external obligations. In such cases, although the country may have no shortage of foreign exchange, it may nevertheless impose exchange controls to prevent capital flights caused by political uncertainties.

Both the country's inability and unwillingness to permit outflows lead to inconvertibility risks for international lenders. Policy risks stem from the country's ability as well as its willingness to meet its external obligations. Policy risks are felt through restrictive measures in areas such as repatriation and other impediments to the smooth operation and transactions of business activities. All three major areas of risk assessment are then integrated to arrive at an evaluation of the country's ability and willingness concerning its debt-servicing obligations. This debt-servicing assessment is then used to set the country's exposure limit and is also used as a basis for evaluating specific loan proposals.

The assessment of the economic environment is based on the set of indicators discussed in Chapter two, such as debt-service ratios based on balance-of-payment data and other national accounts or GNP statistics. These numerical or "quantitative" data can conveniently provide an objective measure of the debt-repayment capability of the country since most of the ratios are developed from the host country's balance of payments and both actual and projected capital inflows and outflows. The assessment of sociopolitical data, on the other hand, is somewhat more complex because of the lack of tangible and objective measures. Some banks are relying on existing models or have developed their own macro-political-risk models focusing on system stability. The shortcoming here is to relate the sociopolitical developments and changes to a country's debt-servicing position. Other banks have proceeded in the direction of installing elaborate political science-based methodology to analyze and forecast the political developments in the countries concerned. One such example is the use of a "political spreadsheet," which incorporates a detailed analysis of the key political actors in the country and their respective stand on issues related to the bank's lending activities.[20] Once the economic and political data are generated, a measuring instrument consisting of an ordinal ranking and weighting system is then developed to derive the country scores. Such country-rating methodologies are similar to the country-ranking instrument depicted in Figure 5.1. Another case study of a major multinational bank shows a systematic approach to country-risk analysis by using sophisticated econometric models in combination with more qualitative studies. In the econometric-model approach, the bank employs discriminant analysis, a type of regression analysis for nonparametric variables, to relate probability of rescheduling to economic variables such as debt-service burden, per capita income, foreign reserves, balance of trade, and domestic-credit creation. These determining or independent variables are selected on the basis of statistical significance with the dependent variable, that is, rescheduling. By entering data into the derived discriminant function (relationship), the model can then be used as an early-warning system for potential lending risks.[21] In a similar vein, another study proposed a country-risk-monitoring system, which incorporates political-risk indicators in the analysis.[22]

In practice, the setting of country limits stems more from economic and marketing information than from political risk assessment. Generally, the country-exposure limit is a function of the market potential and the corresponding level of risk in the respective countries. Market potential depends on the size of the country's GDP and specifically the import component. These two variables are assumed to be primary determinants of the size of the country's loan needs. However, a more detailed analysis of the country's demand for external loans can be made on a sectoral basis using the sector's rate of growth. Sectoral growth rate and national budget plans would provide an adequate basis for projecting the sector's funding needs. Market-potential studies have to be complemented by an assessment of the corresponding risks. A measure of this is usually provided by the ability of the country to generate a stream of cash flow from its export earnings to service its external debt. The purpose for which the loan is applied is a major determinant of the debt-servicing capability of the borrowing unit. The industrial structure of the country should also be another critical factor in assessing the debt-servicing capacity. In general, the more diversified the country's industrial structure, the greater would be its debt-repayment capacity. For instance, in setting exposure limits for Mexico and South Korea, both major debtor nations, the primarily oil-dependent Mexican economy would rate a lower exposure limit, and the more diversified industrial structure of Korea would rate a higher one. This is because the latter's diversified and export-oriented industrial structure would be in a better position to sustain an ongoing stream of export earnings.

The intended purpose of the loan or the nature of the borrower's business could also be used to determine the quality of a loan portfolio for a specific country. The quality of a loan portfolio is a function of its spread, its maturity, and the attendant risk. In general, the greater the spread, the shorter the maturity, and the lower the risk, the better the quality of the loan portfolio. Employing this set of relationships, a indicator of portfolio loan quality can then be developed. Mathematically, the loan-quality indicator can be expressed as a weighted average spread of the loan portfolio divided by the risk-adjusted weighted average maturity of the portfolio.[23]

Integration with decision making. The end result of the risk-assessment function in international lending is directly integrated into the decision process. The process of setting country-exposure limits and the decision on a specific loan proposal are inherently operating line decisions. Thus compared to that with multinationals, which are manufacturing based, the gap that separates risk assessment and operational decision does not appear to be serious. Several studies have outlined how country-risk assessment could be organizationally integrated into bank lending and operating decisions. To integrate risk assessment fully into a bank's operations and planning, one observer proposed a multistage process consisting of the following steps: (1) review the developments in the field of political risk assessment; (2) survey in-house expertise regarding the setting up of the assessment methodologies and information-collection methods; (3) evaluate the option of using outside suppliers of risk information such as consultants and rating services; (4) select an in-house panel comprising country accounts officers, foreign account personnel, and their supervisory management; (5) develop an in-house questionnaire survey and measuring instrument; and (6) synthesize and integrate the results of the various qualitative and quantitative assessment.[24]

CORPORATE POLITICAL RISK INFORMATION SYSTEM (PRIS)

Data Collection

In many corporate in-house risk-assessment systems, information collection is frequently integrated with and is an intrinsic part of the assessment and analysis functions. Analysts are responsible, during country assessment, for generating their own information on an informal basis. The collection of political risk information consists of gathering both primary field information and published secondary data. The major sources of primary field data are the various operating subsidiaries in the respective host countries. Secondary sources of political risk information could range from the news media and international and governmental publications to professional risk-information suppliers. In companies without a formal political risk-information system, the informal and haphazard collection of information would impair the efficiency of the risk-assessment process. An unorganized and nonsystematic information search is time-consuming, costly, and inefficient.

Corporate in-house risk-assessment systems could benefit from a more systematic and organized approach to the data-collection function. The cost of setting up an intelligence system that is disaggregated from the main-line risk-assessment function would have to be measured against the expected benefits from the use and value of the information. The underlying approach to the setting up of a PRIS is to conceptualize it as essentially an intelligence system with systematically established sensory devices. As Figure 5.3 shows, intelligence systems can be designed with a two-tiered monitoring or scanning mechanism: (1) a global scanning capability that would monitor multinational developments affecting a group of three or more countries and (2) a national scanning capability that would monitor developments focusing on a specific country. The scanning systems would collect and generate both primary and secondary data. Primary data sources, collected at the subsidiary and the corporate level, would include a broad spectrum of data ranging from operational data such as production and marketing information to micro and macrorisk data that would include changes in the EMS, economics data, and other sociopolitical developments pertinent to the operations of the firm's subsidiaries.

The main responsibility for the collection and generation of primary data would be the line officers such as the country managers at the subsidiary level and supervising managers at corporate headquarters. The scanning of secondary data could focus on a variety of sources ranging from the news media, syndicated political risk-forecasting services, and governmental and international publications to commissioned reports prepared by outside sources. The mass of information collected would have to be organized and coded in some systematic manner. The information generated by the scanning system could be entered into a two-sectional data base. Following from the micro-macrorisk dichotomy, the data base is accordingly designed with two sectional files, a microrisk file and a macrorisk file. The microfile would contain information on the host country's EMS, especially those developments relevant to the industry in which the firm is operating and developments that would have a specific impact on the firm's projects. The macrofile would focus on macrolevel developments in the areas of political, economic, and sociocultural stabilities of the host country.

FIGURE 5.3
Political Risk Information System (PRIS)/Risk Assessment

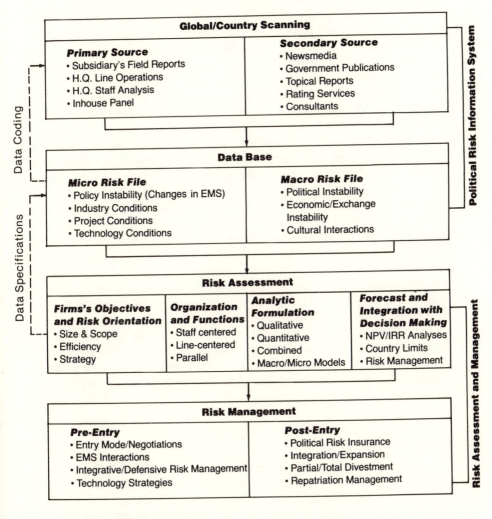

Source: Reproduced with permission of Transource Service Corp., 1986

Integrating Data Collection and Risk Analysis

The output from the data base is then fed into the risk-assessment function or process. Managing the integration of the data base into the risk-assessment function can be approached from two opposing assumptions. The first assumption is to let the nature of the data determine the kind of analytical formulation to be selected. For instance, numerically oriented data are generally more amenable to quantitative analysis, and non-numerical data would have to be transformed into some sort of nonmetric or ordinal variable before quantitative analysis. Data that cannot suitably be transformed would have to be processed by more qualitative analysis. However, letting the nature of the data dictate the type of analysis to use is analogous to putting the cart before the horse, and this approach could miss the entire purpose of risk assessment. This approach of treating the collection of data as a priority or as an end to itself may result in a system being so overwhelmed by a mass of unused data that the original purpose of setting up the system is lost.

An important consideration here is not the adequacy of the data generated but rather the judicious and goal-oriented use of the voluminous amount of information that could potentially be generated by such a system. A more appropriate approach in managing the integration of the data into the assessment function is to streamline data collection and generation on the basis of the selected analytical formulation. In other words, the data-collection function in terms of the form, structure, and amount of data to be collected should be determined by the analytical formulations rather than vice versa. Since the selection of the analytical formulation itself follows from the risk-assessment orientation of the firm and the type of risk it faces, the original objective of setting the PRIS is not lost sight of. Given the assumption that the PRIS should follow from the risk orientation, the risk-assessment functions, and the objectives of the firm, several major forms of risk data can be identified according to nature of the risk facing the firm. The micro and macrofiles in the data base can therefore be further suborganized according to these major categories of risks.

Organizing the Data Base

The major types of risk data in the data base would include information on the three types of uncertainties: economic/exchange uncertainty, political uncertainty, and policy uncertainty, in addition to other micro and macro-risks such as industry, project, and technology conditions and cultural interactions. Along a continuum, economic and exchange-risk data are most "objective" since GNP and balance-of-payments data are essentially numerical. Policy risk data are also relatively tangible, often appearing in the form of changes in repatriation tax rates, in the percentage of local contents requirement, and in percentages of mandated indigenized employment. Political instability risk information is the least amenable to systematic measurement. Although sociopolitical risk models like the PSSI employ frequency counts for political events such as the number of demonstrations and coup d'etats, such measurements are of questionable validity.

Another approach is to transform subjective sociopolitical data into nonmetric measurements such as in the form of a Likert-type scale measuring perceptual data. However, even when it is possible to "quantify" and rank these variables, the same problem remains because the rating and weighting process remains subjective.

Once the data set are organized according to the use for which they are intended, it would facilitate the process of integrating them into the selected analytical formulations. For instance, if the analytical formulation is the determination of country-exposure limits, data collection will be structured and specified according to the type of information needed, such as debt-service ratios and indicators developed from balance-of-payment and GNP data. The analytical formulation would then access the required information from the economic or exchange-risk data of the macrorisk file in the data base. On the other hand, if the analytical formulation calls for the assessment of microrisks to be based on the project-demand model, information should be collected to develop the risk factors specified in the model. The analytical process would then access the policy uncertainty and EMS risk data from the microrisk file in the data base. Or if the PSSI framework is used to assess political instability, data collection and generation would follow from the variables specified in the model. In Figure 5.3, this process can be represented by the dotted line flowing from the risk-assessment box to the data-base box (data specification). From the data base, another line leads into the scanning function, and this represents how the required data should be coded or measured as they are being collected or generated. Such a goal-oriented process allows a better management of data collection, coding, and use.

As depicted in Figure 5.3, the output of the PRIS and the risk-assessment system is the final risk forecast and projected risk scenarios as well as the continuing and ongoing monitoring of the micro and macrorisks facing the firm and its projects. The system output, that is, the risks forecast and the projected risk scenarios, are then integrated into both preentry as well as postentry decision making on a wide spectrum of issues ranging from entry mode, project implementation, and technology strategies to defensive and integrative risk-management strategies and divestment planning.

NOTES

1. Louis Kraar, "The Multinationals Get Smart about the Political Risks," Fortune, March 24, 1980, pp. 86-100.

2. Stephen T. Goodman, "How the Big Banks Really Evaluate Sovereign Risks," Euromoney, February 1977, pp. 105-110.

3. F. N. Burton and Hisaski Inoue, "Country Risk Evaluation Methods: A Survey of Systems in Use," The Banker, January 1983, pp. 41-43.

4. Antoine Van Agtmael, "How Business Has Dealt with Political Risk," Financial Executive, January 1976, pp. 26-30.

5. Dolph Warren Zink, The Political Risks for Multinational Enterprises in Developing Countries (New York: Praeger, 1973).

6. David B. Hertz and Howard Thomas, "Risk Analysis: Important New Tool for Business Planning," Journal of Business Strategy, Winter 1986, pp. 23-29.

7. Steven J. Kobrin, "Political Assessment and Evaluation of Non-Economic Environments by American Firms," Journal of International Business Studies, Spring-Summer 1980, pp. 32-47; idem, "Political Assessment by International Firms: Models or Methodologies," Journal of Policy Modelling, May 1981, pp. 251-270; R. J. Rummel and David A. Heenan, "How Multinationals Analyze Political Risk," Harvard Business Review, January-February 1978, pp. 67-76; Stephen T. Goodman, "Corporate Attitudes," in Richard Ensor, ed., Assessing Country Risk (London: Euromoney Publications, 1981), pp. 111-115.

8. John J. Thompson, "The Poor Man's Guide to Country Risk," Euromoney, July 1981, pp. 182-89.

9. Wenlee Ting, Business and Technological Dynamics in Newly Industrializing Asia (Westport, Conn.: Quorum Books, 1985), pp. 51-69.

10. Joseph V. Micallef, "Political Risk Assessment," Columbia Journal of World Business, Summer 1981, pp. 47-52; Alan C. Shapiro, "Managing Political Risk: A Policy Approach," Columbia Journal of World Business, Fall 1981, pp. 63-70.

11. Gordon Rayfield, "General Motors's Approach to Country Risk," in Ensor, Assessing Country Risk, pp. 129-133. The fictitious generic name International Motors Corporation (IMC), is used to reflect industry-specific risks not only for General Motors but also for the auto industry in general.

12. Ibid., p. 132.

13. Kenneth A. Bollen and Scott T. Jones, "Political Instability and Foreign Direct Investment: The Motor Vehicle Industry, 1948-1965," Social Forces, June 1982, pp. 1070-1088.

14. Thomas E. Krayenbuehl, "How Country Risk Should Be Monitored," The Banker, May 1983, pp. 51-53; P. A. Graham, "Risk in International Banking: Its Meaning for Liquidity and Capital," Journal of the Institute of Bankers, June 1982, pp. 74-76.

15. Pancras J. Nagy, "The Use of Quantified Risk Assessment in Decision Making in Banks," in Ensor, Assessing Country Risks, p. 103.

16. F. John Mathis, "Developing Countries' Foreign Debts: Lessons from Recent Experience and the Risk Outlook," Journal of Commercial Banking, July 1982, pp. 38-46.

17. Lawrence J. Brainard, "Banker's Trust Approach to International Risk Assessment," in Ensor, Assessing Country Risks, pp. 93-98; Joseph J. Tunney, "Bank Perspectives in Measuring Risk," in Ensor, Assessing Country Risks, pp. 83-85.

18. Brainard, "Banker's Trust Approach."

19. Burton and Inoue, "Country Risk Evaluation Methods," p. 41.

20. Tunney, "Bank Perspectives," p. 184.

21. James Merrill, "Country Risk Analysis," Columbia Journal of World Business, Spring 1982, pp. 88-91.

22. Robert R. Davis, "Alternative Techniques for Country Risk Evaluation," Business Economics, May 1981, pp. 34-41.

23. Pancras J. Nagy, "The Use of Quantified Country Risk Assessment in Banks," in Ensor, Assessing Country Risks, p. 108. .

24. David Bruce, "Integrating Political Risk Methodologies at a California International Bank," in Jerry Rogers, ed., Global Risk Assessments, Issues, Concepts," and Applications (Riverside, Calif.: Global Risk Assessment, Inc., 1983), pp. 131-139.

6

Risk-Rating and Forecasting Services

THE NATURE OF RISK-RATING SERVICES

Before the recent resurgence of interest in political risks assessment among multinationals and international banks, risk-rating and forecasting services were already in existence, although their services did not then receive the recognition and awareness they now appear to command. Some of the risk-rating services discussed below predate the Iran and Nicaraguan revolutions. These so-called syndicated risk-forecasting services specialize in the supply of risk information for individual countries presented in the form of numerical or alphabetical rankings and supported by textual summaries. The primary approach of most of the risk-forecasting services is the ranking of countries on a spectrum of aggregated risk dimensions. The risk-rating services usually adopt a methodology that essentially consists of "measuring" a risk factor on a nonmetric categorical or ordinal scale. The risk factor is thus measured as a numerical or "quantitative" variable. Specifically, a Likert-type measuring instrument consisting of a multiple-point ordinal scale is used to measure the various individual risk dimensions, and they are then weighted and aggregated into an overall country-risk score. In addition to the quantitative risk ratings, many of the services also provide narrative and written reports as well as a summary of socio-economic data of the surveyed countries. Since the primary focus of the risk forecasts remains quantitative, the risk-forecasting services therefore run the risk of projecting an illusion of objectivity for what are essentially subjective sociopolitical data. Recently, however, because of the readers' increasing awareness that risk ratings in the form of numbers and letters lack the ability to capture the full range of complex country risks, many of the services are beginning to incorporate more discussion and analysis.

Nevertheless, the major thrust of risk-rating services remains the provision of quantitative and summarized risk information. As noted in Chapter one, certain observers have expressed reservations concerning the conceptual and methodological validity of the risk information provided by risk-rating services. Robert E. Ebel, for instance, commented that the approach to political risk analysis taken by the rating services is highly structured and therefore has the tendency to reduce our perception of complexity to an absolute. In other words, a whole complex of sociopolitical and economic milieu is reduced to a single abstract measure. The author also expressed doubts about whether this reductionist type of political risk analysis can improve the decision-making function. He commented, however, that the structured risk ratings contribute to expanding the decision maker's range of vision and because decision making remains a highly intuitive art, this contribution is important.[1] Other observers similarly noted that although aggregated quantitative techniques are helpful in refining and structuring human judgment, qualitative analyses remain essential because of their greater likelihood of being understood and hence incorporated into decision making.[2] Mainly because of these reservations, some of the risk-rating services have recently begun to expand the textual analysis that usually accompanies the risk ratings.

Moreover, another dimension needs to be considered with respect to the process of risk ratings. Like the other approaches to risk assessment, the act of rating a country and its various risk dimensions is essentially a process of developing and forming subjective risk perceptions. Compared to objective risks, which deal with actual empirical outcomes of risk events, subjective risks basically involve the perceptions of uncertainty in the external environment. Subjective risks are perceptions of uncertainty and are therefore a psychological or mental state involving a conscious awareness of the probable occurrence of risk events. The formation of subjective risks or uncertainty perceptions may be influenced by the range of personal and individual traits of the risk analyst, and this may affect the objectivity of the analytical and decision-making process. The evaluation of the validity and usefulness of risk ratings, therefore, has to be considered in the context of its subjective nature.

MAJOR RISK-RATING SERVICES

The following sections examine the major features and methodology of several better known risk-rating services. The services include the Business International (BI) country-assessment service, Frost and Sullivan's world political risk services, International Reports international country-risk guide (ICRG), and the Business Environmental Risk Information's (BERI's) country-risk-rating service. Figure 6.1 provides a summary of the major features of the risk-rating services, including their rating methodologies, panel composition, and pricing information.

Frost and Sullivan

Frost and Sullivan's political risk service provides a wide variety of country-assessment services. Its two major risk-rating and assessment services are the political risk country reports and the political risk letter (PRL). The political risk country reports present an eighteen-month and a five-year forecast on the three most likely regimes to come to power for more than eighty countries, and they provide analyses and forecasts on both political and economic risks. The presentation is in the form of narrative summaries and analyses on the various risk dimensions and offers more in-depth textual analysis than the PRL. The PRL also presents both eighteen-month and five-year forecasts on several risk dimensions: probability of the most likely regime to remain in power, chances of political turmoil, financial transfer risk, direct-investment risk, and export risk.[3]

In Frost and Sullivan's PRL (see Figure 6.2), *direct-investment risk* is defined as risk resulting primarily from deteriorating political stability rather than more restrictive government policies. It is therefore a measure of macro rather than microrisk. Such an emphasis on macrorisk may be of questionable value to international business decision makers, particularly at a time when a changed global risk scenario has moved significantly toward an entry-management system (EMS) type of policy risk. *Export risks* are defined as those arising from high nontariff barriers and poor credit ratings of the country. The service uses both ordinal and probability-estimate measurements. The most-likely-regime forecast is measured by probability estimates, whereas political turmoil is measured at four levels: low, moderate, high, and very high. The three risk factors are measured on an ordinal scale based on a twelve-grade scale from $A+$ $D-$. The actual scaling and weighting methodology in the risk-measurement instrument used by the service to arrive at the risk ratings is documented, and this could provide a basis for evaluating the usefulness and value of the risk forecasts. The ratings in the PRL are accompanied by summary narratives, which elaborate on the significance of the ratings.[4]

The risk assessment or rating panel used by Frost and Sullivan is generally described as comprising a network of 250 country specialists with functional expertise and foreign contacts working together with in-house advisors. The panel includes academic specialists with a background in political science, economics, and history; independent or research consultants; retired government officials with a background in foreign policy; defense and intelligence agencies; and international businessmen. The background, qualifications, and nationality of the members comprising the panel used by the risk-

FIGURE 6.1

Major Risk Rating Services

PUBLISHER	NAME OF RATING SERVICE	RISK/FACTORS FORMAT PRESENTATION	INDEX/SCORING SYSTEMS	COUNTRIES COVERED	PANEL/ RATERS	UP-DATE INTERVALS	FEE: ANNUAL SUBSCRIPTION	OTHER SERVICES
FROST & SULLIVAN, INC.	Political Risk Country Reports	• 18-month and 5-year forecasts for three possible regimes	Summary narrative on risks	over 80	250 Unspecified Country Specialists and In-house Advisors	• Annual revision • Special monthly up-date	Service Package $4,000. Discount Available	• Int'l Business Environment Rep. • Project Consultation and Analysis • Seminars and Conferences
	Political Risk Letter (PRL)	• 18-mth and 5-year forecasts on: Most likely Regime, Turmoil, Transfer Risk, Investment Risk, and Export Risk.	• 12-grade system: A+ to D– • Probability estimate for most likely regime	over 80		Monthly up-date		
BUSINESS INTERNATIONAL CORPORATION	Country Assessment Service (CAS) and Annual Forecast	• 5-year forecast of 56 factors: 28 risk factors, 15 opportunity factors and 13 operating conditions factors. • Risk/Opportunity Matrix • 7 Country Indices	• Factor Rating: factor score x weight Scale: 0 to10. • Country Rating: sum of weighted factor scores Scale: 0–100	69	Unspecified Country Analysts and Correspondents	• Quarterly issues • Semi-annual up-date	$1,705	• Special Reports • Investing, Licensing, and Trading Conditions Report • Consultation
INTERNATIONAL REPORTS, INC.	International Country Risk Guide (ICRG)	• 1 year forecast on 3 risks dimensions: 13 political risk factors, 5 financial risk factors, and 6 economic risk factors plus Composite Index	• Political Risk: weighted scale 0–2 • Financial Risk: weighted scale: 0–10 • Economic Risk: weighted scale 0–15 • C. Index: scale 0–100	47	Unspecified Country Analysts	• Semi-annual	$2,500	• Country Reports • Internal Regulations Report • Statistical Service
BERI, S.A.	Business Risk Service	• 1–5 year forecast on: Political Risk index, Operating Risk Index, Profit Opportunity Index Repatriation Index	Country-score scale: 0–100	48	• 105 Senior Bank, Business, and Government Officials			
	Forelend	Lenders' Risk: • LR quant: computerized rating on payment capability • LR qual: rating on operating conditions • LR envir: rating on environmental conditions	computerized rating on payment capability	50	• 75 Country Experts on Political Risk	• Tri-annual Issues	$875	• Consultation
	Force	• Scociopolitical Forecast • Economic Forecast • Financial Forecast • Operating Conditions	Summary Analysis and Recommendations	31	• 14 Country Researchers			

Figure 6.2

Frost & Sullivan's Political Risk Letter

For each country, the first line is the 18-month forecast, and the second is the 5-year forecast. Each line includes the REGIME most likely to hold power in that time frame and the PROBABILITY of that forecast, the publishing date of our last country report or our LAST UPDATE note, our risk ratings for level of TURMOIL (from "low" to "very high"), and our risk ratings (from "A +" for the least risk to "D −" for the most) for financial TRANSFER, direct INVESTMENT, and EXPORT to the country. A rating in parentheses shows a change in forecast. An asterisk (*) indicates a non-incumbent regime.

Country & Most Likely Regime	Last Update	Turmoil	Transfer	Invest-ment	Export
Algeria Bendjedid 80%	11/1/85	Low	C+	B−	C
Bendjedid 75%		Low	B	B−	B−
Argentina Alfonsin 70%	3/1/86	High	(C)C+	C+	(D+)C
Alfonsin/Radicals 55%		Moderate	(C−)C	(C−)C	(D+)C−

Privatization Could Be Far-Reaching, But Plan Will Move Slowly. The Alfonsin regime's plan to privatize several state-owned holding companies is an essential part of its effort to streamline the economy. Although not involving public utilities, denationalization will affect steel, petrochemicals, armaments, and shipbuilding. Groups that benefit from the status quo, especially the military, will oppose the plan and slow down its passage, but by the end of 1986, some form of privatization should begin.

Australia Hawke 85%	12/1/85	Low	A+	A−	A−
Hawke 55%		Low	A−	A	B
Austria SPO-FPO 65%	9/1/85	Low	A	A+	A−
*OVP-FPO 50%		Low	A−	A	A
Belgium Christian Dem.-Lib. 65%	11/1/85	Low	A−	B+	A−
Christian Dem.-Lib. 50%		Low	B+	A	A−
Bolivia Paz Estenssoro 60%	11/1/85	Moderate	C−	B+	C
Centrist Civilian 50%		Very High	C−	C+	D+
Brazil Sarney 85%	12/1/85	Moderate	C+	B−	C
*Elected Centrist 75%		High	C	B−	C−
Bulgaria Zhivkov 85%	2/1/86	Low	B−	B−	C+
Zhivkov or Associates 80%		Low	B	B+	B−

High-Level Reorganization Does Not Signify Power Shift. The Zhivkov regime has taken steps to gain better control over economic activities. In order to avoid controversy at the Communist Party congress scheduled for April 2, the government has eliminated four ministries and established three umbrella ministries with wide-ranging powers. These adjustments do not signal a change in either economic policies or who is running the government.

Cameroon Biya 75%	4/1/85	High	C+	B−	C+
Biya 65%		High	C+	C+	B
Canada Conservatives 90%	11/1/85	Low	A	A	A
Conservatives 60%		Low	A−	A	B+
Chile Pinochet 60%	10/1/85	High	C−	B−	D+
*Transitional Military 45%		Very High	D−	D	D−
China Reformers 80%	11/1/85	Low	B	B	B−
Reformers 65%		Moderate	B	B−	C+
Colombia Moderates 70%	12/1/85	High	B−	B−	C+
Moderates 65%		Very High	C−	C	C
Costa Rica Arias 80%	3/1/86	Moderate	A−	A	(C+)B
*PUSC 50%		Moderate	(C+)B−	(B+)A−	(C−)B

Figure 6.2 contd.

Little Change For Business, But Nicaragua War Is A Peril. Oscar Arias' election to the presidency will not have much effect on international investment or the economy in general. Costa Ricans broke a 50-year tradition by returning the National Liberation Party to power. Arias gained support by softening his stand toward Nicaragua, and if the United States increased its direct involvement in Nicaragua, Costa Ricans would be likely to bring mounting pressure to become as uninvolved as possible. In such a situation, Arias might lose needed strength in dealing with the economy.

Czechoslovakia	Centrists 90%	4/1/85	Low	C+	C	C+
	Centrists 70%		Low	B+	B−	B
Denmark	Liberal Coalition 60%	6/1/85	Low	A	A+	A+
	Liberal Coalition 50%		Low	A	A+	A

Source: Frost and Sullivan, *Political Risk Letter,* ed. William D. Coplin and Michael K. O'Leary. March 1, 1986. Reproduced with permission.

rating services should be specified more precisely. If not, this could pose a critical problem for potential corporate subscribers wanting to evaluate the rating service. The validity and accuracy of the risk-rating and assessment reports are only as good as the panel of raters. Without a more precise description of the panel, an objective appraisal of the service and comparison of it with its competitors would be difficult.

Frost and Sullivan's service does offer regular updates of its ratings and reports. The country reports are revised annually, and the risk ratings are updated at monthly intervals. Frost and Sullivan also offer several integrated service packages that include the country-risk-report service and the PRL together with seminars and consultation. Service packages sell for around $4,000 each to corporate subscribers with educational discounts available to libraries and academic institutions.[5]

Business International

Business International also provides an extensive array of international business information ranging from country-rating services to regular reports on investment climates in a selected group of countries. Country-risk ratings are provided through its country-assessment service. Its annual country-forecasting reports consist of more in-depth textual analysis than the CAS. As a result of the preference of corporate clients for narrative analysis, BI intends to integrate its CAS risk analysis with the annual country-forecasting reports. The country-risk ratings, however, will be retained as weekly intelligence reports. The rating service presents five-year forecasts on a total of fifty-six individual risk dimensions. The risk-measuring instrument consists of twenty-eight risk factors, fifteen opportunity factors, thirteen operating-conditions factors as well as economic, political, and financial indices. Examples of individual risk factors include political stability, attitude of major opposition groups, expropriation, ownership restrictions, balance of payments, external debt, and repatriation restrictions. The twenty-eight risk factors thus include a broad range of macropolitical and economic risks as well as micro-EMS-type policy risks. The fifteen opportunity factors include dimensions such as desire for foreign investment, size of middle-class market in terms of GDP, level of foreign investment, and foreign investment profitability. Operating conditions include factors such as the country's legal and judiciary system, bureaucracy and red tape, quality of infrastructure, local contents requirements, and cultural interaction. Proxy indices for the financial, economic, and political factors are the level of corporate taxation, availability of local labor, and expatriate environment, respectively.[6]

Each of the individual factors is measured on a 10-point ordinal scale. The weighting system is dichotomous, that is, a numerical weight of either 85 or 15 is assigned to each factor, with the more important factors weighted at 85 and the less important factors weighted at 15. The weighted factor score is computed for each factor by multiplying the assigned weight with the factor score. For example, if the score for repatriation restrictions is 10, that is, no restrictions, and the weight for this factor is 85, the weighted factor score would be 850 (85 × 10). The weighted factor scores for all factors in a category are added to arrive at the sum of the weighted factor scores. The overall risk rating for the country as a whole is measured on a 100-point scale with a score of 100 representing the least risk. The overall risk rating is derived from the formula: Risk Rating = (Sum of weighted factor scores/Sum of factor weights) × 10. The same formula is used to derive the opportunity and operating conditions indices. In a hypothetical example for Austria, if the sum of its weighted factor scores for the risk dimension is 9,030 and the sum of factor weights for the risk dimension is 1,050, its overall risk rating would be 86 or (9,030/1,050) × 10. In the same example, if the sum of its weighted factor scores is 4,430 for the opportunity dimension and the corresponding sum of factor weights is 575, its overall rating for the opportunity dimension would be 77 or (4,430/575) × 10. A maximum score of 100 indicates the best opportunity. In addition, BI presents a risk/opportunity matrix formed by plotting the risk/opportunity scores of a group of countries on a scatter diagram. Countries falling into the northeast quadrant of the matrix, that is, the low-risk/high-opportunity quadrant, presumably would be the more attractive countries in terms of the investment climate.

One of the many conceptual reservations on the scaling methodology used in BI's risk-measuring instrument concerns its use of a dichotomous weighting system. Assigning numerical weights of either eighty-five or fifteen may be intuitively appealing since it is essentially equivalent to designating each factor as more or less important. However, there could be problems associated with this approach. Given the broad range of factors considered and the possibility that there could be a continuum of importance rather than just two factors, the weighting system is thus not sufficiently sensitive to a more refined and accurate representation of the aggregated factors. The use of a multiple-weights system could perhaps better reflect the more precise relative importance of the factors. In addition, there could be problems concerning the selection of the fifty-six factors. Although the factors represent a broad spectrum of risks, the inclusion of each factor does not appear to be substantiated conceptually. The weighting system and the selection of the factors were described as being based on a survey of one hundred major multinationals and on the subjective judgments of its senior executives and analysts. The rating panel was described as an international network of trained country specialists and correspondents, but their characteristics were not precisely specified. This renders any evaluation of the validity and accuracy of the ratings and forecast tenuous and conjectural.

The country ratings are accompanied by summary narratives of the forces behind the ratings. Such qualitative assessment tends to improve on and reinforce the minimal information provided by the ratings themselves. Currently, the risk reports and the country ratings are issued at quarterly intervals with semiannual updates to reflect any changes and new developments in the countries. Business International intends to incorporate the risk ratings in its country-assessment service with the five-year annual forecast. Approximately seventy countries are covered by BI's risk-forecast service. In addition to providing its risk-rating service, the company also supplies other investment and environmental assessments on a country-by-country basis such as its informative "Investing, Licensing and Trading Conditions Abroad" report (ILT) and Financing Foreign Operations (FFO).

International Country-Risk Guide

The international country-risk guide is a risk-rating service published by International Reports. The ICRG's risk-rating system and methodology is based on the same general approach as that of Business International's CAS. The guide provides rating forecasts on the three major areas of political, financial, and economic risks. The political dimension is composed of thirteen individual risk factors or indicators with the financial dimension consisting of five individual risk indicators and the economic dimension consisting of six. The political risk indicators include risks such as civil war, terrorism, political leadership, corruption, makeup of the legal system and bureaucracy, and racial tensions. Financial risk indicators include loan-default potential, delayed payments, contract repudiations, exchange-rate fluctuations, and expropriation. Economic risks include indicators such as inflation, debt-service capacity, and balance of payments.[7]

The ICRG's risk-measuring instrument consists of a scoring and weighting system that differs from that of BI's country-assessment system. Instead of using a system of weights independent and separate from the scale itself, a system of a weighted scale is used. Hence the weights are built into the magnitude of the scale. The more important the factor considered, the larger the magnitude or points on the scale. The following examples show the weighted scale of selected ICRG risk indicators:

Political leadership	12
Economic-planning failures	12
External conflict risk	10
Racial and nationality tensions	6
Civil war risk	6
Loan-default potential	10
Delayed payments	10
Inflation	10
Exchange risk	5
International liquidity	5

The use of a weighted scale can be more sensitive to the relative importance of the individual risk factors since the factor scores are aggregated into an overall score. The system permits a more precise continuum or gradation of importance to be built into the overall risk rating. Although weighted scales are technically more appropriate, the subjective determination of the weights remains an issue. The ICRG provides no indication of how its weighted scales are determined. Furthermore, apart from the issue of how the weighting process is carried out, there appears to be no substantiation of the inclusion of the risk indicators either conceptually or empirically.

In the ICRG approach, the maximum weighted score for the political risk dimension is 100 points, for the financial risk dimension 50 points, and for the economic risk dimension also 50 points. The higher the score, the less the level of risk. The composite risk rating for a country as a whole is measured on a 100-point scale and is derived from the formula: Composite Risk Rating = 0.5 (total weighted political score + total weighted financial risk score + total weighted economic risk score). For example, if the total weighted score on the political risk dimension for the United Kingdom is 94 and the total weighted scores for the financial and economic dimensions are 44 and 46, respectively, the overall composite risk rating would be 92 (0.5 [94 + 44 + 46]). ICRG's panel of raters is described as an international network of country specialists. The composition and characteristics of ICRG's panel of raters, however, just as in the case of BI and Frost and Sullivan, are not specified. The company also offers a range of supporting services in consultation and special reports. The update interval for the risk-rating guide is on a semiannual basis. The ICRG's risk rating covers about fifty countries.

Business Environmental Risk Information

Business Environmental Risk Information provides three major rating services, each of which is oriented to a particular need. Business-risk service (BRS) offers risk assessment primarily for the international investor, FORELEND specializes in risk ratings for international lenders, and FORCE provides more in-depth narrative analysis on several risk dimensions in summary form. The BRS offers one- and five-year forecasts on four major indices: the political risk index (PRI), the operating risk index (ORI), the remittance/repatriation index, and the profit-opportunity index. See Figure 6.3. The four indices are measured on a one hundred-point scale, with a score of one hundred representing the least risk. The PRI is developed from inputs from 75 diplomats and political scientists, whereas the ORI is developed from the inputs of 105 international business executives. In BERI's risk-measuring instrument, both the PRI and the ORI are derived from a subjectively weighted rating system similar to that of the ICRG and Business International approaches. The remittance and repatriation index is developed from a computerized data base. The BRS risk ratings cover approximately fifty countries.[8]

BERI's other service, known as FORELEND, provides one- and five-year forecasts on risks specific to international lenders and consists of three indices: a capacity-to-pay index derived from a computerized data base (known as LRquant), a composite index measuring a country's resolve to pay, debt profile, corruption and technocratic competence (LRqual), and a composite index measuring sociopolitical, economic, financial, and operating conditions (LRenvir). Just as in the case of the other rating services, there does not appear to be any conceptual or empirical substantiation of the inclusion of specific risk factors in the various risk indices. The panel of raters is comprised of bank executives, government officials, and country experts on sociopolitical risks. The FORELEND service covers fifty countries and is issued three times yearly. The third assessment service known as FORCE provides summary analysis and forecasts on four major environmental scenarios for a host country. They consist of the sociopolitical, economic, financial/monetary, and operating-conditions forecasts. FORCE covers about thirty countries and is also issued three times a year.

EVALUATION OF THE RISK-RATING SERVICES

An examination of the few selected risk-rating services shows both similarities and differences in their methodology, presentation, and range of coverage. The overall thrust of the risk-rating services' approach to political risk assessment is to reduce a whole complex mass of host-country information to a minimal form either in terms of letter grade or numbers that are occa-

FIGURE 6.3

BERI's Business Risk Service = FORCE

Mexico

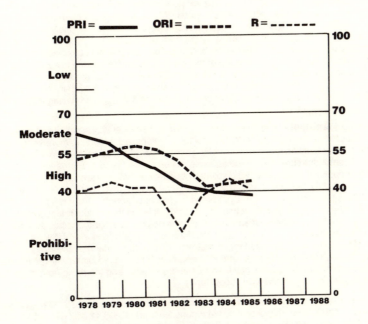

Profit Opportunity Recommendation: 4A

	Combined Score	Political Risk Index	Operations Risk Index	Remittance and Repatriation Factor
1978	156	61	54	41
1979	158	58	56	44
1980	153	53	57	43
1981	146	48	56	42
1982	120	43	51	26
1983	120	40	42	38
1984	126	39	43	44
1985	124	39	44	41
Present	111	38	39	34
***5 Years**	101	36	38	27

Force Report Publication Date:

September 1986

Fig. 6.3 contd.

Profit Opportunity Recommendation. Mexico's economic, social, political, and financial conditions will all deteriorate during the 1980s. The economy responded to fiscal stimuli in 1985 (showing 3.5% growth) but will not again register positive growth until 1989, when it begins a recovery. This downturn will aggravate already-poor social conditions, prompting repressive measures to retain order by late 1986. The opposition PAN party will gain adherents, forcing the ruling PRI party to take more grass-roots steps to arrest the erosion of its monopoly on power. Mexico's foreign exchange reserves are dwindling, falling from US$6.9 billion at end-1984 to the current total of less than US$3 billion. Emergency bridging loans will prevent culmination of a financial crisis this year, but a major restructuring of the entire debt will be needed in early 1987, when the country cannot pay interest without credits beyond the willingness of lenders to extend. Following resolution of the debt crisis, Mexico will experience slow economic growth in the 1990s. Recovery will be limited by persistent oversupply of crude oil and by the impact of having 90 million people and inadequate resources.

Sociopolitical Analysis and Forecast. Social and political unrest will rise sharply by end-1986 in response to declining economic conditions. Unions are becoming more vocal in demands for improvements in living standards, and fringe members of the opposition PAN party are planning street demonstrations. Rising joblessness will be exacerbated by increasing numbers of Central American refugees, who will displace Mexican workers. Thirteen of 31 governorships will be contested in July 1986 elections. The ruling PRI party has never lost a state election; it will lose to PAN in the northern state of Chihuahua in July, but through fraud it will prevent PAN's candidate from claiming victory. This action will provoke violence throughout many northern cities, which will be met by repressive measures. Riots will be on a much larger scale than the protests that greeted the incidents of fraud in local elections at end-1985 (police brutality has been documented). The military will be called into the streets to maintain order in some cities by the end of this year. Through the coming year, foreign relations with the United States will grow increasingly strained over terms of the emergency loan(s), the drug traffic, and the rising number of Mexican immigrants seeking better economic opportunity.

Business Analysis and Forecast. The plunge in oil prices to below US$15 per barrel will lead Mexico into a bleak economic period. Oil revenues fell from US$16.41 billion in 1984 to US$14.29 billion in 1985 and are likely to drop to US$8-US$9 billion in 1986. In previous reports, BERI S.A. noted that even at US$21.00 per barrel, Mexico would not be able to meet its interest obligations abroad. The sharper fall in recent months will prompt a severe economic crisis. Mexico will need an estimated US$8.5 billion in 1986 if it is to keep current on interest and prevent an extraordinarily sharp downtourn in the economy. An emergency loan will be pushed through by the United States to prevent default in the second half of 1986. This will buy time until a more comprehensive solution can be worked out between the major debtor and creditor countries, which will address interest payments as well as the rescheduling of principal over a more extended horizon. Despite emergency loans, Mexico's economy will register declines in economic growth over the coming two years. Following its modest growth in 1985 (less than 1% above population growth), Mexico's economy will shrink by 1.5% in 1986. Mexico's economic performance is likely to be worsened in 1987-88 by austerity conditions tied to the emergency loans. Inflation was 57.4% last year and will exceed 60.0% in 1986 because of excessive gains in money supply.

Outlook for Remittances and Repatriation (R Factor). Falling oil prices have prompted renewed capital flight. Mexicans already are estimated to hold US$25 billion abroad. The scarcity of foreign exchange will force Mexico to place even further restrictions on outflows of dollars. Emergency loans will be rolled over almost immediately to meet pressing interest obligations and will not provide Mexico with sufficient funds to offer dollars on the open market. Peso rates will climb 10% faster than the rate of inflation throughout the coming year. Last year merchandise exports fell 12.5% and imports rose 17.9%. As a result, a small current account deficit occurred for the first time since 1982. Mexico depended on oil for 67% of its export earnings in 1985; this percentage will decline to 55% this year assuming no significant rise in non-oil exports. The new non-oil export plan announced on 17 March to encourage diversification away from a reliance on oil will not have a significant impact on the current account deficits which will be about US$6750 million in 1986. There will be a deficit each year for the remainder of the 1980s.

COUNTRY INFORMATION

	1980	1981	1982	1983	1984
Population (millions)	69.35	71.19	73.01	75.10	76.79
% Change (five-year average)		2.8			
Real GDP (% change)	8.3	7.9	−0.6	−5.3	3.5
Production—Crude Oil (% change)	22.9	13.1	18.8	−2.0	3.9
Consumer Prices (% change)	26.4	27.9	59.0	101.9	65.5
Budget Deficit (% of GDP)	3.1	6.7	16.5E	8.5	6.0
Export Unit Values (1980 = 100)	100.0	109.2	94.3	84.1	81.6
Current Account Balance (US$ millions)	−8162	−13899	−6218	5328	3966
Foreign Exchange Reserves (US$ millions)	2688	4074	834	3913	7272
Average Exchange Rate: (US$1 = pesos (P)	22.951	24.515	56.402	120.094	167.832

12 March 1986: 470.50

Economic Summary: Proven reserves of crude oil total 71.75 billion bbl; 1160 trillion ft³ of natural gas is also proven. Mexico is now fourth largest oil exporter in the world, and the current average is 1.45 million b/d. The economy suffers from insufficient diversification and dependence on imported food; tourism normally contributes an important share of the GDP, but it is currently affected by the September 1985 earthquake and likelihood of growing crime. During the 1980s population growth will outpace economic growth.

Changes in Government: The Partido Revolucionario Institutional (PRI) has dominated Mexican political life in various forms since the Mexican Revolution. The success of the party is based on an elaborate patronage system, whereby favors are granted to supporters all the way down to the municipal level. In 1970 Luis Echeverría Alvarez set the stage for the current economic troubles through his profligate borrowing to support leftist programs. Under the tenure of José López Portillo (1976-1982), great sums were borrowed against anticipated oil wealth. Miguel de la Madrid Hurtado assumed the presidency on 1 December 1982 and has fought to stabilize the economy since then with varying degrees of success. PRI will begin a move to the political left within a year; the opposition PAN party will gain adherents from the middle class and business interests, although it will not achieve the presidency in this century.

Source: Mexico, FORCE, BERI, 1986. Reproduced with permission.

sionally reinforced by summary narratives. Despite both conceptual and practical reservations surrounding the services, they have nevertheless emerged as a notable part of political risk assessment. Since many companies are in fact depending heavily or partially on the rating services for political risk assessment, a more in-depth and systematic examination of their services would be appropriate. Several critical aspects of the risk-rating services have to be examined in terms of their implications for corporate-risk assessment. These dimensions include (1) the inclusion and/or selection of the individual factors in the scaling instrument; (2) a determination of the weighting process; (3) the composition of the rating panel; and (4) the integration of the country-risk ratings and forecasts with corporate decision making.

Inclusion/Selection of the Risk Indicators

Most of the risk-rating services include a broad range of individual risk factors that adequately cover the major categories of sociopolitical, economic/

exchange, and policy uncertainties. However, the selection of the final group of risk factors to be included does not appear to be substantiated rigorously, either conceptually or empirically. Some of the services reported basing their inclusion of risk factors on questionnaire and interview surveys of major multinationals and experienced international business executives. This could be regarded as a kind of quasi-Delphi method in determining the risk factors and not strictly Delphi in approach. Strict application of Delphi techniques requires multiple stages of screening by a group of experts to arrive at a consensus on the most significant risk factors. Apart from using a Delphi approach, another conceptually sound method in determining the list of risk factors to be included is statistical analysis. Specifically, regression or other correlational analyses using time-series or cross-sectional data could be performed to determine the statistically most significant factors contributing to the occurrence of a risk. For example, if political instability is the risk dimension of interest, a representative sample of countries could be analyzed to arrive at a group of factors with which it is most significantly correlated. Similarly, in the case of expropriation, a sample of past expropriations can be analyzed to determine the statistically significant factors. Obviously, the analyst would have to assume that there is a continuity over time in the underlying relationships for the resultant forecast to have any predictive validity.

Other important methodological considerations include the issues of measurement validity and the weighting of the risk factors. *Measurement validity* in general refers to how accurately a certain variable is reflected by the measuring instrument. In risk assessment, in particular, measurement validity refers to whether the intended risk variable is in fact measured by the risk indicators. The design of any scaling or measuring instrument requires the consideration of content validity, criterion validity (concurrent and predictive), and construct validity. *Content validity* refers to the extent to which the items used in the scaling instrument are representative of the area being measured. In risk ratings, for instance, it refers to whether the items or risk factors used in the scaling instrument adequately cover the field of "political risk" or some other risk that it is supposed to be measuring. Content validity can normally be ensured by the judgments of experts. In fact, the Delphi technique is actually a process of attempting to improve the content validity of the scaling instrument.

In the case of criterion validity, the aim is to see whether and to what extent a measuring scale corresponds or correlates with an independent and external criterion, that is, whether and to what extent a risk-rating instrument correlates with another independently developed rating instrument. Thus the risk ratings of Frost and Sullivan can be correlated with that of Business International's ratings for the same period (concurrent) to determine the concurrent validity of each. Cross-validation between the ratings of the various forecasting services may be an appropriate means of judging the accuracy of the services. In practice, however, it may be difficult to cross-validate because different measuring instruments are involved.

Predictive validity refers to the correlation of a measuring instrument with the actual occurrence of an event the instrument is purporting to measure. In short, in risk assessment, it shows how accurately and to what extent the forecasted risk rating had predicted the actual occurrence of a risk event. The usefulness of the many risk-rating services depends the most on their predictive validity. The record of predictive validity of the various risk-rating services appears to be mixed. Most of the predictions seem to stay within the safe boundaries of general perceptions regarding a specific situation. For instance, risk ratings on perceived high-risk countries tend to be reflected in the risk services' forecasts. Perhaps the most demanding criterion to satisfy conceptually is construct validity. *Construct validity* refers not only to whether a scaling instrument accurately measures a given variable but also why. For instance, political instability may or may not be "indicated" by a range of events such as ethnic or national tensions, military ambitions, social unrests, and political repression. Construct validity not only requires these indicators to be accurate measures of political instability but also to provide an explanation of the underlying relationships.

The Weighting System

Perhaps one of the more worrisome concerns in the rating methodology of the rating services is the nature and type of weighting system to use in the measuring instrument. The major decisions here involve what weighting system to use and how the weights should be assigned. The choice of an appropriate weighting system is important in reflecting the relative importance of the risk factors when they are aggregated into an overall risk score for the country. The weighting system of the risk-rating services could range from a basically dichotomous system (less important or more important) to a multiple-weight system that allows a more continuous degree of importance to be assigned to the risk items. An accurate, correct, and appropriate weighting process is therefore essential in contributing to the content, predictive, and construct validity of the overall risk-rating instrument.

The determination of the actual weights to be assigned remains essentially subjective, although the content as well as the construct validity of the overall rating instrument can be improved through rigorous screenings by a panel of experts. For instance, the panel would have to decide whether political instability should be assigned a heavier weight than exchange instability or policy risks in the overall rating instrument. Content validity as well as construct validity would have been met if the degree of importance or weights assigned to the individual risk factors adequately reflected and explained the actual risk configuration for the international investor in the host country. For example, if the cultural interactions dimension is assigned a lesser weight than political instability, is this really descriptive as well as explanatory of the actual situation in the host country being rated?

In addition, another concern in the weighting process is the fact that a set of assigned weights may not be constant over countries. In other words, the relative importance of the four major dimensions of political risks, economic risks, policy risks, and cultural complexity may vary between countries. For instance, the relative weights assigned to political instability for Lebanon or Nicaragua should differ substantially from those of politically stable Japan. Perhaps in the case of Japan a much higher weight should be assigned to cultural complexity so that the importance of this dimension will be adequately reflected in the overall aggregated risk rating. If a measuring instrument does not take into consideration the variation in relative importance of a risk dimension between countries, the aggregated country-risk score will over- or underestimate the actual level risk for a country and this will violate the various criteria of validity. Specifically, criterion and construct validities will not be met if the overall weighted risk score is not descriptive of or able to explain the actual risk configuration of the host country. In general, therefore, the more important a risk dimension is to a country, the greater should be its relative weight in the aggregate measuring instrument. Since the relative importance of any risk dimension may not be constant between countries, the measuring instrument should account for this variation.

A similar consideration is the variation of the relative weights over time within a given host country. Again, in terms of the four major risk categories of political, economic, policy, and cultural interactions, the relative importance of each will change over time for any given country. This variation in relative weights may stem from the constantly evolving environmental dynamics in the host country. In the case of China's recent industrial opening, for example, policy risks emanating from its newly established EMS will be directly more relevant to the foreign investors than political uncertainties as the pragmatic ruling regime further consolidates its power. The risk-measuring instrument therefore should be able to make allowance for such changes in relative weights over time.

Composition of the Rating Panel

Since country-risk rating is essentially an exercise in forming subjective risk perceptions, its composition or makeup critically affects the validity of the ratings and forecasts. The composition of the rating panel is crucial to the predictive, criterion, and construct validity of the country-risk ratings on two levels: the design of the risk-measuring instrument and the actual rating process given the measuring instrument. In designing the measuring instrument, the panel of experts should ensure that the selected risk items and their respective weights in the rating instrument adequately cover and describe the field or scope of the given risk (content validity), ensure whether the selected and weighted items appropriately reflect the same risk as measured by other instruments (criterion validity), and ensure adequate conceptual substantiation of the selected and weighted risk items (construct validity). Second, the panel actually rating the country on a given instrument should be qualified in terms of country knowledge and functional expertise and should remain cost-effective. The qualification requirements also include a consideration of the nationality of the panel members.

The composition of the panel in terms of expertise and professional knowledge may exert a strong influence on the results of the rating. Functional expertise is essential for accurate rating in the respective risk categories, particularly those pertaining to operating conditions. Raters that have stronger backgrounds in international finance will provide substantially more accurate and informed ratings on exchange risks while business executives will have more intimate knowledge of the operating conditions and hence can rate microrisks better. An appropriately composed panel should have a balanced mixture of professionals from the various disciplines as well as business practitioners with a broad spectrum of functional expertise. Trained professionals such as economists and political risk analysts are critical in providing more conceptually oriented inputs and perceptions. Diplomats and journalists, on the other hand, provide crucial perspectives on regionally based information.

In addition, the tenure of the panel members influences the results of the rating. A relatively permanent and ongoing panel is able to provide a continuity of perspective so critical to consistency and measurement integrity in the rating process. Frequent changes in the panel members as in the case of a revolving panel may undermine the measurement consistency of the rating forecast because of raters' biases. Since rating remains a largely subjective exercise, perceptual variation arising from changing panel members could reduce the consistency and accuracy of the rating results. A third crucial consideration in the makeup of the panel is size. Since the statistical universe of raters' perceptions may take the form of a normal distribution, enlarging the size of the panel could produce a more "average" perception regarding a risk dimension.

Finally, the composition of the panel in terms of the nationality of the members also exerts a large degree of influence on the results of the risk rating. This stems from the fact that the nationality of the raters, whether local or foreign, is a major source of rater biases. For instance, panel members who are local nationals tend to be better and more intimately informed as far as country knowledge is concerned. They are also able to interpret the subtle nuances of a complex sociopolitical phenomenon, which may frequently escape even the most astute foreign observer. However, the major shortcoming of using local nationals is their lack of objective perspectives. Their perceptions usually tend to be more emotionally biased. Many nationals of a country, including even highly trained professionals, tend to lack the emotional detachment so essential to an objective assessment of a country, especially concerning sensitive issues such as political instability and ethnic violence. Foreign nationals, on the other hand, have the advantage of being outsiders and hence tend to possess the requisite objective detachment. Their major shortcoming, however, is the lack of in-depth country knowledge, especially in cases in which they are part of a revolving and frequently changing panel. This appears to be a serious drawback of rating services that rely heavily on superficially trained country researchers who are frequently only on temporary assignments. Although less expensive, this approach at best lowers the quality of the rating results and at worst seriously undermines the validity of the ratings.

To minimize the biases stemming from the nationality of panel members, the panel makeup should strive for a more balanced spread between foreign and local nationals. Furthermore, the panel composition could be improved by using more nonlocal nationals who also possess a bicultural expertise and perspective. Such bicultural experts would include foreign journalists on country-specific assignments as well as academics and diplomats specializing in a specific country who have the vantage point of being outside observers while knowing the country intimately. Such a panel should also be balanced by retaining some degree of insider perspectives through using some local officials, business executives, and other knowledgeable local nationals. Rating services that retain a relatively permanent panel comprising a balanced team of the aforementioned members would have effectively provided a high degree of content, criterion, and construct validity in their risk information.

Integration with Decision Making

The most frequently cited reservations concerning risk-forecasting services is the difficulty in using the risk information in corporate decision making. Although many of the rating services do provide sectoral risk ratings for the different categories of political, finance, and policy risks, the ratings are still too general or macro to be of any use for industry- or project-level decisions and strategy. Risk ratings are not able to provide any guidelines for more integrative kinds of risk-management decisions such as a spectrum of project-negotiation issues at the preentry stage. Such issues include decisions on the nature and level of technology transmission, export ratios, and a whole array of project-level issues and entry-management requirements that have to be negotiated with the host country. Since in many instances an investment project "creates" its own risk profile, the general nature of the risk ratings is unable to offer any specific criteria for decisions.

Country-risk ratings appear to be most appropriate for decisions based on a risk-avoidance strategy. They can be used in the initial screening of candidate countries, which will lead to a list of "safe" host countries suitable for investing, lending, or other entry arrangements. This macrolevel screening allows a firm to reduce the number of countries eligible for more in-depth subsequent analysis and investigation. The macrolevel risk ratings that are excellent indicators of sociopolitical instability would also be an appropriate basis for planning a defensive risk-management program consisting of political risk insurance and other political hedging strategies. It could offer guidelines for deciding on the type, contents, and amount of coverage to be provided by political risk insurance in each of the respective host countries in question and also the amount of premiums that would be cost-effective for the protection purchased.

Other uses to which risk ratings and forecasting may be applied is in discounted cash-flow and capital-budgeting analyses. Most companies take political risk into consideration by either adjusting the expected cash flow from the project or arbitrarily adjusting the discount rate upward to reflect a higher degree of risk. Frequently, such cash-flow and discount-rate adjustments are not systematically determined. Many companies add a few arbitrary percentage points to the expected rate of return based essentially on intuitive or subjective judgments. Given possible variations in subjective risk perceptions among risk analysts and managers, such arbitrary adjustment could result in inconsistencies between projects and over time. Although risk ratings can provide a more systematic basis for cash-flow-adjustment procedures, it should be remembered that the adjustment process remains essentially subjective. A possible procedure of using risk ratings for adjusting the discount rate may be performed as follows:

Risk Ratings in Points	Percentage Points Added to the Discount Rate
90-100	+ 0% adjustment
80-89	+ 3% adjustment
70-79	+ 5% adjustment
60-69	+ 7% adjustment
60 and below	+11% adjustment

For proposed projects in countries with ratings between 90 and 100, the discounted rate need not be adjusted, perhaps to reflect the negligible amount of risks. For projects in countries with ratings from 80 to 89, 3 percentage points can be added to the discount rate while adjustments for the other categories of risk ratings can be assigned as shown. Similarly, the different period's cash flow from a project can be adjusted on the basis of the risk ratings. Such a system remains essentially subjective.

ADVANTAGES IN USING RISK-RATING SERVICES

Despite the many shortcomings in their conceptual and methodological foundations and their lack of practical uses for a wide range of more specific international business decision making, there is a definite role for risk-rating services in corporate-risk assessment. Syndicate risk-forecasting services offer certain advantages for corporate-risk assessment when compared to other risk-assessment approaches. For instance, it is less expensive than setting up a formal in-house risk-assessment unit or retaining political risk consultants. Many smaller to medium-size international firms frequently do not have sufficient resources to commit to performing their own in-house risk assessment. For these companies, the risk-rating services provide a relatively inexpensive source of international risk information. As depicted in Figure 6.3, information supplied by the rating services forms an integral part of the political risk data base of corporate-risk-assessment systems.

Moreover, when compared to nonexistent risk assessment or even ad hoc and haphazardly done risk assessment, the deliberately processed and produced risk information generated by risk-rating services provides at least some degree of formal and systematic information for the firms' decision-making process. Some system of risk assessment is better than no system at all. More importantly, since international political risk assessment remains an art rather than an exact science, any information, particularly systematically generated information, would be a welcome reinforcement of an otherwise uncertain assessment process. Risk ratings would be especially helpful even to companies performing their own assessment by providing additional perspectives to and allowing confirmation of the internally generated assessment. The risk information provided by the rating services comes packaged in a relatively easy-to-understand format. Subscribers can easily make country comparisons within a given rating system. Because of the standardized format and rating methodology within a rating service, across-country comparisons can be done with a relatively high degree of validity. Finally, since the information provided by the rating services comes from a source external to a company, it could be regarded as more neutral than risk analyses performed by a specific division or staff unit within the company. Such an independent source of information is usually free of any intracompany biases. Divisional or regional biases that may accompany in-house assessment can then be detected and judged against a neutral source of external risk information. In general, externally produced risk information could potentially help a firm to broaden its perspective on political risks. Therefore, the major task facing companies subscribing to a syndicated risk-forecasting service is to integrate its risk information into the firm's overall risk-assessment function.

NOTES

1. Robert E. Ebel, "The Magic of Political Risk Analysis," in Mark B. Winchester, ed., The International Essays for Business Decision Makers, Vol. 5 (Houston: The Center for International Business, 1980), p. 292.

2. Stephen J. Andriole and Gerald W. Hopple, "An Overview of Political Instability Research Methodologies: Basic and Applied Recommendations for the Corporate Analyst," in Jerry Rogers, ed., Global Risk Assessments, Issues, Concepts, and Applications (Riverside, Calif.: Global Risk Assessment, Inc., 1983), pp. 89-90.

3. Frost and Sullivan Political Risk Services, World Political Risk Forecasts (New York: Frost and Sullivan, 1983).

4. William D. Coplin and Michael K. O'Leary, "Systematic Political Risk Analysis for Planners," Planning Review, January 1983, pp. 14-17.

5. Frost and Sullivan Political Risk Services, Catalog of Services (New York: Frost and Sullivan, 1984).

6. Business International, Country Assessment Service (New York, 1985, various reports and catalogs.

7. International Country Risk Guide (New York: International Reports, 1985), statistical section and various reports by country and by period.

8. Business Environmental Risk Information, Business Risk Service, Forelend, and Force (Long Beach, Calif., 1985), various reports and catalogs

7

Defensive Risk Management

NATURE, CONCEPTS, AND DEFINITIONS OF RISKS

The recent growth in demand for political insurance in international business is part of a process of radical developments in the insurance business that departed from traditional industry conventions. Traditionally, political risks, particularly those stemming from adverse governmental actions, were not considered commercially insurable. This is because the nature of political risks is not strictly in accordance with the classic insurance assumption of the pooling of a large group of more predictable static or pure risks that result only in losses. International investment and lending risks are too diverse and dynamic to lend themselves to the traditional risk-analysis orientation of the insurance industry. Such international risks are part of that category of risks known as speculative risks, the outcome of which may result in both losses as well as gains. The traditional scenario of only insuring pure or static risks is now undergoing rapid and substantial changes in concepts as well as practice. Especially with the growing corporate awareness of political risks after Iran and Nicaragua and the unabated demand for political risk insurance, the role of insurance in multinational risk management needs to be reexamined in the context of the recent changes.

The following sections examine the various concepts of risk. An attempt is made to relate these concepts to the recent developments in the insuring of international business risks.

Objective and Subjective Risks

Objective or *statistical risks* are defined as the relative variation of an actual outcome of an event from some expected outcome. The key focus here is to distinguish one outcome (the actual) from another outcome, usually a benchmark measure indicated by the expected average. Objective risk is usually measured by statistical indicators such as the standard deviation or coefficient of variation. Objective risks therefore involve a strictly statistical definition of *risk* as the variation of outcomes around some expected average. Seen in this context, this definition suggests that the variation in outcome for an event can be either a favorable or an unfavorable deviation from the expected average. This would include uncertainty of outcome in both directions, that is, negative and positive variation. However, from the standpoint of traditional insurance, conventional concepts of risk are usually restricted to a consideration of only unfavorable deviations from expectations, or negative outcomes or losses. *Losses* are defined as the unintentional decline in or disappearance of value as a result of the occurrence of a risk event.[1]

Subjective risk refers to the perceptions of objective risk. As opposed to objective risks, which consider actual or empirical outcomes of a risk event, subjective risks are essentially a mental or psychological state regarding uncertainty. Thus subjective risks can be defined as psychological uncertainty concerning the state of nature and therefore concern a mental state involving a conscious awareness of risks. The formation of subjective risks is a function of personality and risk-taking behavior of individuals. Because of its psychological nature, the personal characteristics and traits of the decision maker may be influential in the perceptions of subjective risks. For instance, various studies have considered the role of personality, age, education, and other socioeconomic factors in shaping the perceptions of uncertainty and risks and hence the nature of an individual's risk-taking behavior. In the context of risk analysis, therefore, it should be remembered that biases arising from personal traits may affect the formation of subjective risks. Subjective risk perceptions of the risk analyst or manager tend to intrude into the analytical process and may affect their judgments and the resulting decision when objective risks are being interpreted and analyzed. For instance, a given level of objective risk may be considered high by some, whereas another may interpret the same level of risk as low.[2]

The nature of political risk generally tends to be more subjective than objective. This may be true because risks such as expropriation, inconvertibility, and other forms of risk arising from adverse governmental actions are not easily amenable to statistical measurement. For example, there is not a sufficiently large number of cases of expropriations to permit any form of average to be developed. As long as statistical averages are difficult to develop, objective risks or statistical variations from the average cannot be easily computed. In addition, most indicators of political risk are formed from the subjective perceptions of the state of political uncertainty in a given country. This is especially true of risk ratings that are essentially ordinal measures of the subjective perceptions of either a rating panel or some risk analysts.

Probability

The concept of probability differs from that of risk. *Probability* refers to the long-run chance or relative frequency of occurrence of some events, whereas *risk* is a concept of relative variation. For instance, if in ten thousand cases of foreign investments, thirty are expected to be expropriated, the probability of expropriation is 0.003, whereas risk in this situation is some number other than the thirty expropriations, that is, a variation either below or above 0.003 probability of expropriation. Therefore, risk can also be defined as the uncertainty concerning loss. Normally, as exposure units increase, objective risk decreases. In other words, as the number of occurrences increases, the actual loss outcome approaches the expected loss; that is, the chance or probability of loss becomes almost known. When the probability of a loss becomes certain or is 100 percent known, risk becomes zero. Accurate prediction of the probability of some specified events is made possible through the operation of the law of large numbers or the law of averages. The law states that the greater the number of observations, the closer will the actual probability approach the expected probability. Thus if a coin is flipped a sufficiently large number of times, the closer will the outcome approach heads 50 percent and tails 50 percent of the time. The increased predictiveness of the probability of occurrence of a risk event made possible through the operation of law of large numbers underlies the fundamental insurance principle of the pooling of risks.[3]

Causes of Risks

Factors or events that may contribute to the probable occurrence of a risk are important in risk analysis and identification. Causes of risks are known as perils and hazards. A *peril* is a contingency or an event that may contribute to an unfavorable deviation from the expected outcome, that is, the immediate cause of a loss. *Hazard* is a condition that underlies the occurrence of a risk. Specifically, it is a condition that may create or increase the probability or chance of loss from a given peril. Normally, the greater the hazard, the greater the probability and severity of the loss. Thus, for instance, the icier and more slippery is the road (hazard), the greater the chance of a serious accident (peril) that could result in serious injury (severity). Both terms are more related to probability than to risks. In the context of political risk assessment, for example, a left-wing coup d'etat in a host country may lead to the probability of expropriation of foreign investment projects more than perhaps a right-wing coup, and if the coup is accompanied by violence, this may increase the chance of expropriation. Here, the violent coming to power of the leftist regime may be considered the hazard, whereas the act of expropriation is the peril.[4]

Static and Dynamic Risks

Besides the aforementioned concepts of risk and probability, other classifications of risks may also be considered. Additional perspectives on the definition of risk can help facilitate a better understanding of the nature of political risks. Two sets of generally accepted classifications may be worth considering. One classification distinguishes between static and dynamic risks, and the other classifies risks into pure or speculative. The two classifications are similar but not identical. Thus static risks may be thought of as similar to pure risks, whereas dynamic risks can be seen as similar to speculative risks.

Static risks refer to risks stemming from an unchanging and stable society or a sociopolitical system in equilibrium. *Dynamic risks* stem from changes in the socioeconomic and technological systems. The latter refers more to the whole spectrum of uncertainties arising from technological changes, industrialization, and other developments stemming from socioeconomic progress. Political risks, which originate from adverse government actions such as expropriation and nationalizations, are essentially static risks and are usually perceived to lead to unfavorable outcome or losses. Such risks, as seen in Chapter two, result basically from a "zero-sum" situation in which a lack of dynamic growth leads frequently to adverse actions taken at the expense of other socioeconomic actors. When the economic "pie" is constant, increased benefits for one group can be attained only by reducing the share of other groups if the system is stagnant and unchanging. In contrast, risk and uncertainties resulting from host-country dynamics and technological developments are dynamic, and they tend to produce both favorable and unfavorable outcomes.[5]

When the host-country-dynamics model is assumed to be prevailing, the scenario envisioned under such conditions usually involves a process of rapid growth and development, especially in the technological and economic system. All economic actors can therefore theoretically share in increased benefits without reducing the share for others. Under such conditions, foreign businesses are accorded status as potential contributors to the process of economic advancement, and the resulting risk exposures tend to be a matter of policy interactions with the host countries. The international investors can benefit from a broad range of incentives and profit opportunities if their policy interactions are considered optimum from the standpoint of the host country's industrial structure. In short, dynamic risks, like entry-management-system risks for specific projects and industry, can produce both profit opportunities as well as losses for the foreign investors, but static risks, like politically motivated expropriations, tend to result only in losses.

Pure and Speculative Risks

Another approach is to classify risks as either pure or speculative. *Pure risk* refers to the uncertainty of loss as a result of a peril. It includes losses due to both natural and man-made perils such as flood, earthquakes, fires, negligence, and sabotage. Thus pure risk normally involves exposure to adversity and the possibility of a loss. The probability of a positive outcome or opportunity for gain is normally not associated with a pure risk phenomenon. Speculative risk, on the other hand, refers to an uncertainty that can produce either a gain or a loss. It therefore includes the whole range of market, technological, production, and competitive risks that provide the potential for profit as well as loss. In terms of the statistical variation concept discussed previously, pure risk may be considered the worse-than-expected outcome, that is, the unfavorable or negative deviation from the expected outcome. In speculative risk, the outcome can either be better than or worse than expected; that is, there is a possibility of a favorable deviation (a gain) as well as an unfavorable deviation (a loss) from the expected outcome.[6]

In the context of international business in general and investment in particular, risks can be either pure or speculative. Political risks such as expropriation and damages sustained by investors during wars, revolutions, and civil strifes would most likely be considered pure risks since these events normally lead only to losses. Classifying political risks as pure risk, however, may be problematic if not confusing. If the international investment process is thought of as speculative because its objective is the pursuit of profit, expropriation and other political risks that are incidental to the basic speculative venture should be considered speculative. For the purpose of this book, therefore, political risks are considered as static risks because of their underlying "zero-sum" assumptions. However, they will not be considered as pure risks because of the dynamic nature of the interactions between the international firm and the host country.

In comparison, the nature of policy risks appears to be more clear-cut. Policy risks, particularly those emanating from the host country's entry-management system, tend to be more speculative. These project-level or industry-specific risks, including both incentives and restrictions, can result in opportunities for gains as well as losses. The international investor may stand to gain if the project is perceived to be a net contributor to economic advancement and may lose if perceived otherwise.

Under traditional insurance industry conventions, pure risk is insurable but speculative risk is not. The underlying reason for insuring only pure risks is that such risks are usually outcomes involving unfavorable deviation or loss. They are therefore relatively more amenable to accurate prediction through the operation of the law of large numbers as the loss-exposure units increase. With greater predictiveness and better knowledge of the certainty of loss, the insurance mechanism can be used as a basis to provide for the pooling and hence the reduction of such risks. In fact, insurance can be viewed as a process of pooling a large number of exposure units to improve on the predictiveness or certainty of loss, which in turn enables the determination of an adequate level of protection from the predictable losses. Pure risks that are considered commercially insurable include property risks, personal risks, and liability risks.

Speculative risk emanates from the dynamics of freely competitive markets and is therefore less amenable to accurate prediction of the outcomes. Thus speculative risks such as market risks (supply and demand uncertainties, product and technological obsolescence, competitive risks) and production risks are not conventionally insurable. As such, speculative risk is usually managed as part of the conducting of normal business strategies and operations. In fact, the bearing of speculative risks is the core function of the entrepreneur, and resultant profits are considered the reward for the speculative risk taking. Recently, the traditional classification of pure versus speculative risk has been gradually weakening due to the changes in the insurance industry's conventions governing the insurability of risks. More and more, insurance coverages are now extended to fields that are essentially considered speculative risks including areas such as municipal bonds, computer-lease contracts, mutual fund shares, mortgage insurance, and, increasingly, political risks associated with international investment. For instance, the insurance coverage for municipal bonds ensures guaranteed timely payment of interest and guaranteed payment of principal at maturity. Apart from pure risks like expropriation, coverages for other international investment risks like contract frustration now similarly offer protection for endeavors that can produce both gains as well as losses.

Pure risks can be classified into three major types: personal risks, property risks, and liability risks. Personal risks include death, disability, and unemployment. Property risks include destruction of, damage to, or theft of property. Liability risks include legal obligations for personal or property losses resulting from negligent behavior. Losses from property risks can be further classified into the loss of the article itself, the loss of income from the use of the property (cash-flow loss), and the additional expenses incurred directly as a result of the loss of the property. In the case of political risk insurance, commonly insured risks are usually confined to property risks such as confiscation, expropriation, and damage to property arising from adverse government actions. At present, political risk insurance has yet to extend into coverages for personal and liability risks. In fact, a common exclusion of political insurance coverages is any loss due to negligent or irresponsible actions on the part of the investors that may provoke the seizure of property or the denial of their rights.

MANAGING RISKS

As seen in Chapter five, a company's risk-assessment and management orientation depends on its perceptions of risk and its risk-taking behavior. Some firms are more aggressive international risk takers because of their size, strategy, or economic-efficiency considerations. Therefore, depending on its size, experience, strategic advantage, management philosophy, and considerations of economic efficiency, a company could adopt a particular risk orientation and pursue a particular risk strategy in its international operations. To implement its chosen risk strategy, the firm can select from a broad range of risk-management strategies and techniques:[7]

1. Risk avoidance
2. Assumption of risk (risk retention)
3. Combining or pooling or risks (insurance)
4. Spreading of risks or diversification
5. Loss prevention
6. Loss control
8. Transference or shifting of risks

Risk Avoidance

Risk avoidance may be one of the most commonly practiced risk-management strategies. In the general context, it involves a decision of avoiding exposure to personal, property, and liability risks by not owning, operating, or entering into a certain field of business or activity. In the political risk arena, risk avoidance is a frequently pursued strategy. Risk avoidance can be implemented at the preentry as well as the postentry stage of the risk-assessment process. If the risk forecast as indicated by risk ratings or the advice of political risk consultants leads to a decision not to invest in a specific country, the firm is essentially following a risk-avoidance strategy. Thus the rejection or acceptance of a country location for a proposed investment in the initial macroscreening process is itself a form of risk-management technique. Similarly, at the postentry stage, the decision to divest either partially or totally from an existing investment in a particular country is also a risk-avoidance technique. Both of these decisions can help the firm avert probable expected losses associated with its investment projects.

Managing political risk in international operations through pursuing risk-avoidance strategies can help a company to allocate its risk-management costs more efficiently. This is especially true for marginal projects in high-risk-country locations. The rejection of such projects may enable the firm better to optimize its investment resources. However, in the case of estimated high-return projects or projects in which the firm has a strategic or technological advantage, country-risk avoidance may lead to suboptimization. In such an instance, that is, a favorable project in an unfavorable country, the company may be better off resorting to other risk-management techniques to realize and preserve the expected profit opportunity.

Risk Retention

Risk retention is another strategy that can be pursued in international risk management. Risk retention can be planned or unplanned. When risk retention is planned, it is known as self-insurance or coinsurance. In most cases, risk is only partially retained by the firm, and the retention is normally used in conjunction with an insurance coverage. This is known as coinsurance. As part of an insurance-policy coverage, the insured company may agree to take back or assume a portion of the risk. In the event of a loss, the coinsured portion, for example, 10 percent of the project value, is not compensated for by the insurer. However, the major attraction of co-insurance or a deductible is that premiums may be substantially reduced, hence resulting in lower insurance costs. When a company consciously assumes 100 percent of the risks, it is effectively acting as its own insurer and may be viewed as providing self-protection. Self-insurance may be accomplished through techniques such as establishing a reserve or a contingency fund to provide coverage for the incurred losses. Reserves funds are useful for larger losses, which cannot be written directly off expenses without drastically affecting net income.

Another approach in the planned retention of risks through self-insurance is the option of either establishing or acquiring a separate subsidiary as a captive insurance firm. This can reduce the costs of insurance for the parent firm and may even generate profits from insuring other outside firms. In some cases, risks are also retained when the potential losses are considered either insignificant or when the benefits of taking the risk are expected to outweigh the costs of insurance. In instances in which losses are considered insignificant they are simply absorbed into operating expenses. When risk retention is unplanned, it is usually when the person or organization is unaware or ignorant about the potential risk in a given business venture, or perhaps it is the result of simple inertia.

In the field of political risk management, risk retention may be practiced in situations when a project's benefits and advantages are more compelling factors than country risks. As noted in Chapter five, many major multinationals continue to invest in countries in Latin America and Africa despite the generally perceived high-risk operating environments in those countries. In addition, international oil firms in particular, with their peculiar need for vertical integration to maintain economic efficiency, are frequently inclined to engage in exploration and production activities in locations ranging from Angola to the coastal waters off Vietnam, seemingly oblivious of political risks. Firms with international operations that practice risk retention out of sheer ignorance or inertia may be rare or even inconceivable, particularly in an era of recent heightened awareness of political risks.

Insurance or Pooling of Risks

Insurance is probably the predominant risk-management strategy pursued by firms in different fields of business. Political risk insurance for international firms, however, is only a recent innovation. The insuring of international political risks is a departure from the traditional industry norms of not insuring dynamic risks. However, with the increasing trend toward insuring speculative and dynamic risks, political risk insurance has become a vital part of the multinational's arsenal of defensive risk-management techniques.

The insurance process is based on the principle of combining or pooling a large number of individual risks to increase the predictability of the risk occurrence. The increased certainty of the risk outcome serves to provide a basis for reducing or even eliminating the risks. Theoretically, if sufficiently large numbers of exposure units having common risks are grouped together, the certainty of loss can be more accurately predicted and known, and hence this provides a basis for spreading the cost of loss. This is known as the actuarial method of estimating potential losses. Risk could thus possibly be reduced or even eliminated. In the case of auto insurance, if a sufficiently large number of accident statistics is collected, it will facilitate the identification of the various risk factors such as age, marital status, and other socioeconomic indicators. The cost of insurance or the premiums are then accordingly determined for the different risk groups to arrive at a proportionate share of the cost of protection for the insured group. In this context, *insurance* can be defined as a socioeconomic device that reduces the uncertainty of loss by making it more predictable by pooling the risks of a large group of exposure units and by spreading the economic burden of the losses proportionately among the exposure units. In short, insurance is a risk-reduction device.[8]

With political risk insurance, the same insurance principle theoretically may be applied to a large group of similar investment or lending risks. If a sufficiently large number of expropriation statistics is available, it may be possible to identify the critical risk factors associated with the project or the host country and hence help to determine the appropriate cost of protection for the different risk groups. The same analysis may also be applied to inconvertibility and contract-frustration risks. However, unlike the more predictable pure risks in the traditional areas of domestic insurance, the interaction between the multinational firm and the host country is dynamic and therefore less amenable to traditional risk analysis and probability estimates.

Underwriting political risks cannot be done easily on an actuarial basis, although some insurers have done so without much success. Some, for instance, have tried to use a risk index with all of its attendant conceptual and empirical problems as a basis for arriving at risk estimates. Many industry observers agree that the most appropriate method of ascertaining potential losses associated with political risks involves a detailed case-by-base analysis. The nature of political risks as it relates to international business is still little understood by the insurance industry and by the risk-analysis profession alike. Partially as a result of this venturing into what is essentially uncharted territory for the insurance industry, the availability of political risk insurance lags far behind demand. Industry observers have noted a lack of willingness to provide reinsurance and coinsurance for underwritten political risk insurance coverages.

To consider the role of reinsurance and coinsurance, another perspective on political risk insurance is to view it as a risk-management method that combines the pooling of risks as well as the transfer of risks and risk retention. Sometimes if outside coinsurance is not adequately available, it may be necessary to establish loss reserves, which is a form of risk retention. Reinsurance and coinsurance provide secondary backing for the original underwritten risks. If Lloyd's of London, a major consortium of reinsurers, assumes the reinsurance of a political risk insurance contract, part of the risks are then transferred to it. In this case, it is acting as risk transferee, that is, the risk bearer onto which the risks are partially shifted. Reinsurance is crucial when the probability of the insured risks cannot be adequately estimated, and this is particularly true of the nature of political risks. Since political risks are not a readily predictable kind of static risk in the classic actuarial sense, part of the insured risks would have to be shifted to other risk transferees.

Diversification and the Spreading of Risks

Diversification is a classic portfolio-management strategy. In the management of a financial portfolio, the diversification principle requires the spreading of risk by investing in stocks, bonds, or other financial assets whose price movements are determined to be independent and not correlated with one another. Portfolio diversification is the basic strategy of investment vehicles such as mutual funds that invest in a diverse range of assets. In the case of corporate investment, diversification is the central strategy of an industrial conglomerate. The conglomerate's objective is to spread risk by investing in a broad spectrum of companies and businesses in different industries. Mergers and acquisitions are in fact considered vehicles for diversification in addition to normal objectives of attaining asset and sales growth.

On an international level, diversification may also be used as a strategy of spreading and hence offsetting country risks. Individual country risks could be offset against each other through market as well as product diversification. Thus by investing over a broad array of independent markets, countries, and products and via a mix of different entry modes, a multinational firm could potentially reduce a substantial degree of its international risks.

Loss Prevention and Control

Additional risk-management methods include loss prevention and loss control. *Loss prevention* refers to actions taken to prevent or reduce the probability of the occurrence of a loss event essentially by reducing or eliminating the associated hazards. *Loss control* or *loss protection* refers to efforts taken to reduce or minimize the severity of a loss. Examples of loss control include the installation of fire-fighting devices such as fire extinguishers or an in-building automatic sprinkler system to curtail the severity of a fire. Examples of loss prevention include the adoption of industrial safety rules and standards and the incorporation of safety features into equipment and products. Another well-known example of loss prevention is the guarantee seal of the Underwriters' Laboratories (UL). The Underwriters' Laboratories was created through the joint efforts and cooperation of a group of insurance companies. Its major functions include the examination and testing of products to determine the hazards involved in their use. The UL seal is an important sign of approval testifying to the product's safety. Loss prevention and control strategies are therefore used in close conjunction with insurance coverages. In fact, the adoption of loss prevention and control is encouraged by insurance companies through their provisions for favorable premium discounts and reductions for adopting such measures.

In the case of political risk, the undertaking of loss control and loss prevention may be considered a part of the firm's integrative risk-management strategy. *Integrative risk management* consists of a set of risk-prevention and reduction strategies achieved primarily by pursuing activities that will increase the indispensability of an investment project. In an era of escalating microrisks stemming from host countries' entry-management systems (EMSs) risk prevention through integrative actions emerges as a crucial strategy for managing such risks. The strategy here is to formulate and incorporate features into the investment package that will maintain the project's worth indefinitely and thus help to forestall any probability of adverse actions on the part of the host country against the project or the firm.

Risk Transfer

Another risk-management technique commonly practiced by firms is risk transfer. In *risk transfer* the taking or bearing of risks is shifted to an outside entity or is externalized. Risk transfer can be combined with risk pooling for the purpose of reinsurance, particularly for risks whose probability cannot be estimated adequately. It is also one of the more common ways to handle speculative risks. Examples of risk transfer in the management of speculative risks include subcontracting, leasing, hedging, extended product-warranty agreements, and surety bonds. In the case of subcontracting, because of the subcontractor's specialization in one phase of the business such as in the installation of the electrical system for the building, a more efficient operation can be attained. This greater efficiency and superior knowledge enable the subcontractor to handle the accompanying risk better and more economically.

Hedging is another popular risk-transfer method. In *hedging*, a firm enters into an equal but opposite transaction to offset the possibility of a loss from unfavorable price fluctuations. By entering into a commodities futures market or the foreign exchange forward markets, for instance, a company can shift some of the price-fluctuation risk on to the other transacting party. Likewise, leasing transfers the risk of ownership to the lessor. Extended product-warranty agreements shift the burden of possible costs of repairs back to the manufacturers. In the case of surety bonds, an independent third-party company assumes the responsibility for a contractor in carrying out his contractual obligations. Should the contractor default in some manner and fail to fulfill the requirements of the contract, the bond company is obligated to make financial restitution on behalf of the contractor.

When applied to international political risks, risk transfers may be achieved through "unbundled" forms of entry arrangements such as equity and contractual joint ventures, licensing, franchising, management contracts, and various forms of countertrade. In such unbundled arrangements, not only is part of the risk transferred to the local nationals but also the risk emanating from nationalistic pressures may be diffused. In the case of contractual joint ventures, part of the production risks and asset-exposure risks are shifted to the joint-venture partner. Similarly, in international franchising, the local franchisee assumes most of the ownership, production, and marketing risks. The franchisor is thus able to partake in the expected profits with only minimal assets and fixed-expense exposures. A management contract may be considered a form of reverse subcontracting. Here, the risks of actual ownership of a construction project, for example, rest with the host-country nationals, while the company, in return for a fee, manages the locally owned assets. In a sense, the firm has "subcontracted" out the asset-ownership exposure back to the local nationals.

DEFINING DEFENSIVE AND INTEGRATIVE RISK MANAGEMENT

In terms of the two-way classification of risk management into defensive and integrative, risk avoidance, insurance, and diversification will be considered defensive risk management, and risk retention, loss prevention and control, and risk transfer will be considered integrative risk management. Chapter eight addresses integrative risk management in greater detail.

With the foregoing discussion of the concepts of risk and risk management we are now in a position to attempt a more exact definition of defensive and integrative risk management. *Defensive risk management,* in the field of political risk, refers to a general set of risk-reduction strategies that will protect against financial loss stemming from adverse and negative government actions in a host country. Defensive risk management for international firms is primarily accomplished by purchasing political risk insurance coverage. It can also be accomplished by pursuing a risk avoidance or a diversification strategy. In short, defensive risk management is any risk-reduction strategy that is undertaken independently of the actual activities of the company with respect to the host country in question. Industry observers have noted that political risk insurance by itself is not a sufficient or satisfactory risk-management strategy. A well-balanced and optimum risk-management strategy requires a combination of both defensive as well as integrative risk-management techniques.

Integrative risk management refers to risk-reduction strategies that are directly linked to the activities of the company in the host country. Integrative risk management can be seen as a general set of actions that are anticipated to bring about an increase in or at least the maintenance of the value or worth of a project from the standpoint of the most-country decision makers. In other words, it includes all actions and measures taken by the firm to raise the perceived "indispensability" of the project or the company's activities in the host country. Such measures could include a continuous injection of current technology into the project or a net-surplus contribution to the country's balance of payments. In comparison, defensive risk-management strategy, because it is undertaken independent of host-country interactions, usually does not have a direct impact on the indispensability of the firm's project or operations. However, it does reduce the vulnerability of the company to financial loss arising from hostile government actions by providing an alternative and parallel mechanism of protection. Defensive risk management, particularly through the purchase of political risk insurance, is a necessary but not a sufficient strategy for managing international risks. The same applies to integrative risk management. Defensive risk management should ideally be used in combination with integrative risk-management techniques since an insurance program provides a kind of "cushion" or fallback position for a company independent of its direct activities in the foreign markets.[9]

CHANGING INSURABILITY OF RISKS

The traditional distinction between pure and speculative risks for the purpose of insurability is now rapidly breaking down. With the recent developments in insurability, coverages are now increasingly being extended to what were heretofore considered speculative risks. Insurance coverage is presently being made available for municipal bonds, mutual fund shares, accounts at depository institutions, and commercial credit. As a result of this blurring of the distinction between pure and speculative risks, these concepts of risks may need to be redefined. One observer proposed that pure risks are really a subset of the more generic speculative risks. Pure risk may be thought of as the loss-producing side of a speculative endeavor that could potentially produce both gains as well as losses. Moreover, pure risks are incidental to the major activities of a business entity that normally exists to undertake speculative activities that have potential for gains as well as losses.

Pure risks are therefore an integral part of the costs of speculative (business) pursuits that tend to have both profit and cost dimensions. Such a proposed revision of the traditional risk concepts may possibly provide some conceptual justification for extending coverages to more speculative ventures. It could also enable the field of risk analysis and risk management to be integrated into the mainstream of the financial management function. Moreover, it could also help to resolve the problem of classifying political risks as either pure or speculative risks. Political risks are essentially dynamic, particularly when viewed in the context of multinational and host-country interactions. Yet these interactions could lead to a pure-risk type of outcome with definite losses for risks such as expropriation and nationalization. Under the revised framework, political risks may then be seen as the negative side or cost dimension of a speculative international venture.[10]

POLITICAL RISK INSURANCE AGENCIES AND SERVICES

The following sections discuss some selected examples of a few better known political risk insurance agencies and firms in both public and private sectors. The major features of their programs and policy coverages are examined in the context of the implications for corporate-risk assessment and management.

QUASI-PUBLIC POLITICAL RISK INSURANCE

Overseas Private Investment Corporation (OPIC) and Export-Import (EX-IM) Bank Insurance

The aims and objectives of the quasi-public insurance agencies that provide international political and commercial risk insurance are basically tied to the foreign policy objectives of the U.S. government. The economic aspects of these objectives generally consist of the promotion of free-enterprise systems, the free flow of international trade and investment, and the industrial development of friendly developing countries. Toward this end, a series of official government and autonomous semiofficial agencies such as the Agency for International Development (AID), the Export-Import Bank, and the Federal Credit Insurance Agency were established.

With the expansion of the political risk insurance market, particularly on the demand side, the role of the OPIC also acquired increased significance. The OPIC, formerly a key federal agency within the AID, specializes in providing political risk insurance and financing assistance for U.S. investors in developing countries. The OPIC was separated from the AID and established as a distinct and autonomous corporate entity in 1971. This was part of the stepped up efforts by the U.S. government in a move to encourage investment in friendly Third World countries by providing political risks insurance for U.S. investors. The OPIC's mandate is to "mobilize and facilitate the participation of United States private capital and skills in the economic and social development of less developed, friendly countries and areas."[11] Therefore, unlike private insurers, which are mainly profit oriented, the OPIC served and continues to serve as an instrument of U.S. policy to promote investment and free enterprise in the developing economies. Its basic objective is to offer relatively low-cost and long-term protection for new U.S. investments that are intended to further economic development in friendly less developed countries (LDCs).

Although beginning life as a bureaucratic entity, the OPIC's structure, programs, and mode of operations have developed along with the growth of political risk insurance. In recent years, as the political insurance market has grown and gained increased sophistication, the OPIC also has altered its orientation. It began to streamline its operations and procedures to make them more responsive to the needs of private business. The OPIC also attempted to bring itself more in line with private-industry conventions, particularly in terms of adhering to the principles of risk management. The agency's associations with private insurance carriers stem primarily from the coinsurance and reinsurance arrangements entered into by the OPIC with both London and U.S. private insurers. To reinforce its relationship with the private insurers, it has instituted a commission program for insurance brokers, making referrals and acting as intermediaries for arranging the OPIC insurance. In addition to providing political risk insurance, the OPIC is also increasingly adjusting and expanding its services to cater to the diverse needs of its clientele by making available a wide range of investment-related services. These services include providing case consultation on a whole range of issues concerned with a proposed investment project; they also include conducting project-feasibility and market studies.

The terms and provisions of the OPIC insurance reflect its overall policy orientation. Its programs include a broad array of coverages. They include coverages for equity and loan arrangements, production sharing, counter-purchase agreements, licensing, technical assistance, branch operations, and other modes of entry arrangements. As part of its investment-promotion service, the OPIC also offers loan guarantees and direct loans to small business. In its political risk insurance service, it insures U.S. investments against five major types of risks: currency inconvertibility, confiscation, expropriation, nationalization and "creeping" expropriation, and property damages sustained as a result of war, revolution, insurrection, or civil strife.

Inconvertibility coverage insures against a company's inability to convert its local currency earnings and funds into U.S. dollars or other hard currencies due to blockage of funds and the imposition of adverse or discriminatory exchange rates. However, the inconvertibility coverage does not protect against currency devaluation and fluctuations. The reason for not covering exchange-rate fluctuations is that they are speculative and thus may result in gains as well as losses. Furthermore, hedging in the forward markets is available to protect against exchange risks. The OPIC's expropriation coverage protects the investor against confiscation or nationalization of assets without fair compensation by the host government. Under the OPIC's definition, "an action taken, authorized, ratified or condoned by the project country government is considered expropriatory if it has a specified impact on either the properties or operations of the foreign enterprises, or on the rights or financial interests of the insured investors."[12] The agency's insurance also protects against *creeping expropriation*, which is defined as a series of adverse actions taken by the host country that has a cumulative effect of depriving the investors of their basic rights in the investment. Creeping expropriation includes measures such as ownership fade-out and mandatory licensing requirements.

The third major political risk coverage offered by the OPIC is for damages suffered as a result of war, revolution, insurrection, and civil strife. This coverage protects against property losses and/or loss of income due to the occurrence of these events. It is of interest to note that the OPIC's definition of civil strife includes acts of terrorism and sabotage but excludes nonpolitically motivated student and labor strikes. Risks arising from student and labor disturbances are separately covered through an extension clause or rider to the basic coverage.

The OPIC's other services include special programs such as providing financing assistance to U.S. investors for overseas projects. Financial assistance programs consist of direct loans for small business and loan guarantees for all other investors regardless of size.[13] Direct loans ranging from $100,000 to $4 million are available for projects sponsored by U.S. small businesses and cooperatives. Under the loan-guarantee program, the OPIC will issue a guarantee for funding obtained from U.S. banks and financial institutions. The loan guarantee covers both commercial and political risks. The OPIC also offers other special programs for contractors, exporters, and lenders.[14] These programs include financial assistance and insurance services for contractors and exporters facing arbitrary government actions in foreign countries and particularly for U.S. firms engaged in energy investments abroad. Most countries require foreign contractors to post bid bonds or performance or advance-payment guarantees in the form of standby letters of credit. In the event of an unfair drawing of such letters of credit, U.S. contractors with the OPIC insurance are protected against such risks. Other areas of OPIC's services range from management consulting, preinvestment counseling, the funding and conducting of feasibility studies for projects proposals, the assessment of foreign investment climates, and the providing of information on specific investment opportunities abroad to a whole array of other informational assistance.

The term of the OPIC insurance for political risk coverages ranges from twelve to twenty years, whereas the OPIC direct loans and loan guarantees extend from five to twenty years. Typical amounts of protection or coverage capacity run from $100 million to $150 million per project and $300 million to $350 million per country. The coverage offers protection only up to a maximum of 90 percent of the total value of the investment, and the investor must assume a coinsurance amount of at least 10 percent of any insured investment. Foreign investments that qualify for insurance can take any form. Coverage is available not only for conventional equity investments and loans but also for investments or exposures of funds and goods and services provided under various forms of contractual arrangements. Coverages for expropriation, inconvertibility and war, revolution, and civil strife are available for licensing, technical assistance agreements, construction and service contracts, international leasing, production-sharing agreements, and special forms of joint ventures provided for under the investment laws of Yugoslavia and China.

Premiums for the OPIC insurance are based on the nature of the investment venture and the project's risk profile but not on the host country in question. Premiums range approximately from a base rate of 30 cents per $100 coverage for inconvertibility to 60 cents per $100 coverage for expropriation. Premiums rates for coverages extended to exporters and contractors required to comply with foreign requirements such as advance payments for bid bonds and performance guarantees are approximately 30 to 40 cents. The insureds are then protected against any unfair calling or arbitrary forfeiture of the deposits by the host government. One of the possible shortcomings of the OPIC insurance is its premium schedule. Since the premiums are not based on the host country, they may not be reflective of differential risk levels in the different countries. In other words, the OPIC's insurance premiums are not cost-effective in terms of the expected or probabilistic value of the protection. This means that a company may have to pay the same amount of premiums for two countries with an unequal probability of risk and will be effectively overpaying for the country with the lower of the two levels of risks.

The OPIC's coverage includes other special features that could be deemed restrictive. One of them is the need for the host government's approval of the investment before it can qualify for the OPIC insurance. One of the reasons for this requirement is perhaps to place the investment project in the context of a government-to-government relationship. It is thus a means of loss deterrence. The involvement of the host government and its blessings for the project mean that a potential loss outcome can be averted even before a claim situation can develop. Moreover, even if an expropriation occurs, a favorable resolution of the dispute with the host government through negotiation may be possible before the taking of any legal actions. The fact that a host government has given its approval for the project may imply a breach of agreement or even a breach of good faith should the project be expropriated. In the event that legal actions or international arbitration becomes necessary, the insured company is required to subrogate all and surrender all of its right to the OPIC when making a claim. This means that the agency would acquire any remaining residual rights the company may have in the project country.

The OPIC insurance stipulates strict eligibility requirements. To qualify, the proposed insurance must be for a new project or venture, and the proposed project must be located in a friendly developing country with a per capita GNP not exceeding $2,950 per annum. The availability of insurance for investments in countries exceeding $2,950 is restricted to projects sponsored by U.S. small business or cooperatives and for minerals, energy, and construction projects. The current list of eligible countries in which the OPIC insurance is available covers approximately one hundred countries.[15] This list includes most of the developing world but excludes the socialist-bloc countries with the exception of China. In addition, the OPIC requires that the project or venture to be insured must be consistent with the economic interests of the United States and must not adversely affect the U.S. economy or U.S. employment. The OPIC insurance is restricted to U.S. citizens, corporations, partnerships and other businesses of at least 50 percent ownership, and foreign corporations and other businesses owned at least 95 percent by U.S. investors. The same nationality restrictions apply to direct loan and loan guarantees.

The Export-Import Bank is another quasi-public agency specializing in a broad range of insurance programs for U.S. companies operating abroad. When the OPIC was restructured by legislative changes in 1978 and some of its programs reformulated, the U.S.-backed EX-IM Bank took over some of the OPIC's former programs, especially those for the higher income countries excluded from the OPIC's coverage. The EX-IM Bank's guarantee program for U.S. contractors offers protection in basically the same category of risks, that is, coverages for inconvertibility of local currency; confiscation of tangible property and bank accounts in the projected country; property damages stemming from war, revolution, or insurrection; and contract disputes resulting in repudiation of payment. The EX-IM Bank's geographical coverage extends to countries that are not under the OPIC's jurisdiction, that is, mainly the more affluent developing countries. Premiums range from 0.3 to 0.8 percent of the insured amount for the different risk categories.

Governments in the OECD countries of the European Community, Japan, and Canada also provide a broad range of government-sponsored insurance programs for both commercial and political risks in their efforts to promote the international operations of their multinationals. Selected examples of a few comparable public as well as private insurance agencies in these countries include the Export Credits Guarantee Department (ECGD) of the United Kingdom, the Compagnie Francaise d'Assurance of France (COFACE), Hermes-Kreditversicherungs (A. G. Hermes) of West Germany, and the Export Insurance Division of the Ministry of International Trade and Industry of Japan (EID/MITI). Most of these programs are not strictly oriented toward political risk insurance for investors per se but are essentially aimed at promoting exports, construction, and turnkey projects. The programs are mainly directed at the reduction of commercial risk exposures for exporters and contractors and include mainly export financing and credit insurance coverages. An interesting departure from the practice of U.S. insurers is the coverage provided by some of these agencies for risks arising from exchange fluctuations and inflation. The program covers losses from adverse shifts in exchange rates that are not covered by commercially available forward-exchange contracts. Under the inflation coverage, COFACE and ECGD offer protection against cost increases exceeding a specified annual rate. Inflation insurance is especially useful in doing business in high-inflation countries. Both foreign as well as local companies are generally eligible for these government-sponsored programs.[16]

PRIVATE OR COMMERCIAL POLITICAL RISK INSURERS

The recent expansion and growth of the political risk insurance market was in no small measure due to the entry of several private insurers into the business. Although the OPIC and other public-sector agencies have been involved in providing political and credit-risk insurance for U.S.-based multinationals since the early seventies and even much earlier, the industry itself did not really take off until the catastrophic events in the middle and late seventies. Critical events such as the 1973 oil crisis, the Middle East conflict, and the Iranian Revolution began to hit home on corporate America, and this brought about a heightened awareness of the need for political risk insurance.

The resultant increase in the demand for political risk coverages at the initial stages of the business could not readily be met by the public-sector capacity alone especially since the OPIC has to, at the same time, deal with an enormous increase in claims. The entry of the private insurers for a while helped to expand the capacity of the industry and therefore make political risk insurance increasingly available. Thus with the combined participation and close collaboration between both the private- and public-sector agencies, the entire political risk insurance industry has been given a substantial boost, particularly with the sudden and rapid rise in demand for coverages as well as the expanded supply. The willingness of the private-sector insurers to extend reinsurance for political risk coverages also played a major role in expanding the capacity of the entire industry at the early stages of growth. The OPIC, for instance, works very closely with the private carriers in establishing coinsurance and reinsurance arrangements. The OPIC also attempts to involve the private insurers in its program through providing commissions payment for insurance brokers arranging the OPIC insurance with smaller to medium-size companies. Presently, however, with corporate demand continuing unabated, even the entry of major insurers has not made it possible to maintain and expand the supply of political risk insurance to keep pace with the strong demand.[17]

Some of the major private insurers that have entered the field of political risk insurance directly as insurers or indirectly as coinsurers include Lloyd's of London, the American International Group (AIG), Chubb, and AFIA. The private insurance carriers extend coverage for most types of political risks such as inconvertibility, confiscation, expropriation, and nationalization. However, they provide only limited coverage for hostilities such as land-based war, revolution, and civil strife. Many of them also offer coverages that are nonpolitical, that is, risks arising from bureaucratic constraints and inactions.

In general, the coverage capacity of the commercial carriers is comparatively smaller than that of the OPIC. Coverage capacity, on the average, ranges approximately from $60 million per project for expropriation to a smaller dollar amount for inconvertibility risks. Length of coverage is relatively short term, about three years. The cost of premiums varies with factors such as nature of the project, location, and other commercial considerations. Unlike the OPIC, which has a policy role to advance economic development in Third World countries and hence restricts coverage to within this group, the private insurers provide protection worldwide for both new and existing investments.

Definitions of Political Risks Normally Covered

Most of the private or commercial insurers providing political risk insurance offer coverage for a broad range of risks. Most of the risks for which coverage is available, however, constitute only a small portion of the diverse range of international risks facing international business.[18] The following are a few selected examples of the risks normally covered by political risk insurance.

Expropriatory action. This refers to a general set of actions such as confiscation, expropriation, nationalization, deprivation, or requisition taken or authorized by the government of the project country (host country) that substantially and effectively deny, prevent, or preclude the foreign enterprise from exercising control or its rights over the use or disposition of a substantial portion of its property, assets, and financial interest or from conducting any significant business activities resulting from the investment. Expropriatory actions also include the denial and deprivation of other fundamental rights such as the disposition of financial securities, rights of disposing of mobile assets, and the repatriation of money generated from the project, which consists of earnings and a return to capital of the foreign enterprise. The definition for expropriatory action is virtually the same for both the private insurers as well as the OPIC.

Other insurers define expropriatory action as a loss of investment caused by an action of a foreign government or the confiscation by a government of all or part of the insured company's interest in a foreign enterprise, which directly deprives, prevents, and restricts the insured from operating with its investment. The insured's interest covered could include land, factory buildings, equipment, and bank accounts.

Civil war and insurrection. These terms refer to a general set of events that include any mass-based, sustained, nonintermittent, and cohesively organized series of actions of insurrection, rebellion, revolution, or civil war in the project country or acts of sabotage or terrorism that derive directly and explicitly as part of the civil war or insurrection in the project country. The definition also includes state-sponsored and government-directed terrorism.

Currency inconvertibility. Two major types of inconvertibility can be distinguished:

1. The actual imposition of a law, decree, or regulation by the host government that prevents the conversion of local currency earnings to the investors' home currency for a stipulated period beyond the normal transfer period. This type of inconvertibility stems from a deliberate unwillingness on

the part of the host government or exchange authorities to convert local currency received as dividends, profits, earnings, and payments for goods sold or services performed into the insured company's home currency or any other hard currency. This process is known as an active blockage of funds, and it also includes the restrictions on the payment of interest and principal on foreign loans and other quantitative limits placed on the amount of repatriation. Active blockage could be imposed for economic, political, or other reasons. Economically motivated blockage may result from fiscal or monetary problems in the host country such as balance-of-payment difficulties or some form of economic disruption. Politically motivated blockage includes a ban on outflows or capital flights arising from political instability in the host country.

2. The second type of inconvertibility refers to the failure on the part of the host government or exchange authority to process an application for conversion properly as permitted under the current laws of the host country for a stipulated period beyond the normal transfer period. This is known as passive blockage, and it implies that although repatriation is allowed by the host-country laws, there is a temporary or prolonged inability to carry out the conversion or exchange process. This general inability by the host government to exchange the local currency earnings and execute the repatriation of funds may result from a variety of reasons. The exchange authorities of the host country may be faced with a temporary shortage or scarcity of hard-currency foreign exchange reserves in the project country. Sometimes the passive blockage may hide more deep-seated economic or political problems. On the other hand, the failure may result simply from bureaucratic inefficiency and delay. Such passive blockage of funds is usually temporary and is not considered as severe as deliberate, active blockage imposed by laws or decrees.

Contract frustration. This refers to a breach or repudiation of a contract between an insured company and a public-sector or government buyer. It also refers to contractual nonperformance by third parties because of interference by either the host or home government. Contract frustration specifically includes the cancellation or nonrenewal of the insured company's export license by the home government or the buyer's import license by the host government, an export embargo, and other arbitrarily imposed import restrictions that prohibit the entry of specific import items.

Wrongful or improper calling of guarantee. This refers to an arbitrary drawing of various forms of financial guarantees such as standby letters of credit or on-demand bonds deposited with the host government. Such guarantees are required of contractors by many host countries and include bid bonds, performance bonds, and advance-payment guarantees. One of the many risks faced by international contractors is the arbitrary drawing of such guarantees that are not justified by the contract or by other legal procedures.

The following sections examine and compare some of the more specific features of the political risk insurance programs of a few selected private insurers that are active in the field. The various insurers offering political risk insurance emphasize different areas of risk. Some, for instance, do not offer coverage for war and insurrection risks, and others concentrate more on commercial risk coverages.

AFIA Insurance

The AFIA's political risk division was established in 1981 to provide for coverage for international business risks in the changed international risk environment, especially in the aftermath of the 1973 oil embargo and the Middle East crisis.[19] The AFIA's entry into the field of political risk insurance was in a major way prompted by the sharp rise in demand for risk coverages that cannot be adequately met by public-sector insurance. Some of major risk coverages offered by the AFIA include contract frustration resulting from capricious government actions, delays in granting export or import licenses, expropriation, and currency inconvertibility. The company does not offer war and insurrection insurance. The AFIA's first real involvement with political risk insurance began with the sharp rise in demand for insurance coverage for on-demand letters of credit in the Middle East, especially after the drastic oil-price hikes in 1973. The drastic increase in energy costs and the resultant balance-of-payment difficulties led to emerging political instability and a large rise in demand for political risk insurance. The lack of ability of public-sector insurance agencies like the Export-Import Bank, the Federal Credit Insurance Agency (FCIA), and the OPIC to cope with the increasing demand for coverage led to the AFIA's and other private insurers' involvement in the field.

The AFIA's underwriting of political risk insurance is essentially based on the usual principles of underwriting such as the spreading of risks and exposure, establishing of loss reserves, and obtaining of reinsurance. However, political risk insurance cannot be based on a strict actuarial method because political risks in terms of host country-company interactions cannot easily lend themselves to any system of numerical or probabilistic estimates. As such, the underwriting of political risk coverage has to be based on more in-depth and detailed analysis specific to a given project or type of international business transactions. The AFIA uses a team approach in its case-by-case analysis to arrive at potential loss estimates. Its evaluation process incorporates both qualitative as well as quantitative information. Overall, like any project-specific risk analysis, a major part of the process is based on informed although subjective evaluation.

The company's continued involvement and future expansion in political risk insurance is closely tied to the overall industry capacity in taking on additional reinsurance and coinsurance coverages. Like other political risk insurers, the AFIA has developed close links to the Lloyd's syndicates and other U.S. insurers. The AFIA's present needs appear to have been adequately met by available reinsurance at its current level of insurance activity. However, further expansion would be limited by the backup support of the reinsurers.

Chubb Insurance

Another private insurer that has made a significant entry into the field of political risk insurance is the Chubb Group of Insurance Companies. The major feature of Chubb's program is its offer of a comprehensive package of coverages for a broad range of perils including political risks as well as limited coverage for actual physical property damage caused by civil war and insurrection.[20] Some of the major features of its political risk insurance include a maximum coverage of $10.5 million per project per country for most perils and a $5.0 million maximum coverage for civil war and insurrection damage. A *project*, as defined by Chubb, is the total activities and assets of the company in the country regardless of the number of businesses or factories.

Other major provisions of Chubb's coverage include a coinsurance requirement, warranty and confidentiality requirements, and policy exclusions. The coinsurance requirement on expropriatory action is the standard 10 percent. This implies that the insurance will pay up to 90 percent of the loss while the insured retains 10 percent. In the warranty and confidentiality agreement, Chubb requires that the insured company take all reasonable actions to comply with the laws and regulations of the host country and not to undertake actions that will unduly expose itself to expropriatory actions. The insured is also required to keep the existence of the policy confidential except when making loan applications. This is intended to avoid any unnecessary attention on the insured project, especially if such protection could itself provoke adverse and negative perceptions on the part of the host country.

Under Chubb's policy-exclusion clause, which is intended to complement the warranty requirements, various kinds of losses are excluded from the coverage. They include losses due to criminal or illegal acts by the insured; noncompliance with and falsification of contracts and agreements undertaken in the project country; property damage or destruction due to nuclear, chemical, or biological warfare; business losses or loss of profitability or market share arising from normal competitive conditions; and bankruptcy. Another important exclusion is losses resulting from any war or military hostilities among the big five powers, that is, the Soviet Union, the United States, China, Great Britain, and France, or hostilities between the project country and the insured's country.

Political risks covered by Chubb include the following:

Expropriatory actions. This refers to the broadest forms of deprivation and denial of the rights and use or removal of assets. Such denial of rights may result from the actions of the government of the project country as well as third-country military blockades including that of the insured's own government. This means that U.S.-based multinationals will be compensated for any loss resulting from a U.S.-imposed blockade on the project country. Under an expropriatory-action coverage, if a fixed investment is confiscated or expropriated by the host government, compensation for the loss is based on the adjusted book value of the fixed assets at the date of the expropriation. Chubb's political risk policy also covers partial loss, such as a forced partial divestment or confiscation. Only the partially lost portion needs to be subrogated to the insurer. In addition, its coverage also provides for relocation expenses resulting from a project's expropriation as well as protection of key personnel. The key-personnel coverage protects senior corporate employees and other specified employees through an extension clause. Coverage includes removal expenses of the insured personnel from the project country, additional tax obligations, interruption of business travel, and loss of and damage to the personal possessions of the insured key personnel.

Currency inconvertibility. This coverage provides for not only inconvertibility of local currency earnings but also for inconvertibility of local currency compensation paid by the host government for expropriation. In the event of an expropriation that is compensated for by the government, the insurance will pay an equivalent amount in U.S. dollars for any local currency compensation that is difficult to convert into either the U.S. dollar or any other hard currency. However, the inconvertibility coverage does not include currency fluctuations, devaluations, exchange controls, or tax restrictions.

Civil war and insurrection. This coverage insures against physical property damage directly due to civil war and internal insurrection. In addition, Chubb broadens the coverage to include property damage and losses resulting from civil commotion such as riots, demonstrations, and strikes that are not politically motivated. This is a departure from the policy of other insurers, which does not normally provide coverage for property damages stemming from civil commotion. Compensation for losses arising from physical property damage is based on *loss value*, which is defined as the "lesser of the replacement or repair cost or actual cash value of the damaged assets in the insured's country on the date immediately before the date of loss." This means that if a U.S.-based company suffered a property damage, the value for computing the loss would be the item's equivalent cash value in the United States. Acts of sabotage or terrorism are covered only if they are part of civil war or insurrection.

American International Group (AIG) Insurance

The AIG is one of the first companies to venture into the field of political risk insurance. It initially began offering coverage in 1974 for expropriation and currency-inconvertibility risks. Its political risk insurance unit is formally known as AIG Political Risk, Inc., or AIG PRI. The company offers several programs, including coverages for overseas investors, contractors involved in private and public projects overseas, suppliers selling internationally, and financial institutions with foreign loans.[21]

Political risks covered by AIG include the following:

Expropriation, confiscation, and nationalization coverages. This coverage offers protection to overseas investors and lenders for expropriatory acts initiated by the host government that prevent the insured from exercising its rights with respect to the investment or assets for a continuous period of one year. The insured company's risk exposure is considered from a "financial interest" basis or an "asset" basis. The former covers all of the financial interest the insured has in the locally incorporated subsidiary and therefore insures not only the equity in the venture but also loans made by the insured company to the local subsidiary as well as any tangible assets such as plant, equipment, and land. In the case of exposure on an asset basis, companies with exposures in cash, inventories, or other movable assets are covered only for the value of these assets. The AIG will pay compensation only for that part of the expropriated assets not adequately compensated for by the host government.

Contract repudiation, license cancellation, and capricious calling of guarantees. The contract-repudiation coverage provides protection for losses sustained by contractors or international sellers conducting business with public or private foreign entities as a result of contract frustration or the cancellation of export or import licenses. The contract repudiation coverage also includes protection for lenders against default or nonpayment of interest and principal by a sovereign borrower. In the area of trade finance, the AIG also extends coverage for improper and arbitrary calling of letters of credit or on-demand bonds for bid, advance payment, or performance guarantee opened in favor of a sovereign entity.

Currency inconvertibility. This coverage offers protection for investors, exporters, and lenders who are prevented by the host government or exchange authority from converting local currency earnings, dividends, interests, or fees into the insured's currency. The AIG extends coverage for losses arising from two types of fund blockage. First, it provides protection against active blockage in which by imposition of law, decree, or regulation the insured is prevented from converting local currency into home currency for a period of sixty days beyond the normal transfer period. Second, the AIG offers protection against passive blockage or the failure on the part of the host government or exchange authority to act on a proper application for converting local currency for a period of at least ninety days beyond the normal transfer period. The insured is paid an equivalent amount of home currency for the blocked funds at the rate of exchange prevailing on the day the inconvertibility began. Currency devaluations and exchange-rate fluctuations are not covered.

Export-credit coverage. A broad line of political and commercial risk coverage is offered through this program. It includes protection against nonpayment by a foreign buyer beyond the normal payment period. Optional coverages under the AIG's export-credit program also include protection against losses arising from cancellation of import and export licenses, war, revolution and insurrection, expropriation of the buyer, embargoes, insolvency, and contract repudiation by a public buyer.

The AIG does not insure against war and insurrection risks for investors. Like most other private insurers offering political risk insurance, the AIG imposes no eligibility requirements in terms of the nationality of the insured or limiting coverage to only certain geographical areas. Host-government approval is not required for the AIG insurance.

Premium rates for the expropriation coverage range from 0.10 percent to 5.0 percent per annum of the insured value and are determined on the basis of the country location, the nature of the investment and project insured, and the AIG's estimates of the risks. Premiums for export-credit insurance are based on limits of liability, average outstanding receivables, or turnover and are subject to a minimum premium of $50,000. The term of the AIG's expropriation policy can extend for an average of up to three years and longer for new investments. Inconvertibility coverage has a minimum term of one year, and export-credit policies can be written for terms up to five years. The AIG insurance requires a waiting period of one year for an expropriation claim to become effective; the waiting period for inconvertibility various with the situation. The waiting period is intended to encourage the insured to pursue negotiations or other remedial actions with the host government to resolve the dispute in question. The coinsurance for all coverage is the standard 10 percent of the value of the loss.

Under the AIG's exclusions, losses resulting from several specified conditions are excluded from the coverage. They include losses resulting from nonperformance by the insured; fraudulent, criminal, or dishonest actions by the insured; noncompliance with local laws; financial insolvency; and currency fluctuations or devaluations. In the case of export-credit insurance, exclusions apply to losses arising from nonperformance by the insured and wrongful and illegal acts of the insured or its agents. War or other hostilities are not covered by the AIG political insurance.

COMPARISON OF THE OPIC AND PRIVATE INSURERS

It is evident from the foregoing discussions that there are major differences between the provisions of the OPIC political risk coverage and that of the private insurers, particularly in terms of eligibility requirements. A comparison of the differences in the OPIC and private-sector political risk insurance would help to identify and draw out some strategic implications for corporate-risk-management strategies. The OPIC, as a semiofficial agency, offers political risk coverages that are closely tied to the foreign policy goals of the United States. Although technically incorporated as a private corporation, the agency is relatively less profit oriented than the private insurers. This basic difference in operating philosophy perhaps accounts for some of the major differences in the programs offered.[22]

The OPIC insurance is more restrictive in its eligibility requirements in terms of the nationality of the insured and in its geographical availability. For instance, eligibility is restricted to investors who are U.S. citizens or companies substantially owned by U.S. citizens. In addition, because it is mainly an instrument of U.S. policy, countries in which the OPIC insurance is available are limited to "less developed friendly countries." This stipulation limits the availability of its programs to approximately one hundred developing countries with a per capita GNP of less than $2,950 (1979 dollars), although exemptions from the per capita GNP restriction of $2,950 are allowed for U.S. small business and for certain approved projects. Another OPIC requirement is the prior host-government approval of the proposed investment project. This is aimed at obtaining the host government's cooperation and acquiescence for the venture perhaps in order to preempt any likelihood of future expropriation. Thus the OPIC is able to offer this loss-deterrence feature because of its vantage position in dealing with host governments. Private insurers impose no nationality restrictions or any restrictions in geographical availability for their political risk insurance. In addition, confidentiality is an important requirement of the private insurers, and this allows the insured to avoid disclosing the coverage to the host government.

Perhaps because of its public-policy considerations, the OPIC's premiums are largely uniform for all of the listed countries it covers, and therefore it makes no distinction between countries as far as country risks are concerned. However, it does set premiums to vary with the nature of the projects. Since micro or project risks are generally not reflective of macro-country risks, the OPIC's premiums thus do not take the differential levels of country risk into consideration. Judged strictly on the basis of a cost-benefit criterion, a uniform premium rate that is not reflective of different risk levels is not cost-effective. This means that a company with identical projects in two countries would be paying the same amount of premium for what essentially are different probabilistic or expected values of protection. In comparison, private insurers set their premiums to reflect not only project risks but also country risks. Premiums charged by private insurers vary according to the country location, the nature of the project, and an estimate of the risks.

Private-sector insurance is generally more flexible, particularly for shorter term projects in most parts of the world. The cost of private commercial coverage tends to be relatively more costly. The OPIC and public-sector insurance, on the other hand, is superior in offering low-cost protection for long-term projects in developing countries. The typical OPIC coverage capacity of about $100 million or more per project exceeds that of the commercial carriers, which typically cover up to $60 million per project. In addition, one of the major features of the OPIC is the availability of relatively unrestricted war, revolution, and insurrection coverages, whereas for the private insurers only limited coverage is available.

Private insurers may be in a position to offer more flexible coverage since they are not required to act under the constraints of policy considerations. Since they operate under primarily commercial considerations, private-sector political risk insurance appears to be able to provide quicker and more flexible response to the needs of the clients. Overall, from the stand-point of corporate-risk-management strategy, the choice of an appropriate and optimum insurance program is a function of the nature of the project and the target host country. An optimum strategy may suggest a well-balanced combination of both public- and private-sector insurance. For a multinational with an array of proposed projects in different host countries, an optimum strategy would suggest the choice of OPIC insurance for a longer term labor-intensive project in high-risk developing countries together with private insurance for more technological intensive projects in higher income and more developed countries.

NOTES

1. C. Arthur Williams, Jr., and Richard M. Heins, Risk Management and Insurance (New York: McGraw-Hill, 1981), pp. 4-20.

2. Mark R. Greene and James S. Trieschmann, Risk and Insurance (Dallas: South-Western Publishing Co., 1981), pp. 3-14.

3. Williams and Heins, Risk Management and Insurance, p. 6.

4. Greene and Trieschmann, Risk and Insurance, pp. 8-10.

5. Ibid., pp. 10-11.

6. Williams and Heins, Risk Management and Insurance, p. 10-11.

7. Greene and Trieschmann, Risk and Insurance, pp. 11-13.

8. Ibid., pp. 20-29.

9. David M. Katz, "Two Ways to Handle Political Hazards," National Under-writers, November 18, 1983, p. 11.

10. Fikry S. Gahin, "Reworking Classic Risk Models to Fit Real World Decision Making," Risk Management, June 1984, pp. 62-70.

11. Investment Insurance Handbook (Washington, D.C.: Overseas Private Invest-ment Corporation, 1984), p. 3.

12. Ibid., p. 12.

13. Investment Finance Handbook (Washington, D.C.: Overseas Private Invest-ment Corporation, 1984).

14. Contractors and Exporters (Washington, D.C.: Overseas Private Investment Corporation, 1984).

15. Country and Area List (Washington, D.C.: Overseas Private Investment Corporation, 1984).

16. Cecil Hunt, "Insuring for Political Risk," in Richard Ensor, ed., Assessing Country Risk (London: Euromoney Publications, 1981), pp. 137-142.

17. John W. Milligan, "Political Risk Coverage Markets, Demand Grows," Business Insurance, October 12, 1981, p. 28.

18. H. Felix Kloman, "Risk Management: 1990 and Beyond," Risk Management, March 1984, pp. 32-39.

19. "Political Risk: Team Approach Leads to Success," Annual Report, AFIA, 1984, pp. 10-15.

20. Chubb Group of Insurance Companies, Declarations: Political Risk (Warren, N.J., 1984).

21. The American International Group, Political Risk Insurance for Overseas Investments (New York, 1984).

22. Felton McL Johnston, "Political Risk Market Expansion Broadens OPIC's Role," Risk Management, February 1984, pp. 18-24.

8

Prospects for Risk
Assessment and Management:
An Integrative Approach

EMERGING INTERNATIONAL RISK ENVIRONMENT

The preceding chapters have presented the thrust of risk assessment and management in the newly transformed international business environment. Although traditional macropolitical risks remain relevant and crucial to international risk assessment and management, the risk environment is moving substantially in the direction of policy or regulatory risks, which tends to impact on companies on a project-specific level. The implications of this development for corporate-risk assessment and management would involve some degree of rethinking on the extant political risk concepts, realignment of the perceptions of the practitioners in the risk-assessment profession, and the introduction of new and innovative methodologies and techniques in risk analysis and assessment.

In many of the newly industrializing countries (NICs) into which the predominant amount of international investment and business activity is now channeled, the traditional mode of political risk thinking can no longer serve as adequate and valid underpinnings of risk assessment. Instead, in an era of prevailing host-country dynamics, old notions of expropriation, confiscation, nationalization, and ideological conflict are alien to the central concepts of technological development and industrialization.[1]

Many of the host countries are driven by economics and technology rather than by political ideology and hence have reoriented their objectives to managing the entry-management-system (EMS) interaction with the foreign investors. The entire spectrum of EMS conditions such as technology requirements, export-ratio requirements, and ownership restrictions are now brought to bear on the host country's attempt to control its interactions and relationships with foreign investors. To deal effectively with these emerging developments, political risk concepts, perceptions, and methodologies may have to be reattuned to the new realities. Specifically, the areas of risk assessment and management in the context of the new risk environment are addressed in the following sections.

INTEGRATIVE RISK ASSESSMENT

Risk assessment is the general process of collecting, generating, processing, and producing information and/or prescriptions on the various risk factors and their interrelationships for business decision making. It would therefore include collection of primary and published political risk data, rating of risk dimensions, forecast of future risk scenarios, and prescriptive statements concerning the projected risk scenarios. In the context of the emerging risk environment, the assessment functions and processes will have to be readapted to a focus on micro or project-oriented risks, entry-management-system restrictions, and other policy risks. Thus instead of a focus on the collection and analysis of political science variables, the risk-assessment function should move to an emphasis on these microrisk variables. Specifically, in this light, the locus of data collection would shift to mainly primary data at the host-country or subsidiary level. The data would generally consist of tracking and monitoring changes in EMS conditions and policy shifts, particularly concerning project technology, industry conditions, and the emergence of project obsolescence.

Referring to the political risk information system (PRIS) outlined in Chapter five, the data base in the context of the newly transformed risk environment would enlarge on the substance of the microrisk file, particularly policy instability and project obsolescence. In the area of risk-assessment functions and organization, a system weighted in favor of a line-centered assessment unit appears to be more appropriate to the collection and analysis of microrisks since line personnel are more attuned to project-level operations and EMS conditions impacting on the project. The line-centered-assessment unit would consist of line personnel with a high degree of country or regional based expertise. Since a line-centered approach does not imply a preclusion of staff analysts, experts in the areas' project negotiations and technology development and transfers should be added to the risk-assessment unit to reinforce the assessment and forecasting process. In addition, since monitoring and analysis of microrisks are conducted mainly on a project basis, the analytical formulation is now especially amenable to quantitative methods such as net present value and other discounted-cash-flow analyses. Also because project-level discounted-cash-flow analyses are in essence decision models, the shift to microanalysis will led directly to a decision output.

Finally, conventional macro-oriented risk analysis should be combined with the new focus on microrisk assessment. Even in the context of a transformed international risk environment, an optimum risk-assessment approach would still have to consider the probability of occurrence of macropolitical risks such as regime changes and sociopolitical uncertainties. As noted in earlier chapters, although macropolitical-oriented models do not provide a direct linkage to a specific impact on projects, broad-range risks such as sweeping expropriatory acts and politically motivated funds blockage would still constitute risk possibilities for the multinational company.

INTEGRATIVE RISK MANAGEMENT

Risk management is the general process of planning for, controlling, and reducing the impact of the incidence of risks including activities and events that are considered causes of the occurrence of the risk. Risk management, therefore, consists of both preventive as well as remedial actions taken in relation to the causes and impact of risks. Based on this distinction, risk management in the field of international political risks can be classified into defensive and integrative risk management.

As discussed in Chapter seven, risk avoidance, insurance, and diversification may be considered defensive risk-management strategies, and risk retention, loss prevention and control, and risk transfers may be considered strategies of integrative risk management. Integrative risk management differs from defensive risk management in that the former is preventive and the latter is remedial. Defensive risk management is considered remedial mainly because it includes actions taken to minimize the impact of the incidence of risks. It focuses on activities that would alleviate the negative impact of a risk after it has occurred.

Defensive Risk Management

Defensive risk management refers to a general set of independent risk-reduction strategies that will protect against financial loss stemming from adverse and negative government actions in a host country. Political risk insurance is undertaken independently of the actual activities of the company or the investment project in the host country. The decision regarding the purchase of political risk insurance, for instance, is usually not based on strategies pursued at the project level such as export-ratio, local contents, or indigenization requirements. Thus, by itself, defensive risk management does not avert or prevent the actual incidence or occurrence of the risk events but rather replaces the risk-induced loss with another form of payments, that is, reimbursing the loss through claims for compensation as provided for under the policy coverage. Political risk insurance is a necessary but not sufficient condition for an optimum risk-management strategy. A well-balanced and optimum risk-management strategy requires a combination of both defensive and integrative risk management.

Integrative Risk Management

Integrative risk management may be considered preventive, and it includes actions and strategies pursued at the project level to minimize or even prevent the possibility of the occurrence of the risk events.[2] In other words, integrative risk management tends to focus on managing the causes or activities that may lead to a risk event. It therefore refers to risk-prevention strategies that are directly linked to the activities and strategies pursued by the company in the host country. Integrative risk-management techniques consist of a general set of actions and strategies such as negotiated compliance with the host country's EMS requirements and the adoption of appropriate technology strategies. Such integrative strategies are anticipated to bring about a more favorable perception of the project or venture by maintaining or increasing the worth of the project as seen from the standpoint of the host-country decision makers. In other words, it includes all actions and measures taken by the firm to raise the perceived "indispensability" of a project. Integrative risk-management strategies include upgrading the technology contribution to the host country through a continuous injection of current technology into the project or making a net surplus contribution to the country's balance of payments through intensive exports.

The adoption of integrative risk-management strategies by international investors is based on the premise that such strategies will lead to a greater probability of minimizing or even preventing the actual incidence of risks, that is, adverse actions taken against the company and the project by the host government. As the international investment environment gets increasingly transformed into the host-country-dynamics model, especially in the newly industrializing countries, integrative risk management may in fact be more appropriate and more relevant under the newly emerged scenario. This is true mainly because in the economics- and industrialization-driven and intensely competitive environment of the NICs, foreign investors are facing mainly micropolicy risks emanating from the host country's entry-management system. Such microrisks involving gradual and subtle changes in the host country's EMS rules and regulations that may impact negatively on a project are in effect not considered insurable risks under political risk coverage. Integrative risk-management strategy is therefore aimed precisely at policy risks through managing the company's and the project's policy interactions with the host country's EMS.

At the pre- and postentry stages, integrative risk management would involve, for instance, adjusting the project in accordance with EMS requirements such as ownership arrangements; export-ratio, indigenization, local contents, and countertrade requirements; and profit-repatriation restrictions. It also includes imparting a technological contribution and a contribution to the host country's balance of payments. Such techniques are all part of the firm's strategy to integrate itself and its project positively and dynamically into the host country's economic and industrial fabric.

Indispensability-Vulnerability Profile

Integrative risk-management strategies can best be explained in terms of an indispensability-vulnerability profile for an investment project. As noted under the obsolescing demand model (Chapter one) for a foreign investment project, the perceived worth of any project from the standpoint of the host country is a function of various risk factors that contribute to a faster or slower obsolescence of the project. The "demand" or desirability of the project tends to decline over time as a result of these combined factors (local firms' competition, technology and foreign exchange contribution, company image, and multinational corporation [MNC] competition). Thus physical, time, perceptual, and especially technological factors begin to set in to render the project less dispensable and more vulnerable to adverse consequences.

If the investor firm in question does nothing to forestall or avert the decline, the project will face increasing vulnerability in terms of tightening restrictions from the host country's EMS. Although outright expropriation is highly unlikely in the nonideological NICs, other adverse measures such as bureaucratic impediments, delays in funds transfers, increased pressures for ownership rearrangements, and withdrawal of tax incentives will increasingly begin to threaten the investment project selectively targeted for punitive treatment. On the other hand, if certain integrative strategies are pursued by the firm to influence the rate of obsolescence, essentially by slowing its progress and maintaining the project's worth, the project can be expected to remain relatively indispensable to the host country's economic, industrial, and technological objectives.

The level of project indispensability can be maintained or even increased by actions and strategies that will integrate the project into the technological and economic fabric of the host country. This set of risk-management strategies can therefore be seen as the integrative rather than the more defensive risk strategies such as buying insurance protection or pursuing expensive diversification strategies. Integrative risk-management strategies that can serve to maintain or raise the indispensability level of an investment project mainly consist of those that meet and conform to the industrial policies and priority technological needs of the host country. Major examples of integrative risk-management strategies include the following:

1. Undertaking joint ventures and unbundling
2. Managing interactions with the host country's EMS

3. Maximizing export intensity of the project
4. Maintaining a technological contribution
5. Expanding into value-added activities
6. Reinforcing the company's corporate image
7. Pursuing social responsibility goals
8. Interfacing with Foreign Corrupt Practices Act (FCPA)-related activities

JOINT VENTURES AND UNBUNDLING

Joint ventures and other unbundled modes of market entry have frequently been cited as appropriate risk-reduction strategies undertaken by sharing ownership, management, and technological expertise with host-country nationals. *Unbundling* refers to the separation and disaggregation of functional systems such as technology, management, and marketing from traditional ownership by the foreign investors. Since the functional systems are now host-country owned, it releases the foreign investors from ownership risks and hence reduces or even eliminates risks. In the case of joint ventures, however, the anticipated risk reduction may be short lived, especially when the local counterparts begin to acquire some degree of expertise as a result of the learning-curve phenomenon. In fact, at some stage the joint-venture arrangement itself becomes a source of risk for the foreign partner as differences in management objectives and philosophy and other cross-cultural conflicts gradually emerge. International joint ventures will always remain an expedient and artificially contrived marriage of convenience between partners that are frequently separated by management orientation and cultural background.

Even within the context of joint ventures, however, the potential for risk reduction may be realized if a high degree of commitment and persistent efforts are provided by both partners. A more lasting arrangement may be designed by establishing a mutually accommodating balance of power within the joint venture. For instance, in most joint ventures, control of marketing implementation and other operational functions are more appropriately vested in the hands of the host-country nationals, and the foreign partners may want to retain and provide more strategic guidance for the venture. Most successful joint ventures usually appear to consist of an arrangement whereby host-country nationals assume operational control while the foreign partner offers a strategic guiding hand in shaping the long-term direction for the business. One of the most crucial areas of concern at the strategic level is appropriate management of the joint venture's policy interactions with the host country's EMS. Later sections in this chapter discuss in greater detail how the foreign investor can formulate strategies concerning aspects of the EMS like local contents, export-ratio, and countertrade requirements using the integrative approach.

Other unbundled entry arrangements such as licensing, management-contract, and turnkey projects also allow foreign investors and multinationals to establish a market presence in the host country through such risk-preventive arrangements. In the case of licensing, for instance, the arrangement allows the integration of an unbundled production technology into the host country's technological systems without any tangible assets exposure for the licensor firm. Similarly, management-contract and turnkey arrangements, because of their disaggregated and unbundled (from foreign ownership) nature, can more easily fit into the recipient country's system than the traditionally bundled 100 percent owned and controlled investment package. In other words, it is easier to fit in the parts rather than the whole. Thus from the standpoint of the host country, unbundled management, technology, and marketing arrangements, without the burden of foreign ownership, are more easily integrated into the recipient systems. Aside from easier integration, unbundled arrangements do not entail substantial fixed-asset exposure for the foreign firm, and they tend to diffuse nationalistic sentiments on the part of the host-country nationals.

MANAGING INTERACTIONS WITH THE HOST COUNTRY'S EMS

The key to risk management in a transformed international risk environment is the monitoring of the project's interactions with the host country's EMS and the devising of suitable strategies to optimize these interactions to the benefit of the project. Only when the international manager's primary focus has been shifted and redirected to the host country's entry-management system is the company able to gain some degree of leverage in its interactions with the host country. The key in managing the host country's EMS is the pursuit of flexibility and the adoption of a strategic perspective. Such an approach would consist of a mix of possible strategies ranging from straight compliance to negotiated tradeoff between various elements of the EMS in order to accommodate the mutual interests of both the foreign investors and the host country.

Although some of more restrictive EMS elements such as local contents, indigenization, and countertrade requirements are themselves sources of operational risks, negotiating compliance with these requirements in the context of overall interactions with the EMS is a strategic option that cannot be ignored. Frequently, a host country's EMS is sufficiently flexible and variable to allow and accommodate different configurations of interactions. The key strategy is to trade off and find a balance between the positive and negative elements of the EMS. For instance, negotiating to locate in the host country's special economic or export-processing zones with its full range of supportive facilities would offset some of the more restrictive EMS elements. In highly complex markets such as in Japan, a strategy of complete indigenization of the management of the local subsidiary is an appropriate mode of cultural and hence market-risk deduction. For example, IBM's 100 percent owned subsidiary in Japan is completely Japanese topdown from the president. In addition, other elements such as percentage equity, technological contribution, and export-ratio requirements can be mutually traded off with the negative elements to arrive at a configuration that can satisfy the needs and requirements of both the foreign investors and the host country.

Another frequently used integrative device in terms of compliance with EMS requirements relates to ownership and management arrangements in the host country. Such strategies are based on technical but not effective compliance with the host-country laws. For instance, some multinationals have design strategies to circumvent the host country's requirement for majority local ownership and management. Certain Japanese companies in Southeast Asia, for instance, have resorted to a "nominee" system in which the stockholders are nominally host-country nationals but effective management control still resides with the foreign company.[3] Although such practices are questionable if not illegal, most host country's EMSs are usually flexible enough to accommodate many shades of interpretation of the legal requirements.

MAXIMIZING EXPORT INTENSITY OF THE PROJECT

A project's potential as a foreign exchange earner offers it perhaps its greatest leverage with respect to its interaction with the host country. A wide spectrum of countries ranging from those afflicted with massive external debts and poor if not depressing economic performance toward the economic powerhouses of newly industrializing Asia all continue to look to export as the panacea for all types of economic ills. Attempts to unleash all of these exports onto already overcrowded, underfinanced, and protectionistic world markets are fraught with risks. Yet this export mania is precisely what pervades the industrial policies of most host countries. Thus any project offering high export potential tends to possess an unusually great degree of clout and leverage in its bargaining position with the host country.

Therefore, an investor's ability to generate exports from its investment project equip him with an almost unmatched instrument of integrative risk management. By contributing to the exchange earnings and hence the host country's balance of payments, the investing firm can potentially keep at bay most EMS restrictions such as inconvertibility, countertrade requirements, and, most importantly, ownership restrictions. Most host countries now tie ownership to export orientation, allowing, for instance, 100 percent ownership for a 100 percent export ratio. High-technology companies such as IBM, for which 100 percent ownership and control are desirable, often find willingness to comply with high export intensity as a convenient and no less profitable means of establishing a corporate presence in countries like Mexico. Companies with established market acceptance and brand recognition usually have no serious problems in exporting their products to the world markets. In addition, once the integrative function has been served, the investors can always use their strong bargaining position, earned as a result of their export contribution, to negotiate for gradual and increased penetration of the host country's domestic market.

MAINTAINING THE PROJECT'S
TECHNOLOGICAL CONTRIBUTION

The other crucial integrative risk-management technique, besides maintaining high export intensity, is a continual injection of up-to-date technology into the project, particularly in the area of light manufactured exports. Continual maintenance of updated project technology in the host country is closely tied to a high export-ratio requirement. This is mainly because for the wide middle range of manufactured industrial products, those with a cutting edge and competitive technologies normally have a better chance of selling to the highly demanding export markets. Thus in conjunction with a high export requirement, host countries are increasingly seeking and showing a preference for technologies capable of producing a broad range of light manufactured exportable products. Companies able to offer the host country an opportunity to participate in the production and export of products like electric appliances or personal computers inevitably find the most conducive operating environment awaiting them even in what are usually perceived as highly restrictive and risky countries.

Aside from export promotion, desirable technology in its own right tends also to command an usually high degree of leverage and bargaining position even in the host country's import-substitution markets. Investment projects introducing technology that offers improvement in efficiency and performance in various sectors and industries tend to integrate themselves more favorably and positively into the economic and industrial fabric of the host country. In addition, the EMS restrictions such as exchange-control, local contents, and countertrade requirements are often reduced if not entirely lifted for such projects.

The technological contribution and subsequent transmissions and integration into the host country's industrial and technological system, however, could present a source risk. As the technology diffuses into the host economy and industries, the process is accompanied by an increasing loss of control of the technology, especially in host countries lacking a strong technology-protection system. This reduction of technological appropriability in terms of the loss of ability to maximize returns from its technological innovation is one of the concerns that the international investor should take into consideration when pursuing an integrative technology strategy. Chapter two has referred to some of the measures that an investor can adopt in minimizing the risks inherent in international technology transmissions.

EXPANDING INTO HIGH-END VALUE-ADDED ACTIVITIES

Expansion into more value-added activities, particularly those that optimize the use of local inputs at all stages of the production process, tends to be viewed more favorably by the host country. It is now a part of the conventional wisdom of political risk assessment that foreign projects that are merely extractive usually face the greatest degree of risk exposure. The perception is that such projects are resource depleting and that no value is contributed to the local economy in terms of substantive and critical learning by host-country nationals. The expropriation of mining and oil projects in the early seventies has already been extensively documented in political risk literature. Despite such lessons, certain multinationals still show a surprising and persistent disregard for history in pursuing activities that add nothing significant and long lasting to the host country.

Thus even among today's international investment flows, a predominant amount of investment still consists of nonintegrated manufacturing activities. Offshore electronics-chip production is a case in point. The labor-intensive parts are usually fabricated in the host countries, and the more sophisticated finishing and assembly operations are done in the home country of the multinational with the result that no substantial and critical industrial skills are imparted and learned. Although such offshore plants help to ameliorate and reduce unemployment in many poor recipient countries, the benefits are temporary and transient. As the multinational investors depart, as many U.S.-based electronics companies are now doing in the Far East, a host country is left stagnated in a technological vacuum.

Much of the blame must be attributed to the host countries themselves in terms of not pursuing more aggressive indigenous technology development and providing a more conducive and receptive environment for self-sustained technology transfers, particularly to the host country's private sector. Neither, however, have the major multinationals recently persisted in providing to other developing countries the kind of technological linkages they have so assiduously developed in the earlier industrialization experience of the NICs, as in Taiwan, South Korea, and Hong Kong. It is, indeed, through such earlier persistence by major multinationals in vendor development and other value-added activities that the multinationals have helped to propel the Asian NICs into self-sustained export-oriented industrialization.

It is no surprise that first-tiered developing countries like Indonesia and China have felt it necessary to pioneer and develop sophisticated counter-measures to force greater absorption, use, development, and participation of the host country's skills and resource potential. Measures such as countertrade and local requirements are essentially directed toward the attainment of this objective. For instance, foreign investors in China are required to export products unrelated to their projects in order to earn sufficient foreign exchange for their own profit repatriation. Similar measures are in force in Indonesia. In the context of such a newly structured scenario, the question facing the foreign investors is whether to preempt and counter forced integration with voluntary integration. The latter strategy is more advantageous to the investor from the standpoint of retaining control over technology and project performance.

Contribution to value-added activities is closely interlinked with the integrative activities of export intensification, technological contribution, and maximization of the incorporation of local contents. For instance, in negotiating a lower export-ratio requirement, the international investor can offer to engage in greater value-added activities and a more substantive technology contribution in exchange for lowering the export of unrelated products over which it has no control. Specifically, the multinational can work toward a goal of developing a set of closely supervised local vendors with the promise of aiding their subsequent export efforts in the highly demanding export markets. On the other hand, the investor can negotiate for reduced local contents and even avoid countertrade by offering perhaps a 100 percent export intensity for its own fully controlled products. Therefore, it can be seen that in designing and structuring integrative risk-management strategies, a multinational investor is given the opportunity to develop and negotiate a fine-tuned project package that will optimize the needs and objectives of both sides at the preentry as well as the postentry stages. As noted in Chapter five, preentry and postentry project negotiation is a crucial precursor to a successful and effective integrative risk-management strategy.

CORPORATE IMAGE, SOCIAL RESPONSIBILITY, AND FCPA-RELATED ACTIVITIES

Finally, we have an interrelated set of dimensions that together furnish an additional mechanism for integrative risk management. The host country's perception of the foreign investor or multinational influences to a great extent the possible actions it may decide to take in regard to the firm's project. Thus another important aspect of integrative risk management is the need to take into account the host country's perception of the company's image. From the standpoint of the host country, a firm's *corporate image* may be defined as the whole range of cumulated facts, information, and perceptions concerning the firm that resides in the social consciousness of the host-country nationals. The firm's corporate image can be subject to variables over which it has no control, but more frequently it is shaped by factors that it can influence and manage. Thus the strategy of the multinational or international investor in regard to its corporate image is to develop and foster the formation of a positive corporate image, particularly in the host country in which it operates. The expectation is that a more positive corporate image will contribute to minimizing any risk exposure the company may face in the host country.

Multinationals such as IBM, ITT, Union Carbide, and Nestle each have a specific corporate image consisting of both positive and negative elements. When negative perceptions predominate, the firm usually carries with it an "image baggage" that may impinge unfavorably on its activities in many host countries. Nestle's travails with its baby formula is a case in point, and Union Carbide's tragic gas-leakage incident in Bhopal, India, is another one. Such negative images may take years to correct. The strategy that must be adopted is to reemphasize the positive dimensions of the corporate image. In other cases, companies may also proactively foster a favorable image, especially with respect to a public it considers vital. Thus the recent spate of exodus of major multinations from South Africa may stem partially from their desire to take a moral stand with respect to that country's racial policies and partially to foster a more positive image with a possible new regime in the event of a change. Such strategies tend to move away from pure profit motivations to the area of social responsibility.

In addition, positive corporate image may be developed through more traditional means such as contributing to charitable and philanthropic causes, establishing scholarship funds, training and employing the hard-core unemployed and the handicapped, and sponsoring social and civil events. The strategic objective is to create a perception of the company as a good corporate citizen and therefore an integral part of the society and community in which it operates. On an international level, reinforcement of the social responsibility image has been carried out with a degree of success. IBM, for instance, has managed to foster a positive reputation for educational sponsorship involving the establishment of training institutes and scholarship funds in many of the host countries in which it operates. Other companies, such as Caterpillar, have issued explicit codes of conduct detailing their expected business and citizen roles and standards of behavior in the respective host countries.[4] All such measures are intended to be a part of a company's attempt to integrate itself not only into the business but also the social fabric of the host country.

One area of host-country integration that remains controversial and is therefore shunned by the risk-assessment profession relates to bribery and graft in the host countries. The FCPA prohibits U.S. firms from engaging in questionable payments in foreign countries.[5] Because of this illicit nature, the role of bribery in risk management has received scant attention in the literature. However, such practices, although illegal under U.S. laws, are pervasive in the majority of host countries. In many countries, these practices constitute the essential facilitating mechanism for both business and governmental transactions. Integrative risk-management strategy therefore suggests that FCPA-related activities perform a vital function in facilitating the smooth integration of the foreign firm into the business and social systems of the host country. The corporate-risk analyst, however, should still consider the legal as well as moral ramifications of FCPA-related activities as an integrative device. Moreover, although resorting to these practices may reduce or eliminate risk in the short run, FCPA-related activities may themselves lead to risks in the long run.

NOTES

1. Wenlee Ting, Business and Technological Dynamics in Newly Industrializing Asia (Westport, Conn.: Quorum Books, 1985), pp. 54-60.

2. Ann Gregory, "Political Risk Reduction Techniques of North American Firms in Southeast Asia," paper presented at the Academy of International Business Annual Meeting, London, November 1986.

3. Franklin B. Weinstein, "Multinational Corporations and the Third World: The Case of Japan and Southeast Asia," International Organization, Vol. 30, No. 3, 1976, pp. 387-396.

4. Caterpillar Tractor Company, "A Code of Worldwide Business Conduct and Operating Principles," undated.

5. Jack Kaikati and Wayne A. Label, "The Foreign Antibribery Law: Friend or Foe?" Columbia Journal of World Business, Spring 1980, pp. 46-51.

Selected Bibliography

AFIA. "Political Risk: Team Approach Leads to Success," Annual Report, 1984, pp. 10-15.

Aharoni, Y. The Foreign Investment Decision Process (Boston: Division of Research, Graduate School of Business Administration, Harvard University, 1966).

Akinsanya, Adeoye, A. The Expropriation of Multinational Property in the Third World (New York: Praeger, 1980).

Aliber, Robert Z. "Exchange Risk, Political Risk, and Investor Demands for External Currency Deposits," Journal of Money, Credit and Banking, May 1975, pp. 161-179.

Altman, Edward I., R. G. Haldeman, and P. Narayaman, "ZETA Analysis: A New Model to Identify Bankruptcy Risk of Corporations," Journal of Banking and Finance, Vol. 1, 1977, pp. 29-54.

American International Group. Political Risk Insurance for Overseas Investments (New York, 1984).

Andriole, Stephen J., and Gerald W. Hopple. "An Overview of Political Instability Research Methodologies: Basic and Applied Recommendations for the Corporate Analyst," in Jerry Rogers, ed., Global Risk Assessments, Issues, Concepts, and Applications (Riverside, Calif.: Global Risk Assessment, 1983), pp. 89-90.

Arnold, Tom, and J. T. McCarthy. Domestic and International Licensing of Technology (New York: Practicing Law Institute, 1980).

Baglini, Norman A. Risk Management in International Corporations (New York: Risk Studies Foundation, 1976).

Bank, Arthur S., and Robert B. Textor. A Cross-Polity Survey (Cambridge, Mass.: MIT Press, 1963).

Basche, James R. Nationalization: The Experience of U.S. Companies in the 1970s, Conference Board Bulletin No. 62 (New York: The Conference Board, 1979).

Beeman, Don R. "An Empirical Analysis of the Beliefs Held by the International Executives of United States Firms Regarding Political Risk Reduction Methods in Developing Nations," Ph.D. diss., Indiana University, 1978.

Bergsten, C. Fred. "Coming Investment Wars?" Foreign Affairs, Vol. 53, No. 1, October 1974, pp. 135-152.

――――. "The New Era in World Commodity Markets," Challenge, Vol. 17, No. 4, September-October 1974, pp. 32-34.

Bergsten, C. Fred., Robert O. Keohane, and Joseph S. Nye. "International Economics and International Politics: A Framework for Analysis," in C. F. Bergsten and L. B. Krause, eds., World Politics and International Economics (Washington, D.C.: Brookings Institute, 1975), pp. 3-36.

Bickelhaupt, David L. General Insurance, 11th ed. (Homewood, Ill.: R. D. Irwin, 1983).

Bierman, Jr., Harold, and Seymour Smidt. The Capital Budgeting Decision, 3d ed. (New York: Macmillan, 1971).

Billerbeck, K., and Y. Yasugi. Private Direct Foreign Investment in Developing Countries, World Bank Staff Working Report No. 348 (Washington, D.C.: World Bank, 1979).

Boddewyn, Jean J., and Etieme Cracco. "The Political Game in World Business," Columbia Journal of World Business, January-February 1972, pp. 45-56.

Bollen, Kenneth A., and Scott T. Jones. "Political Instability and Foreign Direct Investment: The Motor Vehicle Industry, 1948-1965," Social Forces, June 1982, pp. 1070-1088.

Bradley, David G. "Managing against Expropriation," Harvard Business Review, Vol. 55, 1977, pp. 75-83.

Brainard, Lawrence J. "Banker's Trust Approach to International Risk Assessment," in Richard Ensor, ed., Assessing Country Risk (London: Euromoney Publications, 1981), pp. 93-98.

Brewer, Thomas L. "The Instability of Governments and the Instability of Controls on Funds Transfer by Multinational Enterprises: Implications for Political Risk," Journal of International Studies, Winter 1983, p. 147.

Bruce, David. "Integrating Political Risk Methodologies at a California International Bank," in Jerry Rogers, ed., Global Risk Assessment, Issues, Concepts, and Applications (Riverside, Calif.: Global Risk Assessment, Inc., 1983), pp. 131-139.

Burton, F. N., and Hisaski Inoue. "Country Risk Evaluation Methods: A Survey of Systems in Use," The Banker, January 1983, pp. 41-43.

――――. "Expropriations of Foreign Owned Firms in Developing Countries: A Cross National Analysis," Journal of World Trade Law, Vol. 18, 1984, pp. 396-414.

Business America, "Andean Countries Liberalize Foreign Investment Policies," August 5, 1985, pp. 23-25.

Business International. Country Assessment Service (New York, 1985), various issues.

――――. Investing, Licensing, and Trading Conditions Abroad—Brazil (New York, January 1985).

_____. Investing, Licensing, and Trading Conditions Abroad—France (New York, February 1985).

_____. Investing, Licensing, and Trading Conditions Abroad—Korea (New York, June 1985).

_____. Investing, Licensing, and Trading Conditions Abroad—Spain (New York, January 1985).

_____. 101 Checklists for Coping with Worldwide Countertrade Problems (Geneva: Business International S.A., 1985).

_____. Threats and Opportunities of Global Countertrade: Marketing, Financing, and Organizational Implications (New York, 1984).

Business Environmental Risk Information. Business Risk Service, Forelend, and Force (Long Beach, Calif., 1985).

Business Week. "A Forward Market's Long Reach," November 23, 1981, p. 103.

Calvet, A. Louis. "A Synthesis of Foreign Direct Investment Theories and Theories of the Multinational Firm," Journal of International Business Studies, Spring-Summer 1981, pp. 43-59.

Carvounis, Chris C. "The LDC Debt Problem: Trends in Country Risk Analysis and Rescheduling Exercises," Columbia Journal of World Business, Spring 1982, pp. 15-26.

Caterpillar Tractor Company. "A Code of Worldwide Business Conduct and Operating Principles," undated.

Chatterjee, Ashok K. Foreign Direct Investment and Political Risk: A Weak Signal Perspective, Ph.D. diss., New York University, 1982.

"China's Economic Bureaucracy," The China Business Review, May-June 1982, p. 22.

"China's Trade and Investment Law," The China Business Review, November-December 1985, pp. 40-45.

Chubb Group of Insurance Companies. Declarations: Political Risk (Warren, N.J., 1984).

Citibank. "The Multinational Corporation: An Environmental Analysis," Investment Research Department, New York, unpublished, April 1976.

Coplin, William D., and Michael K. O'Leary. "Systematic Political Risk Analysis for Planners," Planning Review, January 1983, pp. 14-17.

Crawford, C. T., R. M. Hammer, and G. Simmonetti. Investments Around the World (New York: Wiley, 1981).

Davies, Robert R. "Alternative Techniques for Country Risk Evaluation," Business Economics, May 1981, pp. 34-41.

Davies, Warnock. "Beyond the Earthquake Allegory: Managing Political Risk Vulnerability," Management International Review, Vol. 21, 1981, pp. 5-9.

Donaldson, Gordon. "Strategic Hurdle Rates for Capital Investment," Harvard Business Review, March-April 1972, pp. 50-58.

Dunn, John. "Country Risk: Social and Cultural Aspects," in R. J. Herring, ed., Managing International Risk (Cambridge University Press, 1983).

Ebel, Robert E. "The Magic of Political Risk Analysis," in Mark B. Winchester, ed., The International Essays for Business Decision Makers, Vol. 5 (Houston: The Center for International Business, 1980), p. 292.

Feierabend, Ivo K., and Rosalind L. Feierabend. "Aggressive Behavior in Politics,

1948-1962: A Cross-National Study." Journal of Conflict Resolution, Fall 1966, pp. 249-271.

Fikentscher, Wolfgang. "The Typology of International Licensing Agreements," in N. Horn and C. M. Schmitthoff, eds., The Transnational Law of International Commercial Transactions (Antwerp, the Netherlands: Kluwer/Deventer, 1982), pp. 211-222.

Financial Accounting Standards Board. Foreign Currency Translation, Statement of Financial Accounting Standard No. 52, December 1981 (Stamford, Conn., 1981).

Ford, David, and Chris Ryan, "Taking Technology to Market," Harvard Business Review, March-April 1981, pp. 117-126.

Frost and Sullivan Political Risk Services. Catalog of Services (New York: Frost and Sullivan, 1984).

Gahin, Fikry S. "Reworking Classic Risk Models to Fit Real World Decision Making," Risk Management, June 1984, pp. 62-70.

Gebelein, C. A., C. E. Pearson, and M. Sibergh. "Assessing Political Risks to Foreign Oil Ventures," paper presented to the 1977 Society of Petroleum Engineers' Economics and Evaluation Symposium, 1977.

Geyikdagi, Mehmet Y. Risk Trends of U.S. Multinational and Domestic Firms (New York: Praeger, 1982).

Gilpin, Robert. U.S. Power and the Multinational Corporation (New York: Basic Books, 1975).

Gladwin, Thomas N., and Ingo Walter. Multinationals under Fire: Lessons in the Management of Conflict (New York: Wiley, 1980).

Goldsmith, Carol S. "Countertrade, Inc.," The China Business Review, January-February 1982, pp. 48-50.

Goodman, Stephen T. "Corporate Attitudes," in Richard Ensor, ed., Assessing Country Risk (London: Euromoney Publications, 1981), pp. 111-115.

———. "How the Big Banks Really Evaluate Sovereign Risks," Euromoney, February 1977, pp. 105-110.

Graham, P. A. "Risk in International Banking: Its Meaning for Liquidity and Capital," Journal of the Institute of Bankers, June 1982, pp. 74-76.

Greene, Mark K. "The Management of Political Risks," Bests Review, Property Liability Insurance Issue, July 1974, pp. 71-74.

Greene, Mark R., and James S. Trieschmann. Risk and Insurance (Dallas: South-Western Publishing Co., 1981), pp. 3-14.

Gregory, Ann. "Political Risk Reduction Techniques of North American Firms in Southeast Asia," paper presented at the Academy of International Business Annual Meeting, London, November 1986.

Guide to Investment in Korea, A, The Korean Chamber of Commerce and Industry, 1983-84.

Haendel, Dan. Foreign Investment and the Management of Political Risk (Boulder, Colo.: Westview Press, 1979).

Haendel, Dan, Gerald T. West, and Robert G. Meadow. Overseas Investment and Political Risk (Philadelphia: Foreign Policy Research Institute, 1975).

Hall, Duane. International Joint Ventures (New York: Praeger, 1985).

Haner, F. T. "Business Environment Risk Index," Bests Review, Property Liability Insurance Issue, July 1975, pp. 47-50.

Hawkins, Robert G., N. Mintz, and M. Provissiero. "Government Takeovers of U.S. Foreign Affiliates," Journal of International Business Studies, Vol. 7, 1976, pp. 3-16.

Heller, H. Robert, and Emmanuel Frenkel. "Determinants of LDC Indebtedness," Columbia Journal of World Business, Spring 1982, pp. 28-33.

Hershbarger, Robert A., and John P. Noerager. "International Risk Management: Some Peculiar Constraints," Risk Management, April 1976, pp. 23-34.

Hertz, David B., and Howard Thomas. "Risk Analysis: Important New Tool for Business Planning," Journal of Business Strategy, Winter 1986, pp. 23-29.

Hill, Eileen. "Protecting U.S. Intellectual Property Rights," Business America, April 14, 1986, pp. 2-6.

Ho, S. P., and R. W. Huenemann. China's Open Door Policy: The Quest for Foreign Technology and Capital (Vancouver, B.C.: The University of British Columbia Press, 1984).

"How Companies Are Coping with the Strong Dollar," Fortune, November 26, 1984, pp. 116-124.

Hunt, Cecil. "Insuring for Political Risk," in Richard Ensor, ed., Assessing Country Risk (London: Euromoney Publications, 1981), pp. 137-142.

"IBM Is Cleared by Mexico to Build a 100% Owned Plant," The Wall Street Journal, July 24, 1985.

Ingram, G. M. Expropriation of U.S. Property in South America: Nationalization of Oil and Copper Companies in Peru, Bolivia, and Chile (New York: Praeger, 1974).

International Country Risk Guide (New York: International Reports, 1985), statistical sections and various reports by country and by periods.

Investment Guide to Korea, Ministry of Finance, Republic of Korea, 1983.

Jodice, D. A. "Sources of Change in Third World Regimes for Foreign Direct Investment, 1968-1976," International Organization, Vol. 34, Spring 1980, pp. 177-206.

Johnson, Howard C. "An Actuarial Analysis," in Richard Ensor, ed., Assessing Country Risk (London: Euromoney Publications, 1981), pp. 31-48.

_____. Risk in Foreign Business Environments: A Framework for Thought and Management (Cambridge, Mass.: Arthur D. Little, 1980).

Johnston, Felton M. "Political Risk Market Expansion Broadens OPIC's Role," Risk Management, February 1984, pp. 18-24.

Jones, Jr., Randall J. "Empirical Models for Political Risks in U.S. Oil Production Operations in Venezuela," Journal of International Business Studies, Vol. 25, 1984, pp. 81-95.

_____. "A Model for Predicting Expropriation in Latin America Applied to Jamaica," Columbia Journal of World Business, Vol. 15, 1980, pp. 74-80.

Kaikati, Jack, and Wayne A. Label. "The Foreign Antibribery Law: Friend or Foe?" Columbia Journal of World Business, Spring 1980, pp. 46-51.

Katz, David M. "Two Ways to Handle Political Hazards," National Underwriters, November 18, 1983, p. 11.

Kelley, Margaret. "Evaluating the Risks of Expropriation," Risk Management, January 1974, pp. 23-43.

Kim, Taeho. "Assessment of External Debt Capacity: An Alternative Methodology," Journal of Economic Development, December 1985, pp. 35-52.

King, John K. "Political Risk Assessment for Food Company Foreign Operations," Food Systems Update, December 1984, pp. 10-17.

Kloman, H. Felix. "Risk Management: 1990 and Beyond," Risk Management, March 1984, pp. 32-39.

Knight, Frank H. Risk Uncertainty and Profit (1921) (Chicago: University of Chicago Press, 1971).

Knudsen, Harald. "Explaining the National Propensity to Expropriate: An Ecological Approach," Journal of International Business Studies, Spring 1974, pp. 51-71.

———. "Expropriation of Foreign Private Investments in Latin America," Ph.D. diss., University of Oregon, 1972.

Kobrin, Stephen J. "The Environmental Determinants of Foreign Direct Manufacturing Investment: An Ex-Post Empirical Analysis," Journal of International Business Studies, Fall-Winter 1976, pp. 29-42.

———. "Foreign Enterprise and Forced Divestment in LDCs," International Organization, Vol. 34, 1980, pp. 65-88.

———. Managing Political Risk Assessment: Strategic Response to Environmental Change (Berkeley, Calif.: University of California Press, 1982).

———. "Political Assessment and Evaluation of Non-Economic Environments by American Firms," Journal of International Business Studies, Spring-Summer 1980, pp. 32-47.

———. "Political Assessment by International Firms: Models or Methodologies," Journal of Policy Modelling, May 1981, pp. 251-270.

———. "Political Risk: A Review and Reconsideration." Journal of International Business Studies, Spring-Summer 1979, pp. 67-89.

———. "When Does Political Instability Result in Increased Investment Risk," Columbia Journal of World Business, Fall 1976, pp. 113-122.

Kraar, Louis. "The Multinationals Get Smart about the Political Risks," Fortune, March 24, 1980, pp. 86-100.

Kransdorff, Arnold. "Multinational Code in Sight," Financial Times, November 24, 1982, p. 16.

Krayenbuehl, Thomas E. "How Country Risk Should Be Monitored," The Banker, May 1983, pp. 51-53.

LaPalombara, Joseph, and Stephen Blank. Multinational Corporations and National Elites: A Study in Tensions (New York: The Conference Board, 1976).

Lasswell, Harold D., and A. Kaplan. Power and Society (New Haven: Yale University Press, 1950).

Lewellen, Wilbur G., H. P. Lenser, and J. J. McConnell. "Payback Substitutes for Discounted Cash Flow," Financial Management, Summer 1973, pp. 17-25.

Lindblom, Charles E. Politics and Markets (New York: Basic Books, 1977).

Lloyd, B. Political Risk Management (London: Keith Shipton Developments Ltd. 1976).

Looney, Robert E. Development Alternatives of Mexico (New York: Praeger, 1982).

MacDonald, Donald L. Risk in the Oversea Operation of American Corporations (Ann Arbor, Mich.: University of Michigan Press, 1979).

Maddison, Raymond. Copyright and Related Rights, Principles, Problems, and Trends (London: Economic Intelligence Unit Limited, 1983).

Magee, Stephen P. "Multinational Corporations, the Industry Technology Cycle and Development," The Journal of World Trade Law, Vol. 11, No. 4, July-August 1977, pp. 297-312.

Mao, James C. T. "The Internal Rate of Return as a Ranking Criterion," Engineering Economist, Winter 1966, pp. 1-13.

"Maquiladoras: Profit for Production Sharing," The Wall Street Journal, September 24, 1984.

Markscheid, Stephen. "Compensation Trade: The China Perspective," The China Business Review, January-February 1982, pp. 50-52.

Mason, R. H. "Conflicts between Host Countries and the Multinational Enterprise," California Management Review, Vol. 17, 1974, pp. 5-14.

Mathis, F. John. "Developing Countries' Foreign Debts: Lessons from Recent Experience and the Risk Outlook," Journal of Commercial Banking, July 1982, pp. 38-46.

Maynard, Cathleen. Indonesia's Countertrade Experience, American-Indonesian Chamber of Commerce, November 1983.

McClelland, Charles A. D-Files for Monitoring and Forecasting Threats and Problems Abroad (Los Angeles: University of Southern California, January 1978), p. 28.

Merrill, James. "Country Risk Analysis," Columbia Journal of World Business, Spring 1982, pp. 88-91.

Micallef, Joseph V. "Political Risk Assessment," Columbia Journal of World Business, Summer 1981, pp. 47-52.

Mikesell, Raymond F. "More Third World Cartels Ahead," Challenge, Vol. 17, No. 5, November-December 1974, pp. 24-31.

Milligan, John W. "Political Risk Coverage Markets, Demand Grows," Business Insurance, October 12, 1981, p. 28.

Moran, Theodore H. "Multinational Corporations and the Changing Structure of Industries Supplying Industrial Commodities," Journal of Contemporary Business, Vol. 6, No. 4, Autumn 1977, pp. 121-130.

_____. "Transnational Strategies of Protection and Reference by Multinational Corporations: Spreading the Risk and Raising the Cost for Nationalization in Natural Resources," International Organization, Vol. 26, 1972, pp. 273-287.

Murray, J. Alex, and Lawrence Leduc. "Public Attitudes and Foreign Investment Screens: The Canadian Case," paper presented at the Academy of International Business Annual Meeting, Cleveland, 1984.

Mytelka, L. "Licensing and Technological Dependence in the Andean Group," World Development, June 1978, pp. 447-459.

Nagy, Pancras J. Country Risk: How to Assess, Quantify, and Monitor It (London: Euromoney Publications, 1979).

_____. "The Use of Quantified Risk Assessment in Decision Making in Banks," in Richard Ensor, ed., Assessing Country Risk (London: Euromoney Publications, 1981), p. 103.

Nehrt, Lee C. "The Political Climate for Private Investment: The Case for Tunisia," in I. A. Litvak and C. J. Maule, eds., Foreign Investment: The Experience of Host Countries (New York: Praeger, 1970), pp. 303-334.

OECD. The Relation of Expropriatory Action by Developing Countries to Foreign Private Investment Flows (Paris, 1972).

Oblak, David J., and Roy J. Heim, Jr. "Survey and Analysis of Capital Budgeting

Methods Used by Multinationals," Financial Management, Winter 1980, pp. 37-41.

O'Leary, Michael K., and William D. Coplin. Political Risk in 35 Countries, 1983 (London: Euromoney Publications, 1984).

Onkvisit, Sak, and John J. Shaw. "An Examination of the International Product Life Cycle and Its Application within Marketing," Columbia Journal of World Business, Fall 1983, pp. 73-79.

Overholt, William H. Political Risk (London: Euromoney Publications, 1984).

Parvin, Manoucher. "Economic Determinants of Political Unrest," Journal of Conflict Resolution, No. 17, 1975, pp. 271-295.

Patents throughout the World. Third Edition, Ed., Alan J. Jacobs. (New York: Clark Boardman Company, Ltd, 1986).

Pfaff, Dieter. "International Licensing Contracts, Transfer of Technology, and Transnational Law," in Norbert Horn and Clive M. Schmitthoff, eds., The Transnational Law of International Commercial Transactions (Antwerp, the Netherlands: Kluwer/Deventer, 1982), pp. 199-209.

Price Waterhouse. Doing Business in France, Price Waterhouse Information Guide, 1985.

————. Doing Business in Mexico, Price Waterhouse Information Guide, 1984.

————. Doing Business in Spain, Price Waterhouse Information Guide, 1982.

————. Doing Business in Venezuela, Price Waterhouse Information Guide, 1985.

Rayfield, Gordon. "General Motors' Approach to Country Risk," in Richard Ensor, ed., Assessing Country Risk (London: Euromoney Publications, 1981), pp. 129-133.

Robock, Stefan H. "Political Risk: Identification and Assessment," Columbia Journal of World Business, July-August 1971, pp. 6-20.

Rossen, K. S. "Expropriation in Argentina and Brazil: Theory and Practice," Virginia Journal of International Law, 1975, pp. 277-318.

Rummel, R. J., and David A. Heenan. "How Multinationals Analyze Political Risk," Harvard Business Review, January-February 1978, pp. 67-76.

Shapiro, Alan C. "Capital Budgeting for Multinational Corporations," Financial Management, Spring 1978, pp. 7-16.

————. "Managing Political Risk: A Policy Approach," Columbia Journal of World Business, Fall 1981, pp. 63-70.

Shubik, Martin. "Political Risk," in Richard J. Herring, ed., Managing International Risk (Cambridge: Cambridge University Press, 1983).

Simon, Jeffrey D. "The Advantages of Danger Files over WEIS as a Crisis Warning System: Some Preliminary Findings," CWSS Pre-Technical Report #1 (Los Angeles: University of Southern California, July 1978), p. 35.

————. "Political Risk Assessment: Past Trends and Future Prospects," Columbia Journal of World Business, Fall 1982, pp. 62-71.

————. "A Theoretical Perspective on Political Risk," Journal of International Business Studies, Winter 1984, pp. 123-143.

Sloan, Michael P. "Strategic Planning by Multiple Political Futures Techniques," pp. 4-17.

Smith, Clifford N. Predicting the Political Environment of International Business," Long Range Planning, September 1971, pp. 7-14.

Sofia, A. Zuhier. "Rationalizing Country Risk Ratios," in Richard Ensor, ed., Assessing Country Risk (London: Euromoney Publications, 1981), pp. 49-68.

Stobaugh, Jr., Robert B. "How to Analyze Foreign Investment Climates," Harvard Business Review, September-October 1969, pp. 100-108.

Stonehill, Arthur, and Leonard Nathanson. "Capital Budgeting and the Multinational Corporation," California Management Review, Summer 1968, pp. 39-54.

Thompson, John J. "An Index of Economic Risk," in Richard Ensor, ed., Assessing Country Risk (London: Euromoney Publications, 1981), pp. 69-74.

_____. "The Poor Man's Guide to Country Risk," Euromoney, July 1981, pp. 182-189.

Thunell, Lars H. Political Risk in International Business (New York: Praeger, 1977).

Ting, Wenlee. Business and Technological Dynamics in Newly Industrializing Asia (Westport, Conn.: Quorum Books, 1985), pp. 51-69.

_____. "New Perspectives on Risk Assessment and Management in Asia Pacific: A Host Country Dynamics Approach," Proceedings of the Academy of International Business South East Asia Meeting, Taipei, Taiwan, June 1986, pp. 778-795.

Torneden, R. L., and J. J. Boddewyn. "Foreign Divestments: Too Many Mistakes," Columbia Journal of World Business, Vol. 9, 1974, pp. 87-94.

Tunney, Joseph J. "Banks' Perspectives in Measuring Risk," in Richard Ensor, ed., Assessing Country Risk (London: Euromoney Publications, 1981), pp. 83-85.

Van Agtmael, Antoine. "Evaluating the Risks of Lending and Developing Countries," Euromoney, April 1976, pp. 16-30.

_____. "How Business Has Dealt with Political Risk," Financial Executive, January 1976, pp. 26-30.

Vernon, Raymond. "The Obsolescing Bargain: A Key Factor in Political Risk," in Mark B. Winchester, ed., The International Essays for Business Decision Makers, Vol. 5 (Houston: The Center for International Business, 1980), pp. 281-286.

_____. Sovereignty at Bay: The Multinational Spread of U.S. Enterprises (New York: Basic Books, 1971).

_____. Sovereignty at Bay after Ten Years," International Organization, Vol. 35, No. 3, Summer 1981, pp. 517-530.

_____. Storm over the Multinational: The Real Issues (Boston: Harvard University Press, 1977).

Weinstein, Franklin B. "Multinational Corporations and the Third World: The Case of Japan and Southeast Asia," International Organization, Vol. 30, No. 3, 1976, pp. 387-396.

White, Gillian. Nationalization of Foreign Property (London: Stevens and Sons, 1961).

Williams, M. L. "The Extent and Significance of the Nationalization of Foreign Owned Assets in Developing Countries," Oxford Economics Paper, Vol. 27, 1975, pp. 260-273.

Williams, Jr., C. Arthur, and Richard M. Heins. Risk Management and Insurance (New York: McGraw-Hill, 1981), pp. 4-20.

Yassukovich, S. M. "The Growing Political Unrest and International Lending,"
    Euromoney, April 1976, pp. 10-15.
Zink, Dolph Warren. The Political Risks for Multinational Enterprises in Develop-
    ing Countries (New York: Praeger, 1973).
Zoller, Adrien-Claude. "Algerian Nationalization: The Legal Issues," Journal of
    World Trade Laws, Vol. 6, 1972, pp. 33-57.

Index

About the Author

WENLEE TING is a member of the faculty of the American Graduate School of International Management in Glendale, Arizona. He is the author of *Business and Technological Dynamics in Newly Industrializing Asia* (Quorum Books, 1985) and numerous scholarly articles on international marketing in leading journals both in this country and abroad. He is also the president and founder of Transource Services, an international business development and consulting firm.

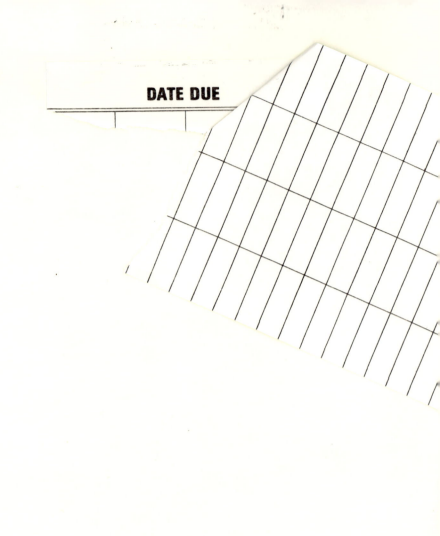

DATE DUE